LANGUAGE AND THE WORSHIP OF THE CHURCH

Language and the Worship of the Church

edited by

DAVID JASPER
*Principal of
St Chad's College,
the University of Durham*

R. C. D. JASPER
Dean Emeritus of York

St. Martin's Press   New York

© David Jasper and R. C. D. Jasper 1990

All rights reserved. For information, write:
Scholarly and Reference Division,
St. Martin's Press, Inc., 175 Fifth Avenue,
New York, N.Y. 10010

First published in the United States of America in 1990

Printed in Hong Kong

ISBN 0–312–03668–X

Library of Congress Cataloging-in-Publication Data
Language and the worship of the Church/edited by David Jasper,
R. C. D. Jasper.
p. cm.
ISBN 0–312–03668–X
1. Liturgical language. I. Jasper, David. II. Jasper, Ronald
Claud Dudley.
BV178.L63 1990
264—dc20   89–36203
                                                                    CIP

Contents

Preface

Few things in recent years have engendered more passion than liturgical change in the various Christian Churches. What has become clear is the importance of familiar and well-loved forms of language to people. Words often repeated or sung in the context of particular liturgical actions represent a stability and a relationship with God and things of ultimate concern, to disturb which arouses the deepest passions.

How is such language to be fashioned and refashioned in a changing world? We need to examine the rhetorical qualitites of the earliest liturgies and the way their language developed under the pressure of theological and social demands. The vernacular liturgies of the Reformation posed new problems of translation. What is quite evident is that no single approach to the difficulties encountered in such an odd use of language will suffice. Professional liturgists can trace for us the history and theology of liturgical forms; poets will make their contribution, as will students of linguistics, philosophers, musicians, literary critics, classicists and theologians. All of these are represented in this volume. They toe no party line, either lamenting or advocating change, but each in their various ways contribute to a fascinating discussion which is central to our religious and literary experience.

D.J.

vii

Acknowledgements

The editors and publishers gratefully acknowledge permission to reprint extracts from the following copyright material.

Gregory Dix, *The Treatise on the Apostolic Tradition of St Hippolytus of Rome,* revised by Henry Chadwick, published by SPCK (1968). Reprinted by permission of SPCK.

Brian A. Wren (1936–), 'When Christ was lifted from the earth' and 'I come with joy to meet my Lord', reprinted by permission of Oxford University Press, London; copyright © USA and Canada by Hope Publishing Company, Carol Stream, Illinois 60188, USA; reprinted by permission.

Brian A. Wren (1936–), 'We plough and sow with tractors', 'Dear Sister God' and 'Wonder of wonders', copyright © 1983 by Hope Publishing Company, Carol Stream, Illinois 60188, USA; all rights reserved; used by permission.

Christopher Idle, 'Now let us learn of Christ', published by Jubilate Hymns Limited, copyright © Christopher Idle.

Michael Saward, 'Through all our days we'll sing the praise', published by Jubilate Hymns Limited, copyright © Michael Saward.

Michael Perry, 'God is our fortress and our rock', published by Jubilate Hymns Limited, copyright © Michael Perry.

Hymns for Today's Church, numbers 144, 264, 280, 283 and 472, copyright © in this version Jubilate Hymns Limited.

Fred Pratt Green, 'The church of Christ, in every age' and 'Jesus in the olive grove', copyright © USA and Canada by Hope Publishing Company, Carol Stream, Illinois 60188, USA; copyright © world outside USA and Canada Stainer & Bell Ltd, London; reproduced by permission of Stainer & Bell Ltd, London.

Fred Kaan, 'For the healing of the nations', reproduced by permission of Stainer & Bell Ltd, London.

Albert F. Bayly (1901–84), 'Our father, whose creative love' and 'O Lord of every shining constellation', reprinted by permission of Oxford University Press.

Timothy Dudley-Smith, 'Remember, Lord, the world you made', copyright © USA 1981 by Hope Publishing Company, Carol Stream, Illinois 60188, USA; copyright © 1978 world outside USA Timothy Dudley-Smith.

Bryn Rees, 'Have faith in God, my heart', copyright © Mortydd Rees.

Colin P. Thompson, 'Christian people, raise your song', copyright © Colin P. Thompson.

Richard G. Jones, 'God of concrete, God of steel', copyright © Richard G. Jones.

Ann Phillips, 'Into a world of dark', copyright © United Reformed Church; reproduced by permission.

Luke Connaughton, 'Reap me the earth', published by McCrimmon Publishing Co. Ltd, Great Wakering, Essex.

Tom Colvin, 'Jesu, Jesu, fill us with your love', copyright © 1969 Hope Publishing Company, Carol Stream, Illinois 60188, USA; international copyright secured; all rights reserved; used by permission.

Ian Pitt-Watson, Psalm 139, copyright © in this version Ian Pitt-Watson.

Every effort has been made to establish the copyright holders of all material used and the editors and publishers wish to apologise for any errors or omissions which may have been made.

Notes on the Contributors

David Crystal is Honorary Professor of Linguistics at the University college of North Wales, Bangor.

Geoffrey Cuming was formerly Lecturer in Liturgy at King's College, London, and at Ripon College, Cuddesdon.

F. W. Dillistone was formerly Dean of Liverpool Cathedral and is a Fellow Emeritus of Oriel College, Oxford.

David Jasper is Principal of St Chad's College and Director of the Centre for the Study of Literature and Theology, University of Durham.

R. C. D. Jasper is Dean Emeritus of York Minster and a former Chairman of the Church of England Liturgical Commission.

George A. Kennedy is Paddison Professor of Classics at the University of North Carolina at Chapel Hill.

Peter Mack is Lecturer in English at the University of Warwick.

Daniel J. Sheerin is a Professor in the Department of Modern and Classical Languages, University of Notre Dame.

Martin Warner is Programme Director of the Centre for Research in Philosophy and Literature and a member of the Philosophy Department at Warwick University.

Raymond Warren is Professor of Music at the University of Bristol.

J. R. Watson is Professor of English at the University of Durham.

Introduction

David Jasper and R.C.D. Jasper

Rapid liturgical change in the twentieth century has raised many questions and engendered much discussion, a great deal of which has been blurred by passionate feeling and deep-rooted affection for familiar words and actions. It is right, nevertheless, that people should feel, but also think seriously about the nature and form of their worship of God. This book takes no sides in the debate between liturgical 'traditionalists' and 'reformers', and to read into it any such partiality is to misunderstand its purpose. Its discussions are not conducted within the limited concerns and experience of one Church – the contributors are from many denominations – and are unconcerned, in this context, with particular arguments within particular communities. The range of disciplines represented by the contributors is broad and it reflects the immensely complex and difficult questions which underlie the establishment of any form of words intended to be repeated time and again in the liturgical activity of the Christian Church. Some of the essays are, of necessity, highly technical, while others are more general in purpose. For example, Daniel Sheerin offers a careful and fascinating analysis of the Greek text of the Liturgy of St John Chrysostom, in contrast to more general discussions by F.W. Dillistone and Peter Mack. Thus the focus deliberately changes as a further reminder that the appraisal of liturgical language and rhetoric is neither simple nor uniform.

We need to become aware of the *rhetorical* aspects of both scripture and the early Christian liturgies in order to understand more clearly later liturgical developments, when Churches began to worship God in the vernacular. And these questions of rhetoric remain with us as we face the problems of how the language of worship develops or ought to develop within its own tradition and in the context of our modern world. Remarkably little work has been done in this way, particularly in English.

The context of worship makes heavy demands upon language. Though judgements about it are almost invariably made from the standpoint of aesthetic appeal, as David Crystal points out, liturgical utterances are not primarily designed with an aesthetic motive.

1

Not only are the functions of such language manifold and complex, but its conditions of use are peculiar and always changing. That is why, for example, two of these essays, those by J.R. Watson and Raymond Warren, are directly about music, and one specifically about hymns. The mystery of music to which Professor Warren refers is an intrinsic element in Christian worship, and the adaptation of language to music is neither simple nor obvious. In addition, such language must conform to communal utterance, to dramatic performance and possibly to widely divergent local requirements. Forms of English will be different in the various cultures of east and west.

Nor can liturgy altogether insulate itself from the serious and profound developments in philosophy as they have influenced our understanding of the nature and possibilities of language, utterance and communication. Such philosophical enterprise has deeply affected not only our perception and study of literature, but theology and the articulation of the matter of religion. It was necessary, therefore, to recognise the difficult but unavoidable questions posed by Martin Warner in his essay.

Within the continuum of history and tradition, formal Christian worship must continue to celebrate in word, act and music – by teaching, exhortation and the metaphors of praise and thanksgiving – the Christian belief in salvation in Christ. Yet even as Christians rejoice in their kinship with the Church through the ages, they need also to acknowledge that they celebrate the liturgy in an age of mass-communication and secular literature, and in a growing sense of the world's fragility. There is no such thing as an ideal liturgy. Different things will work for different people in various circumstances. What we do need to consider very carefully, in the particular forms of words, are the linguistic requirements of what we try to express in common. Our subject is patient of no slick and easy answers: its complexity will not be illuminated without serious attention to at least the range of disciplines represented in this volume, and quite certainly many more. These essays can only represent a start.

1

Liturgical Forms in Word and Act

F.W. Dillistone

I

Language

No topic known to me has aroused more sustained interest, debate, theories or enquiries over the past fifty years than that of language. It has come to occupy a central place in virtually every humanistic discipline: philosophy, sociology, anthropology, politics, theology. It has spawned a whole series of relatively new disciplines: linguistics, semantics, semiology, pyscholinguistics. It has assumed major importance in the world of communications systems. Language has come to occupy a crucial role in the relations between the great world powers. Does any particular leader in international affairs really understand what his opposite number is saying, even when receiving all possible assistance from an interpreter?

Liturgy

No topic in the religious sphere has evoked deeper concern than that of liturgical revision. For centuries a particular text seemed adequate for the worshipping needs of a particular community – international, national or denominational. Then the pace of change in the twentieth century began to quicken. The spread of popular education, the movement of peoples through displacements caused by war and technological advance, the dissemination of information by the mass media all led to a desire for interchange of traditions and for fuller participation by all social classes in organised worship. Was the former ideal of a uniform liturgy any longer attainable? Was it desirable? Could not new liturgies be framed

3

such as would express more meaningfully the religious aspirations of those living in new environments and new circumstances?

Language

What kind of language is now under discussion? We naturally think of language as recorded in books, articles, journals and pamphlets. (At the time of writing a printed pamphlet has recently been delivered to every home in Britan intended to deal as simply yet as vividly as possible with the menace of AIDS.) Is this kind of language guaranteed to convey a necessary and unmistakable message to all who can read? Then there is spoken language – the language of rhetoric, of exhortation, of instruction, of description, of warning, of promise. Can this be guaranteed to awaken a proper response in an audience or a fellow-individual? Then there is body-language: movements of arms, hands, legs, eyes, facial muscles. Perhaps no medium has contributed more to the potentialities of this kind of language than television. (Last evening I watched a programme in which three men and two women participated, the subject being a clutch of recently published books. The talk was lively, sometimes critical, sometimes enthusiastic. What was often far more in evidence than the verbal sentiments was the movement of face and arms. Hands in particular accompanied words in an obviously unconscious fashion. Had there been no sound of voices one would still have watched an animated scene in which approval, deprecation, emphasis and questioning were being portrayed.) The essence of successful television is the relaying of drama, and the language of drama is that of bodily activity combined with expressive speech. The language of those presenting the drama needs to find an echo or a resonance in the experience of an audience using the same general language. Speakers and hearers, both possessing the repertoire of a common language, can together progress towards some new apprehension of a common aim – though in a church or theatre the audience is often inert.

Liturgy

The 'liturgy' of an ancient Greek (leitourgia) was a public service – outfitting a ship, production of a drama – performed for the state by a wealthy man . . . Theology is a liturgy in the more usual modern sense, a public ceremonial setting forth, for the corporate participation, the wholeness of the common faith.

Wholeness is a large word: it is not in the attainment of one language. Theology in its inherited sense suffered and caused suffering because it aspired to an unattainable completeness as well as an unattainable accuracy. Theology is complete only as it is enacted in all modes of symbolic speech and act . . . Thus the authority of theology is never in itself but in its use to a service beyond its own decisions. It is offered as liturgy and sacrifice.[1]

According to this judgment theology is constructed, not primarily by means of propositions or dogmatic statements, but rather through liturgy and sacrifice. It is in performing a liturgy at a particular time, in a particular place, in the contingencies of a particular situation, that we 'do' our theology and direct ourselves towards that wholeness which belongs to God Himself.

Language and Liturgy

In a perceptive comment on the development of modern Hebrew during the past century, C.H. Sisson has written:

The violent resuscitation of Hebrew a hundred years ago must have given the language a traumatic new start. How have all the changes of the centuries been reflected in the modern language? No doubt it has, like many other languages, borrowed a host of technical expressions from Anglo Saxon or other contemporary sources. Such developments are superficial. What one would like to know . . . is what was imported into the modern language by the linguistic and other experience of those who learned to speak it. What effect had the new wine on the old bottles? Liturgy is a great preserver of meanings . . . but new people and new times are always pressing on all languages and relentlessly demand subtle changes which it is one of the functions of literature to suggest. The vigour one senses in Amichai's work . . . seems to indicate profound tensions between old words and new meanings.[2]

Liturgy preserves: but 'new people and new times are always pressing on all languages and relentlessly demand subtle changes'. It is this interrelationship between the constant pressure of language changes and the equally constant resistance to change on the part of liturgies that is the general subject of this essay. Nowhere has this interrelationship received more frequent illustration than through the immigration into Canada and the United States of America of representatives of scores of European national cultures during the past two hundred years. In new territories a multiplicity of liturgies has been used and these have often been expressed in and through the languages of their places of origin. Yet gradually the pressures of the English language have made their influence felt in the worship experience of particular Church groups. Older people have clung to the familiar liturgy expressed in what to them has seemed sacred language. Younger people's ties have gradually loosened, especially as they have become integrated into a new educational system. The urge to translate has become increasingly powerful. Often a musical accompaniment remains intact while the new language is adjusted to it. But, to use Sisson's phrase, can the new wine be preserved in old bottles?

One final distinction may be made concerning language in general. At all times and in all places language is the instrument of *connection*. 'Only connect' has become one of the most frequently quoted phrases in modern literature. Yet connection always implies duality. There are languages of *expression* from individuals or groups towards objects in the natural world, beings in the social world or beings in the superhuman world. Similarly there are languages of *impression*, directly or indirectly, from the total environment within which any individual may dwell.

In the former category of communciations are spells, myths and, above all, prayers; in the latter category are covenants, stories and commands. All are examples of communication between humans and their encompassing environments, the direction of the former being outwards, that of the latter being inwards. Moreover, whereas the spokesperson of language may in the first case act as representative of a wider community, in the second a leader will act for God, society or nature in transmitting information or demands to individuals or groups in whatever situation they may be. The roles of priest and prophet have been of crucial importance in transmitting languages in liturgical forms.

II

With all the stirring of interest in language – its origins, its ways of development, its function in communciation and its power to represent reality – there has certainly been no agreement about its *use*, its variant styles and its adequacy to convey meaning. Can language perhaps be viewed as a *game*, with fixed rules but with an infinite variety of possible implementations? Can it be viewed as a *tool*, useful for the accomplishment of certain human tasks but limited by its scope of adjustment to human needs? Can it be viewed as a *weapon*, suitable for human defence or attack against hostile forces, whether subhuman or human or superhuman? What is the function or functions of language in the history of mankind?

As would be generally agreed, it is quite possible to speak of *animal* language. A cat can purr with satisfaction, it can miaow with entreaty, it can hiss with alarm when confronting an enemy. But its forms of language are severely limited. The same is generally true of other animals. Fright, loneliness, separation, sexual desire, aggression, hunger can receive some form of vocal expression. But these expressions appear to be instinctive, the property of particular animals or birds, with no possibilities of development into a wider range of activities or more efficient means of permanent recording. At some stage in the whole evolutionary process the power of humans to speak *symbolically* emerged, that is, the power to use gestures, signals, sounds and displays in order to exercise some kind of control over the natural environment and to initiate some kind of communication with the social environment. Humans, like animals, can exercise *force* in relation to these two environments and this force may take a large variety of forms such as no animal could exert. Far more significantly, however, humans may use *symbolic forms*, whether manual, facial or aural, to effect immediate purposes and to develop these by constant trial and error. Gradually a symbolic world is created in which the possibilities of relations to the natural world and the social world become unlimited in extent, symbolism being in constant tension with the static, the fixed, the one-track, the final equilibrium, the lifeless certainty.

However there are clearly variations in any spatial environment and, still more, temporal changes in the realm of social relationships. These variations have had a profound effect on human efforts to exercise control over the conditions in which men and women live. The primary concern is indeed to *live*, to *survive*, and this means obtaining an adequate supply of food and drink. Two sources for each of these may be found. For tribes which have come to be known as 'gatherers', a fertile area provides water and land products: fruit, vegetation and roots. For tribes known as 'hunters', there must be a constant search for some kind of reservoir or stream to provide water. In addition a never-ceasing hunt ensues for whatever animals may inhabit a particular area. This fundamental division between the settled and the mobile, those dependent on a section of land and those dependent on a species of animal, those with a regular supply of water and those whose journeys must always be oriented towards some hoped-for source: this dual character of early humanity is of outstanding importance for its effects not only upon sheer survival but also upon the symbolic language systems which came to be developed within each social context. The gatherers were essentially centripetal communities, concentrating their desires and hopes upon the constituents of their bounded home; the hunters were essentially centrifugal communities, ever stretching out towards new adventures and new experiences, more at risk, less able to rely upon the regularities of a more settled habitat.

I have made the distinction which, as far as we know, appeared in the very earliest history of the human race: the distinction between settlers devoted to a particular land area and hunters going out to unfamiliar regions and unknown experiences in search of subsistence for themselves and their families. Yet I recognise that such a distinction cannot be regarded as *absolute*. From any enclosed region some may venture forth in search of the new: a roaming band may discover a settlement providing a permanent residence for at least some of its members. Human history discloses innumerable instances of accommodations and mixtures and mutual influences between the more settled and the more mobile, between the happily established and the hopeful migrants. My concern is to discount the idea of any *unitary* pattern of human existence or of human symbolic forms. Languages of all kinds are sometimes virtually static, sometimes dynamic, sometimes the reflection of a settled existence on a long established tract of land, sometimes the consequence of movement towards a goal conceived as more desirable and more promising than anything previously experienced. The tension between the relative continuity of a cyclic return and the relative novelty of penetration into unknown territory belongs to any comprehensive understanding of human history, and it is this which I am eager to illustrate by reference to the worshipping activities of humans. In certain cases these have developed into seemingly invariant liturgical forms, while in other cases the whole emphasis has lain on free expression within a minimum of liturgical uniformity.

III

I return to the question of symbolic forms within the two types of society that I have briefly described. Within the community able to survive through dependence on the resources of a particular territory, there tends to be a sense of regularity, of repetition, promoted by the regular movements of the heavenly bodies, by dependence on predictable rainfall and by the rhythm of the annual seasons. Humans and the natural order are thus closely allied. The dance is a natural expression of solidarity: so too is the procession to the accompaniment of drums. There is continuity from generation to generation as rhythmic chants are intoned. The spoken language relates to the continuing processes of regular living: birth, puberty, marriage, death; and, with the development of agriculture, to sowing, irrigating and harvesting. Common speech is used to deal with these recurring events in the life of a society, the major variation being the invocation of the gods to share in and to prosper the labours of those responsible for the welfare of the society.

In contrast to the sedentary, repetitive pattern characteristic of a settled society, there exists another pattern expressed by an outward-moving goal-seeking social group. The motive for going out into the unknown may be born of sheer necessity, the need to find fresh food and drink in an area where climatic conditions or dangerous animals have made existence hazardous. Or it may be the result of an awareness of booty to be acquired through stratagem or cunning. In barren or in inhospitable places man's chief rival is the animal, and his conquest of the rival became infinitely more possible through the discovery of the means of producing fire. In the hunt all regular and smoothly ordered methods were of no avail. A sudden appearance, an unexpected confrontation, a period of suspense, use of crude weapons – all found a place in a successful hunt. And when the prey had been captured the opportunity came to celebrate symbolically by dramatic reconstruction of the contest, by song or by story-telling. The great event had been made possible, it was generally assumed, by divine assistance. The language used would be partly that of shouts and cries in the midst of the struggle, partly thanksgiving and celebration of divine power when success had been attained.

The double character of ancient societies is illustrated by their languages, which may be either relatively smooth, rhythmic, celebrating recurrent processes, or relatively sharp, ejaculatory, celebrating some notable event in which the possibilities of life and death seem equally to hang in the balance. There were indeed plenty of heroic episodes in Ancient Greece, rivalries and tragedies. But these came to be set against a background of an equable climate, regular seasons and the fruits of labour in the fields. Work on the land never ceased. Mediterranean societies could rely on the natural cycle to bring them sufficient to eat and drink and even to allow them to enjoy leisure pursuits. It was a very different story for the Hebrews, who seemed always to be exposed to dangers of one kind or another. Drought and floods, storm and fire, raids by hostile tribes and subjugation by imperial powers meant that the Hebrews could never enjoy a quiet existence in their own land. Their astonishing achievement was that of reciting orally and recording in more permanent form their adventures and crises and above all the acts of Yahweh by which He had delivered his chosen people out of bondage or defeat. The literature encoded in the Old Testament is totally different from that of Greece. In the former there is promise, expectancy, disappointment, disaster, renewal of faith and hope; in the latter the regular passing of the seasons with an unbroken sequence of life on the land led to the production of writings embodying the knowledge acquired by interpreters of the natural and social orders, within which a civilised existence became possible.

IV

A brief description of the life of religion in Greece and Israel with special reference to liturgy may illustrate this contrast. Of fundamental importance in both cases was the correlation between the pattern of social living and the style of the language which members of the society used. This correlation is one which runs through the whole record of human history. There may be a recurring pattern of actions with a mythological accompaniment of words, spoken or chanted or sung; or there may be sudden, unforeseen events, celebrated by words or reverie, expressing surprise or wonder. Recurring ritual actions, together with sacred words expressing the regularities of the natural order, represent one possibility; verbal recall of a surprising event, together with dramatic action confirming the significance of the event, constitutes the other possibility. The slaying and eating of an animal appears originally to have been an experience bonding together communities drawn from either gatherers or hunters. But whereas the gatherers discovered common bonds through a continuous supply of the fruits of the earth and of domestic animals and thereafter linked this experience with a mythical story of heavenly provision for their needs, the hunters discovered their bonding as they strove together to track down their prey, always hoping that the record of what had been done on an earlier occasion could encourage them to make further efforts. Thus, in religious theory and practice, there has been a signal divide. On the one hand ritual action and vocal prayer constantly repeated; on the other hand a story (recording some surprising event) and dramatic celebration. In the one case religious exercises have been directed towards superhuman powers whose nature has been revealed in and through the wonderful constancies of the created order: birth and death, seedtime and harvest, the regular supplies of water and the control of fire. In the other case they have been directed towards the power who has guarded a particular people through the vicissitudes of their historic experiences, sustaining them by surprising deliverances in the past and promises for the future, such deliverances and promises being dramatised by means of ritual activities.

Among the Greeks, Walter Burkert has affirmed, 'the essence of the sacred act, which is hence often simply termed doing or making sacred or working sacred things, is in Greek practice a straightforward and far from miraculous process: the slaughter and consumption of a domestic animal for a god'. He proceeds to give a vivid description of the sacrificial ritual. The victim is to be offered within a strictly defined circle; there are ceremonies of purification by water; all participate in throwing barley groats from the sacrificial basket before the actual slaying of the animal.

The ritual of animal sacrifice varies in detail according to the local ancestral custom, but the fundamental structure is identical and clear: animal sacrifice is ritualized slaughter, followed by a meat meal. In this the rite as a sign of the sacred is in particular the preparation, the beginning on the one hand and the subsequent restitution on the other: sacralisation and desacralisation about a central act of killing attended with weapons, blood, fire, and a shrill cry.[3]

The whole movement is circular or cyclical. The circular site, the devotees dancing around the central altar, the smoke curling skywards, the rhythm of slaying and feasting. Everything is designed to promote and stabilise a settled tribal community. 'The order of life, a social order, is constituted in the sacrifice through irrevocable acts; religion and every-day existence interpenetrate so completely that every community, every order must be founded through a sacrifice'.[4] And what was true of Greece was equally true of Rome. The founding of a house, the launching of a military expedition, the celebration of victory: every notable event had to be marked by an appropriate sacrifice. In course of time variations arose concerning the portions of the sacrifice shared by gods and their devotees. But in general the essential act of religion in the Mediteranean world was the offering of *animal sacrifice*. It was the task of a priest to preside over and carry out the details of every such ceremony.

The ritual *action* was central. What then can be said about accompanying *words*? Did the words recited express the feelings of the participants? Only, it appears, when at the moment of the actual killing blood began to flow. Only then did the women of the company emit a shrill cry. It was the priest who at an earlier stage recited an invocation, a desire or a vow. This was essentially a *prayer*, an address to a god or heavenly being such as would appropriately designate the nature of the critical action being performed. After his vivid description of sacrifice and blood rituals, of the offering of first fruits and of vows, Burkert has this to say about Prayer:

Libation, sacrifice, first-fruit offerings – there are the acts which define piety. But each of these acts must be attended by *the right word*. Any wrong, evil, coarse or complaining word would be harm, *blasphemia*, and so the good speech, *euphemia* of the participants consists in the first instance in holy silence. Out of the silence there rises up the apostrophe to an Opposite, an invocation and entreaty, the prayer.[5]

Thus in Greek religion the primary and all important element was the ritual *act*, taking the form of *sacrifice*, normally of an animal but, with the development of agriculture, sometimes of fruit or cereals. This was accompanied by words of invocation and supplication, words which hardened into formulae which could be repeated or chanted by those participating in the ritual. But I find no suggestion that a *story* was ever rehearsed or recorded at the time when the ritual was being performed. There were cries, ejaculatory prayers, even repetitive formulae, and in some sense this was a *liturgy*. It was performed by a priest in the presence of bystanders, the wording corresponding to the particular god invoked and the particular result to be effected by the worship-act. Perhaps one could use the term liturgy to describe the total performance, but with the proviso that the sacrificial action constituted the central moment of the liturgy, words accompanying it being more varied and related to the actual need and desires of the worshippers. The pattern of ritual act accompanied by a set formula became even more regulative within Roman religious practice. Thus Cyril Bailey summarises its character in the following way:

> In all the records we have left of the old religion the salient feature . . . is exactness of ritual. All must be performed not merely 'decently and in order' but with the most scrupulous care alike for every detail of the ceremonial itself and for the surrounding circumstances. The omission or misplacement of a single word in the formula, the slightest sign of resistance on the part of the victim, any disorder among the bystanders, even the accidental squeak of a mouse, are sufficient to vitiate the whole ritual and necessitate its repetition from the very beginning. One of the main functions of the Roman priesthood was to preserve intact the tradition of formulae and ritual, and, when the magistrate offered sacrifice for the state, the pontifex stood at his side and dictated the formula which he must use. Almost the oldest specimens of Latin which we now possess is the song of the Salii, the priests of Mars, handed on from generation to generation and repeated with scrupulous care even though the priests themselves, as Quintillian assures us, had not the least notion what it meant.[6]

In all recorded examples of Mediterranean religion, then, the

outstanding feature was the centrality of the sacrificial action. How
this came about remains matter for speculation. What seems certain is that humans asserted their superiority over and control of
animals either by capturing them, and holding them in thrall, or by
actually wounding and killing them. A carcase could then be taken
(the blood being manipulated) and subjected to fire before the
appropriate parts were eaten by members of the community. With
the development of agriculture, particularly in the Mediterranean
world, there came the transition from a bloody sacrifice to the
unbloody offering of cereals and wine. However, the action still
remained that of sacrificial offering and the elements so offered
could still keep the associations with animal life (flesh and blood)
which had so long dominated the religious consciousness of
human worshippers. The background pattern of Christian liturgy
in the Western European world is thus derived from the religion of
Greece and Rome, in which sacrifice was the central and essential
ritual act and in which prayers and thanksgivings, though a necessary feature, only attained formal shape as the community itself
took shape. It then expressed its worship in words growing out of
and related to its own structure as a primarily *agrarian* society
whose worship was directed to the God of all creation, holding in
His hands the issues of life and death.

V

The background of Hebrew religion was very different from that of
Greece and Rome. An initial reading of the Old Testament is likely
to impress the reader by records of sacrifice being offered and, as
in the book of Leviticus, being strictly regulated in a variety of
forms – sin-offering, guilt-offering, thank-offering, whole burnt-
offering, peace-offering. But the question arises as to how far these
are regulations designed (after contacts with other peoples) by a
priestly caste to reinforce their own status and to centralise a
legally imposed culture and how far they were ever really intended
to apply to a pilgrim people which owed its very identity to
patriarchs and prophets whose primary concern was to promote a
word-culture rather than a *nature*-culture. Patriarchs and prophets
were essentially men of the open pastures and desert places,
shepherds and dwellers in tents, rather than occupants of settled
fields and villages. They had visions, it is true, of some future

haven in which they could enjoy rest and security, but these visions never gained more than a temporary realisation. On their journeyings they might erect an altar and offer a sacrifice, but these acts of worship never constituted a regular celebration of some recurring ritual pattern. The concern of Israel's leaders, whether patriarch or prophet, was to bring all members of their select community into a willing dependence upon and obedience to the Divine Overlord who had first called them into existence and who had destined them to fulfil His righteous purpose. So in their treks and wanderings the all-important feature of their social life was the *word*, the promise, the call to go forward under divine protection towards the fulfilment of their rightful destiny.

Response to the divine call is, in the Old Testament, represented by the term translated *covenant*. This is a remarkable verbal designation of a social arrangement in which a god and the members of a community are bonded together through *words* rather than primarily through ritual actions. The words were indeed designed to summon to action, but it was action of an ethical character, action based upon social relationships rather than upon material necessities. In desert places, or in what the Exodus story called the wilderness, there was no possibility of dependence upon regular organic resources. Only through agreements and compacts and mutual exchanges could a non-landed society survive. Here were the beginnings of that covenant-existence which has been the formative influence in the life of the Jewish people, a feature which has at times been perverted into a rigid legalism or a grasping commercialism but which at its best has made it possible for societies to walk together in the pursuit of a common goal.

In the classical examples of covenant-making recorded in the Old Testament, bonding through words and verbal promises was sealed and confirmed by some kind of sacramental action. It might be a bodily mark establishing membership in the covenant-community, it might be participation in a joint covenant-meal, it might be a dramatic remembrance of benefits formerly bestowed upon those within the covenant. Whatever its nature, a ritual action followed upon a verbal recital of that which the act was intended to confirm. Members of the community were summoned to an awareness of their duties and destiny within the provisions of the covenant; they responded through a verbal assent and, on appropriate occasions, through a dramatic re-enactment of the genesis of their calling. For the Hebrews an intensely dramatic remembrance of their call and liberation was performed annually through Passover, while through their weekly Sabbath the covenant could be similarly renewed.

Probably the other most notable examples in history of communities regarding themselves as chosen to fulfil a divine purpose and to that end relying almost exclusively on their marching orders, the directions communicated through prophetic leaders to guide them in their endeavours, were, in the sixth century AD, the dynamic movement of Muhammad's faithful followers and, in the seventeenth century, the passage of the Pilgrim Fathers and their families across the Atlantic Ocean. In each case there was almost barren territory on which to encamp and establish some kind of foothold; in each case there were hostile natives who must be subjugated or dispersed or liquidated; in each case there was a holy *book* whose injunctions bore ultimate authority for social life. The nature of the physical world and the resources of the land were regarded as largely irrelevant to the pursuit of the ordained mission. As long as nature could be made subservient to human needs, all that mattered was to obey the divine will and to live in loyal relationship with one another.

For Islam's development over the centuries the indispensable guide was Muhammad's legacy, the holy Quran in the Arabic language. This specified undeviating rules for religious observance and for social conduct: the confession of faith, the daily discipline of prayer, fasting, pilgrimage and almsgiving. These obligations are related to the *time*-cycle but have little reference to *land*-culture. Similarly the Puritan New Englanders depended unreservedly on the Holy Bible and its instructions, especially as far as the organisation of their new societies was concerned. But forests had to be felled, the land exploited and the search for daily food carried on relentlessly. The Book, it was believed, held all the secrets of living under divine blessing. There was little need for sacramental observances except in so far as it was man's proper duty to acknowledge God's bounty and to give thanks by word, by charity and by the enjoyment of common meals.

Other examples of religious systems in which the focus of attention, of reverence and of authority has been a holy book may be seen in Sikhism, in Mormonism and in Fundamentalist sects of Reformed Protestantism. In all these, as in Islam and in orthodox Judaism, a fixed canon was rigidly defined, this being regarded as the unique revelation of God through one or more prophets. The revelation in each case related to the social experiences of a particular people as preserved in writing by faithful scribes. In worship exercises the book was given all honour and devotion, its words being recited or paraphrased or explained or directed to particular human needs: the *liturgy* was primarily a recital of passages from the holy book interspersed with human responses in prayer, in confession and in song. The pattern was essentially that of proclamation or declaration, with responsive speaking or singing. Sacramental *actions* must be regarded as secondary (for example, in Reformed Christendom, baptism, the Lord's Supper and the offering of alms). The *Word of God* was primary and the purpose of the liturgy of the people was to honour that Word, to listen to its reiterated proclamation, to respond to it with thanksgiving and penitence and intercession, and to resolve to put into practice what its commands required.

All this is derived from a view of religion as primarily the response to divine orders in the social experience of humankind. This is not to deny that the world was created by a divine artificer or that the world's processes are controlled by divine wisdom. But this is not the primary concern. To be fully human it is necessary for men and women to *communicate* with one another and to establish structures for their common welfare. Intercommunication and structures for civilised living depend for their realisation on *language*, interpreted in a wide sense (that is, through gestures, through artefacts, through visual aids, through music and above all through spoken words). Language is essential for human intercommunication and so for the upbuilding of social structures. Until some two hundred years ago it was assumed (however much it might be neglected and occasionally denied) that such communication and upbuilding were dependent upon *divine* activity and inspiration. Humans might discover new ways in which this divine overlordship was being exercised, but they did not in general doubt that a divine order had been established in the world for all humankind and that it was for humans to accept this order and to seek to adjust their behaviour to it.

This, I have suggested, was true of the social order and of the attempt by the strictly monotheistic religions to relate themselves to the divine purpose by learning about it through His *Word* and by responding to that revelation by means of language or languages stirred into expression by social experiences. (The rise of the European nations and the development of their vernacular languages represented not only political but also religious movements.) The vital questions were: What is God's purpose in all these changes and how is it to be expressed verbally in commands and promises? But the vast and altogether revolutionary change began to take place when the leaders of society decided that it was within their power to create their own covenants and constitutions, to frame them in their own languages, to amend them as occasion required and to allow the structure of society to be formed not by the authoritative word of God but through debate and discussion couched in terms produced in ordinary life and conforming to the constraints of human activities.

VI

I have focused attention on human language as a tool or weapon, on its functional use and its corporate employment. What does this entail for *liturgy*? As we conceive liturgy today it denotes an ordered pattern of words and actions, sometimes relatively fixed and invariable, sometimes more flexible and allowing for many variations. It is possible to concentrate on the actual verbal qualities of liturgy as expressed in written (or printed) form. A definite pattern is presented and it is then expected that a community will follow this prescription in its regular worshipping activities.

But although the prescription of written verbal forms and rubrics is valuable and may seem to be essential for the proper ordering of a congregation's worship, I think that it is legitimate to stress the importance of a *speech community* for the creating and sustaining of intercommunication. The corollary would seem to be that in every provision for liturgical revision the first necessity is that of being sensitive to the *speech community* which is helping to create the liturgical form and for whose more vital worship the form is intended. This implies that there is a constant dialectic within a speech community, a dialectic in which the members create communication and are at the same time created by the communication.

Herein surely lies the central problem of language and liturgy. The aim of those who formulate liturgies is to create a pattern of words and actions which will faithfully re-present and recall patterns of a formal nature handed down by a leading figure in the past. This leader has bequeathed an acceptable pattern. The question is whether the pattern is to be fixed exactly, using the best possible translation into the language of the worshippers; or whether it is to be regarded as so sacred that it may only be used just as it is; or whether the major aim is to be to relate the original words to the context in which their modern recital is to take place. In Western Christianity, once the words of institution had been translated into Latin and had been made central within a prayer of thanksgiving, the tendency was to regard this total prayer as so sacred that it must not be altered in any respect. On behalf of all the worshippers a sacred official (the priest) was authorised to offer a sacrifice (liturgical action) and to accompany it with a sacred formula (liturgical words). The words were to be in a fixed Latin form, the whole procedure being regarded as effective on behalf of the people in their relations with God. They might not understand the words contained in the formula; they might not apprehend the full significance of the manual actions performed by the celebrant; but in accordance with the long tradition of Roman religion, acts and words together could be deemed to effect whatever particular outcome was being sought in the relations between humans and God.

Writing about Roman religion before the advent of Christianity J.H.W.G. Liebeschuetz has said:

> Roman life was accompanied by innumerable ritual acts, each of which had to be accompanied by precisely the right form of words. The implication is that words have power. This implication may be rejected by the wisest as far as their individual beliefs are concerned, but collectively all men have always had confidence in the power of words, even though sometimes unaware of it. Belief in the power of religious words was maintained by a complex of feelings, aesthetic, associational and even empirical, the sense that Rome had fared well while these formulae had been used.[7]

This basic conviction in ancient Roman religion was, it seems to me, carried over into the Roman Christian Church as it became the religious guardian and sustainer of the Roman Empire. Wherever Latin held sway as the official, legal, scholastic language, there the ecclesiastical liturgy was performed according to the pattern established by authority. Action and Word were regarded as of universal efficacy, to be performed on behalf of the people to secure their eternal welfare.

This conviction has been steadfastly maintained within Roman Catholicism until comparatively recently. It received a severe challenge in the sixteenth century, but the Counter Reformation sternly resisted liturgical change. Those nations whose languages were deeply influenced by the Latin tradition were most successful in rejecting change, while others, in the course of promoting new vernacular forms, still drew heavily on the classical Latin pattern. Not until the twentieth century and the reforms inaugurated by Vatican II did a revolutionary change take place, with the emergence not only of the use of the vernacular in the central service of worship but also of actions by priests and layfolk by which the essentially corporate nature of the Eucharist could be openly displayed. Today, for instance, in the island of Gozo with which I am familiar and where the mainly agricultural population retains a deep allegiance to the Church, Mass is celebrated in Maltese (the only Arabic-based European language) by the priest facing the people over a simple table and performing the sacred actions in their view. This revolutionary change has led, I am informed, to no resistance or corporate objection. Words and actions of priest and people together are the means by which the ordinary words and actions of this island people are lifted heavenwards and sanctified.

Amidst all the changes that we associate with the Reformation, one thing stands out clearly. It is that pre-eminently in England and in Germany there was a marvellous enthusiasm for expressing the new consciousness of national identity and destiny in the vernacular. In poetry, in drama, in worship, in song, the language of the people found ever fresh outlets and there were not lacking men of genius to create distinctive forms through which the vernacular could be expressed. In England it was Cranmer with his *Book of Common Prayer*; in Germany it was Luther with his translation of the Bible. In both countries – and indeed in other countries where Reformers were in the ascendant – the major concern was to establish a form of worship in which the nature of sacrificial action could be re-interpreted and in which the words of the Bible could be given fullest possible prominence. The central action of the community was to be that of feeding upon a sacrifice once made, not that of offering sacrifice anew; the central speech of the community was to be that of the Bible in the vernacular, not that of legends and stories of saints. Any reading of Reformation formularies indicates how strong was the influence of the vernacular, of the printing press and of the media expressing national aspirations.

The use of the English language has never been superseded in the past four hundred years, but in the twentieth century determined efforts have been made to revise the liturgy. Partly this has been due to a growing concern that language should be that of the modern 'speech community' rather than that of sixteenth-century scholars; partly it has been due to a revised understanding of the nature of sacrifice in a fully Christian context. Moreover the heavy stress on uniformity within the Church of England has been relaxed and the same has been true of dogmatic formularies in Germany. The question necessarily arises whether there is any longer a place for uniformity or for unchanging liturgical language. In a period of mass media, with an immense variety of language forms being heard over the air and a wide variety of actions and events being seen through television, what place is there for any central authority to determine forms of worship? A particular Christian denomination, for example, may be represented in a number of national contexts and its liturgy may be translated into the language of each. But within every nation there exist wide varieties of vocabularies, dialects and interpretations. How can there be a wide consensus either in language or in ritual form? Even the media of radio and television in Britain are constantly relaying messages in *four* distinct forms and, although there may be an occasional attempt to concentrate on a single event, in general broadcasts are adapted to the known interests and needs of a sectional community and expressed through their languages and activities.

Thus we are made constantly aware of a double movement in the world today. On the one side there is the movement towards a global uniformity expressed through scientific means and purveying scientific information. In every nation efforts are being made to obtain knowledge of the material world and to employ that knowledge for the control of forces in the natural environment. The fundamental language is that of mathematics; the fundamental activity is that of the manipulation of energy by electronic means. On the other side there is the movement towards an ever widening diffusion of human speech and action through the interaction of cultural traditions. These interactions produce both creative co-operation and internecine struggle. The recurring question is how the resources of the material order are to be used: in ways making for construction or in ways leading to destruction? Even in the religious world (which many wish to be independent of the natural and scientific order) a basic ambiguity cannot be avoided. Is God to be worshipped through a liturgy language of which is the unchangeable, bound to the demands of the natural world, and through actions which are prescribed, uniform, bound to what appear to be undeviating natural laws? Or is God to be worshipped through a liturgy ever open and sensitive to changes in the human response to ultimate reality and ever willing to express such a response through a redemption of that reality and through a transformation of corporate activity? The most effective safeguard against absolute liturgical uniformity is to be found in communication, at whatever cost, within a living 'speech community' and in co-operation directed towards some constructive end rather than in a rivalry directed towards the destruction of the stranger.

VII

I shall finally attempt to draw together the enquiries I have made concerning the use of language and particularly its employment in liturgical activities. I want to summarise my conclusions by linking them with the earliest division which anthropologists have made in their survey of human history: the division between gatherers and hunters, between the centripetal and centrifugal, between what I propose to call the dominantly *feminine* urge to draw together into a centre, a hearth, a nest, a home, an ordered system, and the dominantly *masculine* urge to adventure outwards, to anticipate, to seek a better location, a desired treasure, a greater exercise of power. Focusing on liturgy, I shall speak of a liturgy in the round and a liturgy on the road.

Liturgy in the Round

It is scarcely possible to imagine a time when the daily existence of humans has not been dangerous. There have always been hostile forces, most obviously animals, human strangers and superhuman spirit-powers. Even today every human community is concerned with *defence* and with the establishment of some kind of protective wall which can be effective in dealing with any sudden aggression. Within some kind of circular order, providing relative security, humans can share the fruits of the earth, can begin to build shelters, can promote an *esprit de corps* by song and dance, and can maintain continuity with ancestors whose spirits still surround them. The whole aim is to preserve unity and continuity, an aim which can be achieved only by sustaining friendly relations with superhuman powers which are believed to be constantly active in human affairs.

Such an early pattern of existence came to far more extended expression through the development of agriculture and the resultant construction of settlements near water sources in order to make possible the growing, tending and storing of crops. This form of human activity was still centripetal but could now be regarded as part of a far wider circular movement. Sun and moon, the stars and planets, winter and summer, birth and death, all belonged to one vast circular movement with which humans could identify themselves in work, in leisure and in worship. Thus the whole pattern of earthly activities could be regarded as the earthly mirror (or perhaps shadow) of the heavenly cycle. It was incumbent on humans to express their own conformity with the heavenly cycle through a liturgy in which gestures and vocal accompaniments could be combined. In short, offerings through ordered actions and appointed words constituted the pattern of liturgy in the round, not only in pre-Christian agricultural societies but also in those societies which, accepting the Christian faith, continued to direct their worship through ritual actions and words which linked them to the rhythmic order of nature and the activity of God Himself. After the Incarnation of the Divine Son, gestural and verbal tools have been used by humans to express and re-express, to celebrate and re-celebrate, to perform continuously a dramatic re-presentation on earth of the divine activity which sustains the whole created order in heaven and which was supremely revealed through the outward manifestation within humanity and so within the earthly scene of the Divine Logos, the One who unfolds the meaning of the total divine economy.

Liturgy on the Road

In spite of the dangerous character of human life and the natural instinct to establish communities within protective walls – a cave, a wall of fire, a wall of stone, a wall of water, even today a proposed wall impenetrable by ballistic missiles – there has always been another urge to leave behind the safe and the settled centre and to go into the unknown in search of some anticipated treasure: a new land, a new source of livelihood, a new kind of society, a new kind of freedom to *trade*. If there are dangers for those who seek to defend familiar territory and established life-styles, there are equally dangers for non-conformists who break with the accustomed round. The career of Abraham and his descendants has been perhaps the supreme wonder of human history, for it has provided the paradigm for pioneering and reforming groups ever since. 'By faith Abraham obeyed when he was called to go out to a place which he was to receive as an inheritance and he went out, not knowing where he was to go. By faith he sojourned in the land of promise, as in a foreign land' (Hebrews 11: 8–9, RSV). 'Called, obeyed, inheritance, not knowing, sojourned, promise, foreign': all these describe a man on the move, trekking, uncertain of the immediate, yet embracing the future, believing that something better lay in store, ultimately braving all manner of hazards and testings, yet enduring because (like Moses later) 'seeing him who is invisible'.

Can there be a liturgy on the road? Only, I think, when there is consciousness of a call, a challenge, a promise, a hope. Obedience to such a call requires action and celebration. The *action* is comparable to walking, a steady movement towards a destination. For Jesus it meant setting his face steadfastly towards Jerusalem while still on the road. When Jerusalem came into sight he wept over it but still went on until the city seemed to destroy all anticipation and hope. But it was not the final destruction: others began joining themselves with him on the road to Emmaus and the future. A new liturgy was being celebrated, from the past to the future, from the failure of all hope to the prospect of a new mission in which a liturgy of God's saving acts would be recorded through word and song.

Such a liturgy, while seeking to bear faithful witness to the gospel of Jesus' death and resurrection, must always seek a new language (as in the great vernacular translations of the sixteenth century) and new hymns (as in the outbursts of hymnody in Germany and England in the seventeenth century) and once again new languages (as in the era of Bible translation in the nineteenth century) and new forms of popular preaching (as in the late nineteenth and early twentieth centuries) and new adaptations to the techniques of the mass media (as in the twentieth century).

There are many dangers on the road, as Christian found in *The Pilgrim's Progress*, but the goal is the Heavenly City and changes of human language must be accompanied by changes in liturgical forms if life on the road is to remain in dialectical relationship with life in the round. The writer of the Epistle to the Hebrews held both together with amazing dexterity. There remains a sabbath *rest* for the people of God under the great high priest who has passed through the heavens; yet our only safety lies in getting on the road and running with patience the race that is set before us, looking unto Jesus, the pioneer and perfecter of our faith. Christian liturgy cannot be monochrome. It employs language in the round and language on the road. Through a process of describing and re-describing, of enacting and re-enacting, of forming and re-forming, through this dialectical process language and liturgy and the society to which they belong avoid the equilibrium of death and discover ever new sources of ongoing life.

Notes

1. John W. Dixon Jr, *The Physiology of Faith* (New York, 1979) pp. 209f.
2. C.H. Sisson, *London Review of Books*, 18 December 1986, p. 22. (Review of C. Block and S. Mitchell, *Selected Poetry of Yehude Amichai*, 1986).
3. Walter Burkert, *Greek Religion: Archaic and Classical* (Oxford, 1985) p. 57.
4. Ibid, p. 59.
5. Ibid, p. 73.
6. C. Bailey, *The Religion of Ancient Rome* (London, 1921) p. 24.
7. J.H.W.G. Liebeschuetz, *Continuity and Change in Roman Religion* (Oxford, 1979) p. 35.

2

The Rhetoric of the Early Christian Liturgy

George A. Kennedy

Much has been written about the historical conditions which encouraged, influenced or impeded the spread of Christianity in the early centuries of the Roman empire; much has also been written about the influence of Jewish and classical thought upon Christian theology and ethics, and about the influence of Roman administrative organisations on the ecclesiastical structure of the Church. Somewhat less has been said about external influences which may have shaped the forms or reception of the early Christian liturgy. Yet it seems likely that persons converted to Christianity brought with them expectations and assumptions, probably largely unvoiced, which affected their attitude towards and understanding of the new religion and which conversely may have influenced some actual practices and rituals of Christianity. Certainly Jews converted to Christianity brought with them expectations about worship developed within the synagogue, and it was indeed in the synagogues and within Jewish worship that some of the important utterances of Jesus, Paul and other apostles were voiced. Can we discover anything about how gentiles may have understood or reacted to the liturgy? A possible approach comes from the discipline of rhetoric, which pervaded the Greek-speaking world and which in recent years has provided productive insights into the study of the Bible and early Christian writings. The objective of this essay is to suggest some possible phenomena which those interested in liturgical questions might wish to explore in greater depth than can be done here. Both the Reformation and our own time have seen the liturgy affected by rhetorical forces outside the Church, and it is not unlikely that such forces existed in ancient times as well.

This is not the place to try to examine the many problems met by scholars in describing the evolution of the Christian liturgy. It is clear that practices differed in different places. In Bithynia in the early second century Pliny the Younger seems to have found the Christians meeting at dawn on Sunday to sing an antiphonal hymn to Christ and to bind themselves *sacrimento* not to steal or commit adultery or take false oaths or deny a debt (*Epistle* 10:96). Pliny does not mention reading of the scriptures or preaching, and it is not clear if the group partakes of the Eucharist or if that comes later with the communal meal, which he also mentions. Paul had forecast a need to separate the Eucharist from the *agape* (1 Corinthians 11:29–34), and that development certainly occurred either in the late first or early second century. Pliny of course did not personally see or fully understand the Christian service, and he thought of it as analogous to the meeting of a club or guild, something much distrusted by Roman officials as subversive.

The earliest account of the liturgy in any detail occurs in the *First Apology* of Justin Martyr, written in the middle of the second century. Justin describes the rite of baptism (chapter 65) and the liturgy of the Sunday service (chapter 67). The elements of the latter are the assembling of the congregation from the city and outlying districts, the reading of the 'memoirs' of the apostles (gospels, but not necessarily our canon) or the writings of the prophets, 'as long as there is time'; then the one who presides speaks, admonishing and exhorting the imitation 'of these fine things'. After that the congregation stands and offers prayers. The administration of the Eucharist then follows, together with prayers and thanksgiving. All say 'Amen', and the service ends with a collection of contributions for the poor and needy. Though in the reading of scripture, followed by moral exhortation, there is certainly a similarity to Jewish synagogue services, there is no reading of the Pentateuch. The preaching is derived from the texts and to that extent is homiletic, but its function seems to be moral instruction (*paraenesis*).[1] This can be assumed to involve some degree of exegesis, depending on the text chosen, as well as paraphrase. Nothing is said about singing.

The basic features may be divided into two parts. One, Jewish in origin, is the reading of a text and its explication and application by a speaker; the other is the ritual re-enactment of and sharing in the Lord's Supper. The two parts are already found in the apostolic period in Acts 2:42, though the punctuation of the King James Version at this point wrongly suggests three parts: 'in the apostle's doctrine and fellowship, in breaking bread, and in prayers'. For the Eucharist too there are Jewish precedents in the Passover celebration, but also a resemblance to mystery religions of the classical and near-eastern world, such as the Eleusinian mysteries in Greece and banquets with the gods celebrated in Greek and Roman cities. There is little similarity to official pagan cults, which consisted of a procession, the dedication of sacrificial animals, their slaughter and examination of the entrails by priests. Though pagan ceremonies included chants and hymns, and often ended with feasting, they did not include the reading of texts or preaching, and the objective was to appease the god, not to instruct the onlookers in how to live.

For non-Jews the formal experience closest to belonging to a Christian community was going to school. In the time of the Roman empire elementary and secondary education was available in Greek or Latin or both in every town; by the second half of the second century it was at least partially subsidised by local town councils.[2] We do not know what percentage of the free population had formal education, but the evidence from inscriptions and papyri is that basic literacy was very widespread, even among humble people. Given Roman hostility to any kind of club or special-interest organisation, school was the only communal experience for the average individual, at least before entering military service. What he or she (for girls could receive elementary education) found in school was an authoritative teacher, the *grammaticus*, prepared to enforce his rules with the whip or the rod or in the final analysis to cast the student out into ignorance and darkness. The method was everywhere the same: the teacher read out the texts of classical writers – the Homeric poems in Greek, or the *Aeneid* in Latin, or other literary works – , explained the grammar and meaning, word by word, and told the student what to imitate and what not to imitate in the text. The students copied what he said onto their waxed tablets and memorised and recited it, and they took turns reading aloud from the text for the teacher's criticism. Everything was done aloud, often in a sing-song, almost antiphonal way. Much attention was given to memorising. The schools were the only secular institution in which there is an analogy to the regular recitation of a text from memory, such as a psalm or a creed in Christian worship.

Progress in elementary school was slow: learning the letters, then the syllables, then the words and their inflexion, then connected passages; but after a few years the students began exercises in composition, what were called *progymnasmata*.[3] The easiest exercise was the fable. The teacher read or told a simple fable, such as one by Aesop, and explained it. The students then wrote up the fable in their own words and drew the moral. The scriptural counterpart of a fable is a parable. If the priest or elder in an early Christian congregation read parables of Jesus and applied them to the lives of the congregation, he was engaging, in a formal sense, in very much the same action. A slightly more advanced exercise was the narrative. The teacher read or told the students some story from myth or history. The students then wrote out and recited their own paraphrase of the story. If the leader of an early Christian congregation read the story of the birth, ministry or death and resurrection of Jesus, and then paraphrased it for his hearers, he was engaged in a process he had learned in school.

One of the most interesting of the grammatical exercises was the *chria*, sometimes translated 'anecdote'. In a *chria* the teacher supplied the students with information about something a person said or did or both and the students were expected to work out or develop the meaning. For example, 'Isocrates said that the root of knowledge is indeed bitter, but the fruit is sweet'. The saying is morally edifying for the students and applicable to their situation, but to be understood it needs to be 'worked out'. This was done by explaining how wise Isocrates was, then telling the anecdote, providing an explanation of it, giving some contrasts and an example, and citing the authority of others. The *chria* provides on a small scale a model interpretation of a text. It encourages the writer to bring in other citations, other passages in texts which can be compared, contrasted or cited as authorities, and it emphasises the moral message and suggests its application by the student. Values and beliefs (*pistis*) were inculcated by the schools, sometimes blatantly, sometimes subtly. These were of course the traditional values of Hellenic culture. Especially in the more advanced school exercises and in those taught by the rhetoricians, persuasion, conviction and the awakening of an emotional response from an audience were the skills aimed at, and they have been useful to preachers throughout history.

Some *chrias* combined a saying with an action: 'When Diogenes saw a youth behaving shamelessly, he struck the pedagogue with his stick, saying "Why have you taught him so?"' This can be worked out in a similar way, explaining both saying and action. When an early Christian who had had a grammar school education heard the words of Mark's Gospel (14:22–5, AV), how did he hear them?

And as they did eat, Jesus took bread, and blessed, and broke it, and gave to them, and said 'Take, eat: this is my body.' And he took the cup, and when he had given thanks, he gave it to them: and they all drank of it. And he said unto them, 'This is my blood of the new Testament, which is shed for many. Verily I say unto you, I will drink no more of the fruit of the vine, until that day that I drink it new in the Kingdom of God.'

The text is central to the life and faith of Christians, but if we confine ourselves to criticism of form, to the social and psychological experience of an average person with a grammar school education, somewhere in the back of his mind sounded the authoritative voice of his schoolmaster assigning a *chria* and awakening unconsciously those processes of interpretation and application in which he had been drilled as a boy. The second feature of the Sunday liturgy, the Eucharist, is in this sense the dramatisation of a *chria*.

The Eucharist and baptism were parts of the early liturgy which involved dramatisation, but the experience of attending the theatre or of reading dramatic literature was probably not an important influence on the liturgy, though it was perhaps to become such in other periods. In early Christian times the legitimate stage was in decline; it was no longer a moral force, as was school, but worldly, sensuous entertainment. None of the Fathers had anything good to say about it, whereas most accepted the need on the part of Christians for basic literacy, elementary education and even some knowledge of secular literature: though they warned against the dangers of paganism, the Apologists and their successors saw in Greek poetry and philosophy some dim apprehension of truth, and even Saint Paul quotes Greek poets.

There are other grammatical exercises which might be studied, and which may have influenced the compositional units of scripture and religious writing and thus the way an audience heard a text, as they certainly did in the case of secular literature. I leave these for others to explore. It should be emphasised, however, that the grammar school, like the liturgy, was entirely text-centred. Students learned, rather unsystematically, something about mythology, religion, history, politics and even science, but only incidentally by elucidation of passages in literary texts, and not as separate disciplines taught in separate classes. Something similar was presumably true for Christian catechumens in learning Jewish history and Christian theology: it was induced from the text.

Beyond the grammar school, for some, lay the rhetorical schools and beyond these, for the few, the schools of the philosophers. In my book *New Testament Interpretation through Rhetorical Criticism* (1984) I tried to give a picture of how rhetoric was conceptualised and taught in the New Testament period and of how this may have affected the way in which books of the Bible were composed and perceived by audiences. Rhetoric was thought of as consisting of five parts, representing stages in the speech act. The theory of invention dealt with the contents of the discourse: how the speaker or writer presents his moral character ('ethos') or, what is often of greater importance in the New Testament, his authority; how the emotions of an audience are moved so that they will act as the speaker urges; and how logical argument is used. In the New Testament, as in much religious discourse, authoritative proclamation plays a major role, but there is also use of inductive argument, based for example on citations from the Old Testament, and of deductive argument in which a proposition is given support by a reason or the semblance of a reason. This creates what in rhetoric is known as the enthymeme, the counterpart of a syllogism in logic. The Beatitudes are enthymemes: 'Blessed are the poor in spirit, *for* theirs is the kingdom of heaven'. The rhetoric of Matthew's Gospel turns out to make much use of enthymemes, in contrast to that of Mark, where there are very few. Inventional theory also identifies three species of rhetoric: a work or a passage is judicial if it asks the audience to make a judgement about an action in the past, as Paul does in 2 Corinthians. It is deliberative if it seeks a decision about future action, as do the Sermon on the Mount and the Epistle to the Romans. It is epideictic if it employs praise or blame and seeks to inculcate a belief or attitude, but does not focus on specific action. The thirteenth chapter of 1 Corinthians and the eleventh chapter of Hebrews are good examples. The determination of the rhetorical species is sometimes crucial in the interpretation of a work. Is Galatians essentially a judicial piece, offering a defence of Paul, as Hans Dieter Betz has argued in his recent commentary, or is it deliberative, as I believe, seeking to persuade the Galatians to take certain actions in accord with Paul's understanding of the gospel? Each species of rhetoric has its distinctive topics and distinctive structure.

The theory of structure is associated with the second part of rhetorical theory, 'arrangement'. Ancient audiences often expected, and biblical writers often followed, a standard structure in which a *proemion* seeks to gain the attention, goodwill and openness to instruction of an audience. This is often followed by a narration, setting out a statement of facts from a speaker's point of view. Either before or after the narration is usually found a proposition, the kernel of the work, and much of what follows constitutes a proof or refutation. At the end there tends to be a recapitulation, and often the introduction of some emotional elements. This rhetorical structure, or some adaptation of it, is found in speeches in the New Testament and often underlies Pauline epistles.

The third part of rhetorical theory is style, the casting of the thought into words within the outline structure of the whole. Style involves study of both diction, or word choice, including the use of metaphor, and composition, or sentence structure, which includes figures of speech and rhythm. In *De Doctrina Christiana*, Book IV, St Augustine analyses figures and rhythms of portions of the Bible. The two remaining parts of rhetorical theory are memory, which explores mnemonic devices useful to one who is going to speak in public, and delivery, consisting of rules for voice and gesture. These are less useful to us in seeking to understand written texts.

Two features of classical rhetoric deserve special attention in considering how biblical texts were perceived by early Christian audiences. One is that texts were invariably read aloud, even by individuals studying them alone. From a literary point of view this means that sound was always associated with sense; one result was an awareness of word play, regarded by many ancient critics as having a deep significance inherent in the relationship of sign to signified. From a more psychological point of view it means that texts were heard from a living, present voice. Since ownership of texts was probably rare among early Christians,[4] many of whom were poor, for many the Bible was known only from hearing it read in public worship. The experience of worship was thus a rhetorical experience, further increased by the central role of preaching, primarily in the form of the exegetical and paraenetic homily. In certain cases preaching approximated to epideictic oratory, and by the fourth century the epideictic sermon is an important form, but more commonly within the liturgy preaching belonged to the tradition of the schools, not of public address. If a text is orally perceived it is perceived linearly. A hearer cannot turn back to see how it began and cannot compare passages, and even a solitary reader with a written text found it cumbersome to do this as long as books took the form of scrolls. The development of exegesis among Christian scholars is closely associated with the change from the scroll to the codex, and the latter of course was more convenient for reading select passages for the day from a large Bible. Linearity is probably an important feature of all audience reception, including the reception and participation in the liturgy. As outlined by Justin, the dynamics of the liturgy seem to move from outside, closer and closer to the individual participant. The reading of the scriptures comes first. However meaningful, and I argued above that it was directly meaningful, this still involves a progressively retreating series of voices from outside: behind the voice of the reader is the voice of the human author of the text, which may include the voices of characters represented in the text, and behind those ultimately is the voice of God. These voices are then brought within the congregation by the personal exegesis of the preacher, physically present, and his application to the lives of the others present at the moment. Then and only then comes their reaction and participation in prayers and thanksgivings and, as the high point of the service, their sharing in the body and blood of Christ, no longer an external force, but physically present among them. Transubstantiation or consubstantiation is part of the dynamics. Having received, the congregation is then ready to give, and the collection and offering comes last. Some other liturgies have different dynamics, which I leave to others to explore.

Rhetors and philosophers conducted their classes from a chair (*cathedra*), which is at least one antecedent of a bishop's throne and in both cases a symbol of authority. The philosophical schools certainly influenced Christianity, especially the Stoic and Platonic schools, which helped to mould Christian theology and ethics, but their influence on the liturgy is probably largely indirect, as seen in concepts such as the Logos. The Stoic and Cynic diatribe was not as significant an influence on Christian preaching as has sometimes been maintained, in that we now realise that a diatribe was, strictly speaking, an answer to the questions of students delivered

in a dialectical way.[5] The teacher–disciple relationship of the philosophical schools perhaps has some similarity to the relationship of
Jesus to the disciples and of the disciples to their followers. It has
recently been argued that the Gospel of Mark derives its form from
expectations and disappointments in the teacher–disciple relationship as perceived in the schools, but this, if true, would only be
indirectly influential on the liturgy in helping to condition an
understanding of the gospels on the part of the well educated.[6]

It seems likely that the formation of the New Testament canon
was influenced by the needs of public worship.[7] Though the evidence of Papias, preserved by Eusebius (*Church History* 3:39:15–16),
has often been distrusted, it remains possible that Mark or even other
gospels were written down on the basis of the teaching of some
apostle to be used by a congregation when he moved on to a
different church.[8] The letters of Paul were sent to congregations,
clearly intended to be read aloud in services and then doubtless
shared with other congregations. From a purely pragmatic point of
view the canon may thus be thought of as the corpus of those
works which were found appropriate for use in the liturgy. Something similar had happened with literary texts. The grammarians
developed canons of those writings regarded as genuine, inspired
and valuable for teaching; for example, seven select plays each of
Aeschylus, Sophocles and Euripides. A great deal of what was not
included in the canon of the schools was then lost.

There are a number of features of the New Testament and the
early Church which may have reinforced the feeling of Greeks that
entering a Christian community was like going to school. Had not
Jesus said 'except as ye become like children you will never enter
the kingdom of heaven'? He himself is often called *pais* (literally
'child', but also 'servant'), for example in *Didache* 9–10. Christianity
is a 'teaching'; Christ is a 'teacher' and is seen 'teaching'. The
specific origins of this tradition are of course in Jewish schools and
in the figure of a rabbi, but Greeks had been to school too, had
known a 'master' and had thought of themselves as 'disciples'.
Before baptism, whatever their age, those preparing for entrance
into the Church usually spent an extended period in instruction as
catechumens. The *Apostolic Tradition* of Hippolytus (17) suggests
three years, which was about the length of time spent in a rhetorical school. There was regular instruction in the faith by a teacher,
and at services the catechumens sat, like a class, apart from others.

To many people rhetoric means style: choice of word, composition, tropes (of which metaphor is most important), figures, rhythm and the like, often connected more with the emotional quality of a text than with its cognitive contents. This definition represents a limitation on rhetoric as understood in the classical period, when invention (content, argument, topics), arrangement, memory and delivery were, together with style, regarded as five canonical aspects of the subject. But word choice and composition, and thus style, are certainly important elements both of the liturgy and of rhetoric. Among early Christians there seems to have been a pull between two opposed tendencies. On the one hand there is a preference for natural, simple and contemporary language in the New Testament and thus in those parts of the liturgy derived from it. The New Testament and Christian writing and speaking generally, at least before the Apologists, is in the *koine*, the common spoken Greek of the Hellenistic and Roman period. With certain exceptions, periodic sentences, the use of the optative mood, literary prose-rhythms and the more artificial figures of speech are not employed.

Christian communities contained many simple people who, even if literate, probably could not have read and understood the dialogues of Plato with ease. Preaching and praying in the early Church was largely a matter of free composition by the speaker. The effect of the liturgy on early Christians, to a considerable extent, was to hear radical 'good news' couched in everyday language. Until perhaps the fourth century there was little of what became the powerful 'rhetoric' of Orthodox, Catholic, Lutheran and Anglican Christianity, derived from the aesthetic and emotional effect of ecclesiastical architecture, religious art, complex music, beautiful vestments, elaborate dramatisation and a ritual cast in a foreign or archaic language. The experience of the early liturgy was far closer to that of evangelical sects today, dependent on a sense of fellowship both within the congregation and between clergy and laity, lacking learning and sophistication, differentiated from the wider contemporary society by values and beliefs, but not by language.

The rhetorical force of the liturgy was directly derived from that inherent in the scriptures, the radical rhetoric of proclamation on the basis of authority, made more attractive and immediate by parable and metaphor drawn from nature and daily life. For many

Christians authority was not difficult to accept; they lived in an authoritarian society. The schools and government implanted it, and their will to believe was enhanced by the promises of the new religion. The challenge was somewhat greater for the educated than for the simple, and it was greater in the Latin-speaking west than in the east, in that the scriptures in Latin, at least before Jerome, sounded strange, lacking the natural rhythms of the language, employing unusual metaphor. Augustine is of course the great spokesman for this original unfavourable reaction to the scriptures (for example in *Confessions* 3:9), and it is significant that for him the liturgy and ritual of the Church seem to have nothing at all to do with his conversion. It was in the final instance the preaching of Ambrose, with its use of allegorical interpretation, that made it possible for him to accept Christianity.

On the other hand, there is from the beginning some pull in an opposite direction, toward the exotic as a feature of sacral language. This is characteristic of religious discourse in most cultures; for Christianity its historical beginnings are found in the Septuagint, the Hellenistic Greek translation of the Old Testament. Though its diction in narrative passages and its grammatical structure is largely that of the *koine*, the attempt to translate a work from the Hebrew, a very different language in a rather different culture, produced features strange to the Greek ear. Unusual meanings are given to Greek words to approximate to the Hebrew, the imagery of the psalms and prophets, though largely comprehensible, over-reaches and strains Greek metaphorical conventions, and the result seems oriental, bizarre, but also suggestive of divine inspiration. God would not necessarily speak in ordinary language, and perhaps this language is His. The language both veils and partially reveals truths too great for direct human utterance. These features, associated with the inspiration and authenticity of the text, were carried over and imitated in Christian preaching and praying as vehicles of its inspiration.

Though less poetic, the New Testament continues the imagery of the Old and thus confirms its place in Christian rhetoric. A striking element are Aramaic words and phrases found in the New Testament which are taken up in the liturgy: *abba, maranatha, hosannah* and so on. The most important are those attributed to Jesus himself, spelled out in the Greek text as a seal of sanctification: *mammon* (Matthew 6:24; Luke 16:9, 11 and 13); *ephphatha* (Mark 7:34); *talitha koumi* (Mark 5:41); *Eli, Eli, lama sabachthani* (Matthew

27:46). This is sacred language, and it is not surprising to find some of it in the early liturgy, as for example in the prayer for the end of the Eucharist in the *Didache* (10:6): *maran atha. amen.* Christine Mohrmann described the whole of the earliest eucharistic terminology in Greek as 'deliberately isolated from the language of everday life', not only in using Aramaicisms, but sometimes in Greek as well: 'κλαίω τὸν ἄρτον, "to break bread", is certainly not a common expression for taking part in a meal, and the modern liturgists who would like to view the earliest eucharistic celebration as a "gathering round the kitchen table" certainly do not find support in the testimony of the earliest terminology. The term *eucharistia*, as we know, is derived from the Jewish prayer tradition.'[9] In pagan ritual and magical incantations saying the right words was often crucial to the success of the rite, and though early Christians did not dogmatically adopt that view, they felt its pull, especially in the crucial acts of baptism and Eucharist. Other more general stylistic features natural in Hebrew poetry but more strange in Greek appear as well, especially pleonasm and parallelism. Perhaps more philosophical in origin is the fondness for a series of compound adjectives using the alpha privative as in the *Anaphora* of Serapion: 'unborn God, inscrutable, ineffable, incomprehensible'. The greatness of God is defined by an accumulation of what He is not.

A feature of the Christian liturgy from the beginning, and still continuing today, is the way it tends to encapsulate the historical narrative of the Old and New Testaments in preaching and prayers. Sometimes the references are brief, only reminders of God's plan in history, but the underlying pattern makes possible almost any degree of amplification. The basic elements are the covenant of God with the patriarchs, the prophecies of the Messiah, the birth of Jesus and his death and resurrection in that order, sometimes carried on into the future and the Second Coming. This schema is already evident in many of the sermons in Acts (2:14–36; 3:12–26; 10:34–43; etc.). The speech of Stephen in Acts 7 shows amplification of the Old Testament antecedents and suggests that this element originated in the effort to explain Christianity to the Jews, but it remained a feature of Christian expression among the gentiles as well, sometimes in very vestigial form. In the eucharistic prayer of the *Didache* it is present only in the two references to David. Whatever the reading for the day, these themes could be introduced to help give structure and meaning. The Easter sermon of Melito of Sardis takes its text from the account of the Hebrew exodus and leads to the resurrection; the Christological sermon known as the *Second Epistle* of Clement takes its start from a verse in Acts (10:42), but weaves in and explicates Old Testament prophecies. Christian sermons and prayers, ancient and modern, are often a pastiche of quotations from the scriptures, and many, it must be admitted, proceed as a train of consciousness, one image or concept reminding the speaker of another. But the scriptures as a whole, at least partially known to the audience, provide a narrative intertext and thus an underlying pattern of order in the minds of the faithful.

Let me conclude these observations with a brief rhetorical analysis of a piece of liturgy, the prayer on the consecration of a bishop found at the beginning of Hippolytus' *Apostolic Tradition* and dating from the early third century. This particular part of the work survives in Greek, though much of the rest has to be reconstructed from Latin, Coptic and other versions. I will first quote the translation of the prayer from the edition of Gregory Dix and Henry Chadwick, preserving their use of quotation marks to indicate passages of scriptural language.[10] Some are not verbatim quotations, and the reader will detect additional words with a scriptural ring; the point is the significant amount of the prayer which is scriptural in style. I will then apply to the prayer the method of rhetorical analysis recommended in my recent study of the New Testament.[11]

1 'O God and Father of our Lord Jesus Christ, Father of mercies and God of all comfort', 'Who dwellest on high yet hast respect unto the lowly', 'Who knowest all things before they come to pass';

2 Who didst give ordinances unto Thy church 'by the Word of Thy grace'; Who 'didst foreordain from the beginning' the race of the righteous from Abraham, instituting princes and priests and leaving not Thy sanctuary without ministers; Who from the foundation of the world hast been pleased to be glorified in them whom Thou hast chosen;

3 And now pour forth the Power which is from Thee, of 'the princely Spirit' which Thou didst deliver to Thy Beloved Child (*pais*) Jesus Christ, which He bestowed on Thy holy Apostles who established the church which hallows Thee in every place to the endless glory and praise of Thy Name.

4 (Father) 'who knowest the hearts of all' grant upon this Thy servant whom Thou hast chosen for the episcopate to (feed Thy holy flock and) serve as Thine high priest, that he may minister blamelessly by night and day, that he may unceasingly behold and propitiate Thy countenance and offer to Thee the gifts of Thy holy Church,
5 And that by the high priestly Spirit he may have authority 'to forgive sins' according to Thy command, 'to assign lots' according to Thy bidding, to 'loose every bond' according to the authority Thou gavest to the Apostles, and that he may please Thee in meekness and a pure heart, 'offering' to Thee 'a sweet-smelling savour',
6 through Thy Child Jesus Christ our Lord, through Whom to Thee be glory, might and praise, to the Father and to the Son with the Holy Spirit now and ever and world without end. Amen.

The prayer is a *rhetorical unit*, with beginning, middle and end. This is further indicated by the context, for the prayer is introduced by 'and shall pray as following, saying' and followed by 'and when he is made bishop'. The *rhetorical situation* is described in the context. The bishop has been chosen by the people. Other bishops, the presbytery and the people have assembled on a Sunday. All keep silent until one of the bishops present speaks the prayer. A holy silence, broken by the voice of one in authority, was familiar to a classical audience. The most famous literary reference is Horace, *Odes* 1:1–4.

The *rhetorical problem* is not acute, in that there is no hostility or prejudice in the audience which the speaker must face; however, the prayer needs to integrate three audiences, which is the chief challenge of the occasion. The speaker needs to invoke the blessing of God and thus effect the consecration; thus the prayer is throughout addressed to God. But there is a secondary need to use the occasion to declare to the new bishop what is expected of him, what his powers will be and in what spirit he should execute these powers, and as a public ceremony the prayer should, thirdly, be instructive to the congregation about the nature of the faith and the Church. The latter two functions are accomplished by clauses inserted into and amplifying the address to God. God does not need to be reminded, or in the final analysis even asked, for these blessings, as indeed the prayer acknowledges ('who knowest all things'). They are indirectly expressed for the benefit of the new bishop and the congregation as teaching. The *rhetorical species*, as a result, is double. As an address to God the prayer is 'deliberative', for He is asked to take specific actions; as addressed to the new bishop and the congregation it is 'epideictic': no specific action is called upon and the thrust of the prayer is to outline general categories of action by the bishop and to strengthen his authority and the faith and belief of the congregation. The *stasis* is qualitative.[12] Specifically, as an address to God, the prayer is an example of *deprecatio*, in which the speaker throws himself at the mercy of the tribunal. Conceived as epideictic, the prayer is still qualitative, but in the form of *remotio* or *translatio*, where fundamental responsibility is referred to another (here, to God).

All of these rhetorical features are common to much prayer, ancient and modern. Since prayer performs the function of instruction, the line between praying and teaching is often an arbitrary one in the Church; the formal difference is that in preaching the audience is passive, in prayer the audience is drawn into the emotional process of communication with God. It is a central doctrine of the Greek rhetor Isocrates (for example in *Antidosis* 274) that one becomes noble by saying noble things repeatedly and thus eventually believing and acting upon them, and much of the moral instruction in schools was based on this psychological premise. Classical hymns and prayers are often instructional; a good example, close to Christianity, is Cleanthes' *Hymn to Zeus*, which develops the Stoic understanding of God. It differs from a Christian prayer in using literary language and thus building faith on the traditions of Hellenism as taught in secular schools rather than on Jewish traditions through scriptural language, but the process is a similar one.

The 'arrangement' of the prayer follows the general pattern taught in the rhetorical schools, though inherent in much natural rhetoric in all traditions. The opening sentence is a *proemion* or *exordium*, invoking God and seeking His goodwill by recognition of his 'mercies', 'comfort', 'respect unto the lowly' and knowledge of all things. But these qualities, which formally would seem to be influencing God to listen, are actually part of the indirect address, reminding the other audience of the nature of God. Then comes, as might be expected, a 'narration' (section 2), which briefly recounts what God has done in the past. Consistent with what I said above about the tendency of Christian preaching and prayer to encapsulate the narrative of the scriptures, there is reference to Abraham, after which the speaker jumps to Jesus, his apostles and the present moment in the Church. The prayer has a strong sense of continuity, and one of its major themes is that the Church shall not be left 'without ministers'.

The narration is followed by petitions which constitute in rhetoric the 'proposition': 'And now pour forth . . .', and then a second proposition: 'Grant upon this Thy servant . . .'. What follows each proposition is the formal counterpart of the 'proof', but it does not take the form of logical reasoning. There are no 'enthymemes' (statements with supporting reasons), though enthymemes can occur in prayer (as in 'Father forgive them, *for they know not what they do*'). The absence of enthymemes, and thus of logical argument, is a sacred element in religious discourse, characteristic of its more radical, authoritative forms, as in the Gospel of Mark (in contrast to the more argumentative language of Matthew). Instead, we have clauses with emotional connotations: 'princely Spirit'; 'beloved Child'; 'endless glory and praise of Thy Name'. In rhetoric this is 'pathos', which together with 'ethos' (or moral character) and logic makes up the three basic modes of rhetorical persuasion. But some reasons why it is in the 'interest' of God to act are touched upon indirectly. The fundamental argument of deliberative rhetoric is that the action is in the self-interest of the addressee. Here God is assured that the new bishop will 'propitiate Thy countenance' and 'offer to Thee the gifts of Thy holy Church' and later will please 'in meekness and purity of heart, offering to Thee a sweet-smelling savour'.

This is the Christian version of pagan sacrifice of incense to the gods as the basis of a contractual relationship: the gods' favour in return for things they are thought to desire. A subtle contractual relationship has continued in Christian prayer, even though the churches have often taught that God cannot be 'bought'. But as epideictic the passages also have an ethical effect on the bishop and people, teaching them values and qualities they should manifest and implying God's grace if they conform to the pattern. Again, prayer is a form of teaching. In the proof the duties of the new bishop are pointed out to him: 'to serve as Thine high priest', 'to have authority to forgive sins . . . to assign lots . . . ' and to make offerings.

The prayer could be said to be cultic, in that its linear pattern seems to lead up to the offerings, 'a sweet-smelling odour'. This is the culminating inducement offered to God, comprehensible to both former Jews and former pagans, and the culminating injunction to the audience. With it the 'proof' ends. What follows is the epilogue (peroration, conclusion). An epilogue recapitulates ('glory, might and praise') and gives a final emotional twist to a speech. It often invokes God or the gods and is the place in public address where a prayer is most frequently found. Here, within a prayer, we find instead reference to Jesus and the Holy Spirit. They might also be thought to function as 'witnesses', giving testimony, as frequently in public address. Throughout the speech there is, indeed, some evocation of witnesses and implied use of examples. What God has been to Abraham, Jesus and the apostles creates a pattern and precedent for His action now.

The most striking feature of the *style*, to a reader of the English translation, is the consistent use of the archaic second person singular. But this represents a modern attempt to find some stylistic feature of sacral language which is a counterpart to other features in the original. It is definitely not a sacral feature of the original text, where the use of the second person singular is entirely colloquial. God is addressed in exactly the same grammatical forms as would be the humblest of those present; nor did Hippolytus have available to him the visual rhetoric of upper-case letters. Nor are there exotic metaphors: even 'feed Thy holy flock' comes from the later Latin version, not the Greek original.

Yet the original has a sacral quality. This comes almost entirely from scriptural quotation and allusion, which introduce terms and concepts with special meaning within Christianity, largely derived from Judaism. Burton Easton judged the Jewish background of the prayer as 'extremely marked' and thought the second section might have been taken from some synagogue formula.[13] The prayer is conceptual and cognitive, rather than imagistic and concrete, and this may be attributable to the taste of Hippolytus himself, trained in the philosophical schools. It is also largely from the scriptural allusions that the effect of pleonasm and parallelism is derived: the various names given to God, the run-on sentence structure, accumulating clauses. There are alpha privatives in section four. There is mild paradox, often found in Christian language, in the statement that God on high has respect unto the lowly. There are doublets, which emphasise a point by lingering on it: 'glory and praise'; 'by night and day'; 'in meekness and a pure heart'. These features somewhat intensify emotion, but compared to some other Christian writing, and compared to Saint Paul at his most expansive, they are restrained.

For all its sacral language the prayer, taken as a whole, is simple, intimate, familiar, belonging to that period or that tradition in the Church which eschews affectation, pomp and elaborate ceremony and seeks its effect in clarity, sincerity, scriptural authority and dignity. The faithful had been taught to expect this in their instruction as catechumens. Text was central to their religion, and for that Jews had been prepared in the synagogue and gentiles in the secular schools.

Notes

1. Classical sources on *paraenesis* relevant to Christianity have recently been collected by Abraham J. Malherbe, *Moral Exhortation, A Greco-Roman Sourcebook* (Philadelphia, 1986).
2. The best general work on a Graeco-Roman education is still H. I. Marrou, *A History of Education in Antiquity*, trans. George Lamb (New York, 1956); see especially pp. 358–418.
3. For an overall account and discussion of sources see George A. Kennedy, *Greek Rhetoric under Christian Emperors* (Princeton, 1983) pp. 54–72.
4. But Hippolytus, *Apostolic Tradition* 36, assumes that Christians by the early third century had 'holy books' for private use.
5. See Stanley Kent Stowers, *The Diatribe and Paul's Letter to the Romans*, SBL Dissertation Series, 57 (Chico, California, 1981).
6. Vernon K. Robbins, *Jesus the Teacher: A Socio-Rhetorical Interpretation of Mark* (Philadelphia, 1984).
7. See C.F.D. Moule, *The Birth of the New Testament*, 3rd edn (New York, 1982) pp. 39–40, 241–5.
8. See George A. Kennedy, 'Classical and Christian Source Criticism', in *The Relationship Among the Gospels*, ed. W.O.Walker Jr (San Antonio, 1978) pp. 147–8.
9. Christine Mohrmann, *Liturgical Latin, its Origins and Character* (Washington, 1957) pp. 25–6.
10. Gregory Dix, *The Treatise on the Apostolic Tradition of St Hippolytus of Rome*, revised by Henry Chadwick (London, 1968) pp. 4–6. See also Bernard Botte, *Hippolyte de Rome, La tradition apostolique d'après les anciennes versions* (Paris, 1968) pp. 42–7.
11. George A. Kennedy, *New Testament Interpretation through Rhetorical Criticism* (Chapel Hill, 1984) pp. 33–8.
12. On *stasis* see George Kennedy, *The Art of Persuasion in Greece* (Princeton, 1963) pp. 303–21, and *Greek Rhetoric* (n.3 above) pp. 73–86.
13. Burton Easton, *The Apostolic Tradition of Hippolytus* (Cambridge, 1934) p. 67.

3

The Anaphora of the Liturgy of St John Chrysostom: Stylistic Notes

Daniel J. Sheerin

EDITORS' NOTE

The Liturgy of St John Chrysostom became the principal rite of the Orthodox Church by AD 1000 and has remained so until the present day. The structure of the 'anaphora', the central prayer of the eucharistic liturgy, is identical with that of a large number of other West Syrian anaphoras, including those of the *Apostolic Constitutions* (book 8), St Basil and St James. It may well represent the form used in Antioch during the episcopate of St John Chrysostom in the late fourth century, although whether the text can be attributed to the saint himself is an open question. But by the time Chrysostom came to Antioch texts were becoming standardised, and he may have found a rite already in existence, which he used and modified. The text used here is from the Barberini manuscript of the late eighth century.

The English version of the Greek text provided here is simply a literal translation indicating the content of each line for the benefit of those readers who have little or no knowledge of Greek; but even this version does give some idea of the kind of stylistic pattern the author (or authors) was trying to create.

DJ & RCDJ

This is an essay in the fundamental sense of the term: an attempt to talk descriptively about selected stylistic features of the anaphora of the Divine Liturgy of St John Chrysostom.[1] Limited stylistic studies of the Greek anaphoras have been provided, in a general way by Antoniades and with more specific focus by Engberding.[2] It also seems useful, however, to consider selected stylistic features, not of several anaphoras at once, or category by category, but of a single anaphora viewed as a whole, that of the liturgy of St John Chrysostom (henceforward referred to as CHR). CHR is considered in this study in its earliest recoverable form,[3] and illustrative and comparative texts from certain other Greek anaphoras are quoted and referred to in the commentary.[4] This study consists of a graphic arrangement of the text of CHR, a brief commentary on it and concluding observations.

The anaphora of CHR has been broken down into the sections established by modern scholarship. The several sections of the text will be presented in order, each followed by a commentary keyed to the line numbers in the left-hand column. In the case of cross-reference to a section other than the one under consideration, the Roman numeral of that section will precede the reference by line number within the section (for example, V.4–6). The sentences of these sections have been further divided into clauses and phrases which have been arranged graphically in order to illustrate stylistic phenomena. This arrangement of the text resembles the presentation of text *per cola et commata* familiar to ancient and modern scholarship, but the *mise en page* here is not intended to restore ancient colometry or to show how the text was composed and/or delivered, but only to facilitate the visualisation and discussion of the phenomena which are the subject of this study.[5] The lines of the text could obviously be arranged in a variety of ways to bring out this or that feature. Thus the length of lines in terms of number of syllables (given in parentheses in the right-hand column) would vary with the arrangement of the text, and in some instances alternative arrangements are suggested.

What is presented to the reader here is a text-with-commentary which is an interpretation, an admittedly subjective one. Any examination of a text from a particular point of view, however scientific the method, necessarily involves the reflection of the text in a mirror that is more or less distorted.

The following comments are made without reference to questions of chronology, authorship or intentionality. Indeed, some matters which will be remarked upon might be dismissed as accidental or coincidental to the nature of the idiom in which CHR was composed or redacted. But the point of this work is simply to describe selected stylistic phenomena in CHR and their probable, or at least possible, effects. These comments may have bearing on the sorts of questions just listed, but that must await more profound study of liturgical Greek and its relationship to a variety of Greek literature, both pagan and Christian.

I have tried to avoid needlessly technical language, but there is no point to re-inventing the wheel, so some traditional terms for figures of speech are employed. A brief definition of each will be provided in parentheses after its first use.[6] For reasons of economy the secondary literature cited here has been kept to a minimum; citations appear for the most part in parentheses in the commentary.[7]

I DIALOGUS

  Ἡ χάρις τοῦ κυρίου ἡμῶν Ἰησοῦ Χριστοῦ (13)
  καὶ ἡ ἀγάπη τοῦ θεοῦ καὶ Πατρός (11)
  καὶ ἡ κοινωνία τοῦ ἁγίου Πνεύματος (13)
  εἴη μετὰ πάντων ὑμῶν (8)
5 Καὶ μετὰ τοῦ πνεύματός σου (8)
  Ἄνω σχῶμεν τὰς καρδίας (8)
  Ἔχομεν πρὸς τὸν Κύριον (8)
  Εὐχαριστήσωμεν τῷ Κυρίῳ (10)
  Ἄξιον καὶ δίκαιον (7)

I DIALOGUE

The grace of our Lord Jesus Christ
and the love of God and Father
and the fellowship of the Holy Spirit
be with you all.
5 And with your spirit.
Let us lift up our hearts.
We have them with the Lord.
Let us give thanks to the Lord.
It is fitting and right.

I THE DIALOGUE

1–4: The first three lines of the Opening Greeting[8] exhibit considerable balance through isocolon (succession of phrases of about
equal length). Note within this symmetry the crescendo effect of
the length of the leading nouns χάρις (2 syllables), ἀγάπη (3),
κοινωνία (4), a feature of the scriptural original in 2 Cor 13:13. Line
4 is reduced in length to 8 syllables. Lines 3 and 4 could be treated
as a unity, yielding a line of 21 syllables. This would close the
series with an appropriately long line, but the resulting asymmetry
is unattractive. The effect of the reduction of length in line 4 and in
a number of other instances we shall see is a kind of truncation
which leaves a feeling of incompleteness and expectation of what
is to follow: in this case, the people's reply. The parison (successive
phrases having the same general structure) of the scriptural original is carried over, as are, incidental to it, the epanaphora (repetition of the same word[s] at the beginning of two or more
successive lines) and polysyndeton (repetition of conjunctions) in
lines 2 and 3, as well as the homoeoteleuton (successive lines
ending with the same sound) in 2–3. The polysyndeton of 2 and 3
both links the members of the series and, by the inclusion of the
conjunction before the second member of the series, gives that
member a greater prominence (A + B + C) than it would have had
if only one conjunction had been used in the series (AB + C).

4–5: These lines are equal in length (isocolon) and, with their
prepositional phrases, mainly parallel in structure (parison). The
initial Καὶ of line 5 provides an additional link, heightening the
responsiveness of line 5 to line 4. Line 5 contains a substantial
ellipsis (omission of words easily understood), for its subject and
verb must be supplied from lines 1–4. The response in line 5 is not,
however, a mere *tautologia*, the repetition in different words of the
greeting of line 4 (see Taft pp. 320–2).

6–7: These lines, also equal in length, are connected by the
repetition of σχῶμεν in ῎Εχομεν,[9] heightened by their chiastic
structure whereby ῎Εχομεν, answering to σχῶμεν, moves to the
initial position and πρὸς τὸν Κύριον, the amplification and specifi-
cation of ῎Ανω, is postponed. Note too the ellipsis of τὰς καρδίας.

8–9: The endings of lines 7 and 8 create antistrophe (successive
lines ending with the same word) and polyptoton (repetition of
the same word in different cases). The exhortation of line 8,
Εὐχαριστήσωμεν, introduces a new theme, and the reply in line 9 a

new pattern in the Dialogue. Lines 5 and 7 are true responses. Line 9 is, by contradistinction, not strictly speaking a response to the exhortation of line 8, but a comment on it. The precise isocolon prevailing through lines 4–7 is broken by line 8, its slightly greater length heightened by the hexasyllabic verb. But any expectation of a movement to a longer line or lines to conclude the series is frustrated by the truncation of line 9, which again leaves an expectation, provides a point of departure for what follows.

The Introductory Dialogue is, then, characterised by considerable symmetry (isocolon, parison) and a variety of linkages (conjunctions, epanaphora, antistrophe, ellipses) which stitch it together into a coherent whole until the brief comment of line 9, which propels the text into the following section. It should also be observed that the interweaving repetitions and, in particular, the ellipses of the Dialogue retain the flavour of dialogue in popular speech. They point to the Dialogue's origins and give energy and the illusion of artlessness to this interchange of congregation and celebrant.

II LAUS: GRATIARUM ACTIO

Ἄξιον καὶ δίκαιον   (7)
   σὲ ὑμνεῖν   (3)
   σοὶ εὐχαριστεῖν   (5)
   σὲ προσκυνεῖν   (4)
5   ἐν παντὶ τόπῳ τῆς δεσποτείας σου   (11)

   σὺ γὰρ εἶ θεὸς ἀνέκφραστος   (5+4)
     ἀπερινόητος   (6)
     ἀόρατος   (4)
     ἀκατάληπτος   (5)
10   ἀεὶ ὤν   (3)
     ὡσαύτως ὤν   (4)
   σὺ καὶ ὁ μονογενής σου Υἱός   (10)
   καὶ τὸ Πνεῦμά σου τὸ ἅγιον   (9)

   σὺ ἐκ τοῦ μὴ ὄντος   (6)
15   εἰς τὸ εἶναι ἡμᾶς παρήγαγες   (10)
   καὶ παραπεσόντας ἀνέστησας πάλιν   (12)
   καὶ οὐκ ἀπέστης πάντα ποιῶν   (9)
   ἕως ἡμᾶς εἰς τὸν οὐρανὸν ἀνήγαγες   (13)

καὶ τὴν βασιλείαν ἐχαρίσω τὴν μέλλουσαν (14)

20 ὑπερ τούτων ἁπάντων εὐχαριστοῦμέν σοι (13)
    καὶ τῷ μονογενεῖ σου Υἱῷ (9)
    καὶ τῷ Πνεύματί σου τῷ ἁγίω (10)
ὑπὲρ πάντων   ὧν ἴσμεν (7)
    καὶ ὧν οὐκ ἴσμεν (5)
25   τῶν φανερῶν (4)
    καὶ αφανῶν εὐεργεσιῶν σου (10)
    τῶν εἰς ἡμᾶς γεγενημένων (9)

II PREFACE

It is fitting and right
    to hymn you
    to thank you
    to worship you
5 in all places of your dominion.

For you are God, ineffable
               inconceivable
               invisible
               incomprehensible
10   existing always
               in the same way,
you and your only-begotten Son
    and your Holy Spirit.
You brought us out of not being
15   into being,
and when we fell you raised us up again
and you did not cease to do all things
    until you had brought us up to heaven
    and granted us the Kingdom that is to come.
20 For all these things we give thanks to you
        and to your only-begotten Son
        and to your Holy Spirit.
For all things of which we know
        and of which we do not know,
25   your seen
        and unseen benefits
        that have come upon us.

II PRAISE AND THANKSGIVING[10]

1: This line is a verbatim repetition of I.9. (Note that CHR and SER repeat the people's statement without comment, while CA, BAS, JAS, MARK, BASAlex ane GREG all amplify it in varying degrees.) Thus I.9 provides the point of departure for Section II not only by the anticipatory truncation of its length, but also by its very words. The infinitive in line 3 recalls Εὐχαριστήσωμεν of I.8, framing it, in lines 2 and 4, with an elaboration of part of its meaning. Thus Section II opens without prologue and is bonded on to the preceding Dialogue.

2–4: These phrases are asymmetrical (3,5,4 syllables). The interpolations into this series in the later CHR (σὲ εὐλογεῖν, σὲ αἰνεῖν in the second and third positions in a series of five) yield a no less symmetrical series of 3,4,3,5 and 4 syllables. The six phrases in the corresponding passage of BAS are a series of 3,3,4,4,5 and 4 syllables, more of a crescendo, with slight truncation in the last member. JAS, however, achieves crescendo and climax by saving the crucial εὐχαριστεῖν for last. The moderation of CHR in the number of members of this series over against the contemporary CHR, BAS and JAS is worthy of remark (see Ledogar, p. 17), as is the slight truncation of the last member, preparatory to the cadential extension of line 5. Lines 2–4 are a tight congeries of infinitive phrases marked by asyndeton, epanaphora (with polyptoton: σὲ, σοὶ, σὲ), parison and homoeoteleuton (three perispomena [circumflex on last syllable] in -εῖν). This congeries creates a sense of mass, but also of considerable compression by the employment of the devices just mentioned, especially asyndeton, which presses the members together, making them less distinct. The epanaphora achieved by repeating and by leading with the pronoun keeps the focus on the second person. Contrast αἰνοῦμέν σε εὐλογοῦμέν σε . . . of the Greater Doxology, where the enclitic pronoun is diminished.

5: The series is concluded, after the truncated final member, with this longer scriptural extension (see Wagner, pp. 73–5; contrast the far more lengthy cadential extensions in BAS and MARK) which provides relaxation and closure after the tight congeries of 2–4.

6: The juxtaposition of σου of 5 and σὺ of 6 produces anastrophe (one clause beginning with the last word of the preceding clause) with polyptoton, and links the first and second sections of the *oration theologica* of section II together, as does the particle γὰρ. Some closure is achieved through a final rendering explicit of what was bound up in Ἄξιον καὶ δίκαιον, for it has been made clear what it is fitting and right to do in lines 2–5, and now why it is so in lines 6ff.

6–11: This famous series (see discussion in Wagner, pp. 75–84) is somewhat asymmetrical. The corresponding vocative series in SER (6,4,6 syll) and in BAS (3,4,5,5,5 syll) are more symmetrically managed. Lines 10 and 11 could be regarded as a longer unit of 7 syllables, but I think they contain two closely related but different ideas, and lines 12–13 provide a reprise (σὺ) and an extension for this module. This is another congeries with asyndeton, but linked internally in several ways. The first four alpha-privative words are joined by the assonance of the initial alphas, and by their homoeoptoton (series of words in same case) and homoeoteleuton (all proparoxytones [acute on antepenult] in -ΤΟς). Lines 10 and 11 are joined to 6–9 by the initial alpha of ἀεὶ, and to one another by antistrophe and the assonance on omega.

12–13: These are the extension of 6–11, and by length of line, repeated conjunctions and formulaic character relax the tension created by the preceding asyndetonic series. This is the first of a series of trinitarian formulas in CHR (see also II.20–2, IV.4–6, IX.4–6) after the trinitarian theme established in the opening greeting. All occur in contexts of praise and thanksgiving, all with repeated conjunctions as here. Those at II.20–2 and IV.4–6 also repeat the chiastic arrangement μονογενής . . . Υἱός (AB)/ Πνεῦμα . . .ἅγιον (BA) which we see here. The initial σὺ of line 12 recalls the second person pronoun series of 2–4 and the initial σὺ of line 6. In addition, the initial σὺ of line 14 completes the series in 6 and 12, providing an extended epanaphora through the mid-section of II, and supplies a slight hypostrophe (catches up the thread of the narrative after a parenthesis and makes a fresh start by either repeating the subject or adding a demonstrative) after the trinitarian parenthesis of 12–13.

14–19: This module is neatly symmetrical. If considered as arranged here, with 14 separated from 15 to point up the antithesis, we have a series of 6,10,12 and 9,13,14 syllables, that is, two sets of three lines of expanding length. On the other hand, if we combine 14 and 15, we have a series of 16,12,9,13,14 syllables, diminishing towards the cryptic summary statement in line 17 (see Wagner, pp. 88–9) in the middle and expanding as it continues. Interesting features in these lines include the antithesis with parison of the prepositional phrases of 14 and 15, the alliteration of initial π from the end of 15 through 16 and 17, the forward shifting of verbs in 15–17 and back again in 18–19, the paronomasia (a similarity of sound of words of the same root, plus a dissimilarity of sense) of παρήγαγες and ἀνήγαγες, ἀνέστησας and ἀπέστης, the antithetical juxtaposition of πασήγαγες, παραπεσόντας and ἀνέστησας, and the pleonastic (joining of several words or phrases which have about the same meaning) use of πάλιν in line 16 (cf. VI.8) and the polysyndeton of repeated καὶ. Note the hyperbaton (a transposition of words from their natural order) in line 19 whereby the separation of μέλλουσαν from βασιλείαν provides a frame for ἐχαρίσω, and its postponement to the strong position at line end frames lines 14–19 with ἐκ τοῦ μὴ ὄντος and μέλλουσαν, thus embracing the entire course of human existence.

20–7: Line 20 resumes the *eucharistia* theme from I.8 and II.3. Its opening words sum up the details of 14–19. Lines 21–3 are a reprise of the trinitarian formula of lines 12–13, with the same polysyndeton and chiasmus and, through the series σοι, σου, σου, an additional internal polyptoton. The opening prepositional phrase of line 23 creates a virtual epanaphora with 20, and provides a hypostrophe after the trinitarian parenthesis of 21–2, resuming ἁπάντων of 20 and anticipating εὐεργεσιῶν of 26. The central core of 23–6 is a pair of pleonastic antitheses in a congeries of phrases. The first antithesis (23–4) is connected internally by the conjunction and by the antistrophe on ἴσμεν; the second (25–6) has the same conjunction and is further connected by the paronomasia of φανερῶν ἀφανῶν. The last two words of 26 provide closure to the long hyperbaton πάντων . . . εὐεργεσιῶν, and a resumption of the second person pronoun. Line 27 is virtually a gloss on 26. Note the chiastic arrangement εὐεργεσιῶν σου (AB)/εἰς ἡμᾶς γεγενημένων (BA). In addition, line 27 summarises and specifies 23–6 and provides some relaxation after the tension created by the 'A not A, B not B' antitheses of 23–6. Lines 23–7 are an abstract recapitulation of lines 16–19 and, being abstract, an amplification.

Section II is characterised by sets of congeries, each with a cadential extension to conclude and resolve the tension: 2–4 + 5, 6–11 + 12 & 13, 23–6 + 27. Contsast is provided by the summary narrative of 14–19, with its longer lines and paratactic (parallel, non-periodic) style. In addition, if we set aside lines 1–5 as the celebrant's elaboration of the people's final response, an ABA pattern emerges in the remainder of the section, a pattern of abstract (6–11), concrete (14–19) and abstract (23–7), with trinitarian formulas intercalated like a refrain.

III A. INTRODUCTIO AD SANCTUS B. SANCTUS

A. Εὐχαριστοῦμέν σοι καὶ ὑπὲρ τῆς λειτουργίας ταύτης   (16)
   ἣν ἐκ τῶν χειρῶν ἡμῶν δέξασθαι καταξίωσον   (15)
   καίτοι σοὶ παρεστήκεισαν χιλιάδες ἀρχαγγέλων   (8+8)
     καὶ μυριάδες ἀγγέλων   (8)
5   τὰ χερουβείμ   (4)
      καὶ τὰ σεραφείμ   (5)
      ἑξαπτέρυγα   (5)
      πολυόμματα   (5)
      μετάρσια   (4)
10   πτερωτά   (3)
   τὸν ἐπινίκιον ὕμνον ᾄδοντα   (11)

B. Ἅγιος ἅγιος ἅγιος Κύριος σαβαώθ   (15)
   πλήρης ὁ οὐρανὸς καὶ ἡ γῆ τῆς δόξης σου   (13)
     ὡσαννὰ ἐν τοῖς ὑψίστοις   (8)
   εὐλογημένος ὁ ἐρχόμενος ἐν ὀνόματι Κυρίου   (18)
     ὡσαννὰ ἐν τοῖς ὑψίστοις   (8)

III A. INTRODUCTION TO SANCTUS B. SANCTUS

A. We give you thanks also for this ministry,
   vouchsafe to receive it from our hands
   even though there stand before you thousands of archangels
     and ten thousands of angels
5   cherubim
      and seraphim
        six-winged
        and many-eyed
        flying on high
10   singing the triumphal hymn:

B. Holy, holy, holy, Lord of Sabaoth

Heaven and earth are full of your glory.
Hosanna in the highest.
Blessed is he who comes in the name of the Lord.
Hosanna in the highest.

III INTRODUCTION TO THE SANCTUS AND SANCTUS

A.1–2: Line 1 continues the *eucharistia* theme (I.8, II.3,20) and in doing so forms a chiasmus with II.20 (prepositional phrase, verb+object/verb+object, prepositional phrase); the καὶ etc. provides both cootinuity and increment-specification through reference to this specific liturgy, a reference peculiar to CHR at this point. The relative clause of line 2 inserts an imperative request, also peculiar to CHR here. An analogue might be the request for our inclusion in the angelic praise towards the end of the Introductio ad Sanctus in SER and GREG (see below on VI.1).

3: Line 3 introduces the more common material of the Introduction, but in an unusual way suggested and/or required by the reference to this liturgy in line 1 and the sentiments of line 2. The adversative particle καίτοι links 1–2 to what follows and explains the need for the request in line 2 reinforced by the antithesis of human hands in 2 and the throngs of angels in 3.

3–6: These lines provide a congeries of angels in paired phrases. The first pair exhibit homoeoptoton and homoeoteleuton in both words effecting a double rhyme. In the second pair, the exotic character of the names, the names' equal length, alliteration, assonance and homoeoteleuton bind the two together. CHR, then, exhibits at this point two tight angelic 'modules', as opposed to the catalogues of angelic choirs in AC (9 choirs), SER (7), BAS (9), JAS (9) and GREG (6). Similar restraint is shown in the employment of the numerals in 4–5, for CHR cuts back tie numerical congeries of Dan 7:10 (χίλιαι χιλιάδες . . . μύριαι μυριάδες).

7–11: What follows is a tightly linked congeries of five adjectives with asyndeton throughout. The first two describe the appearance/attributes of cherubim and seraphim in chiasmus (ABBA), for the seraphim are six-winged and the cherubim are many-eyed (cf. BAS, MARK, BASAlex, GREG). These two compound adjectives are paired by their equal length and homoeoteleuton (both proparoxytones). The next three, describing angelic activity, are not so closely joined. They are linked, of course, by homoeoptoton and a limited homoeoteleuton, but their accents vary and the insertion of the first three words of line 11 retards, if it does not break, the flow of the series. Advantages, however, accrue from these disassociations: the oxytone (acute on last syllable) πτερωτά may be viewed as announcing the conclusion of the series with a final cadence. The greater length of line 11 swells the cadence to the diminishing series of adjectives, but line 11 is more than a cadence, for ᾄδοντα concludes the adjectival series, returning to the proparoxytone of 7–9. In addition, ᾄδοντα is a bridge, adjectival in looking back to the preceding congeries, verbal as governing τὸν ἐπινίκιον ὕμνον, linking it to and announcing the chant of the Sanctus. Lines 7–11 are a good instance of compressed handling in CHR in contrast to the amplification found in comparable texts. Contrast the economy of 7–10 with the elaborate accounts of seraphic activity borrowed from Isa 6 in BAS, JAS, MARK and GREG. Contrast too the sobriety of line 11 with the congeries of participles found in BASAlex (3 participles), BAS (4), JAS and MARK (5), and GREG (6). Note the later insertion into CHR after ᾄδοντα of a participal series which forms a congeries balancing the adjectival congeries of lines 7–10.

The structure of the Introductio ad Sanctus shows marked contrast between the longer, relaxed, paratactic lines of 1–3, each linked to what precedes (καὶ . . . ἦν . . . καίτοι), and the congeries of tense staccato phrases which follow. The increased length of line 11 provides some closure and relaxation of tension, but the overall effect of the tension in 7–11 which leads up to the participle ᾄδοντα may be viewed as creating a sense of expectation of the Sanctus which follows.

B: The Sanctus is, of course, a scriptural cento, but a few words on some of its features are in order. The accentual pattern of the anadiplosis (repetition of the same word in the same clause) of ἅγιος is reinforced by Κύριος, providing a propulsive series of four trisyllabic proparoxytones. The oxytone σαβαώθ creates a strong contrast and an anticipation of what follows. The base text from Isa 6 is elaborated (contrast CA, SER, MARK) with the addition of lines 3–5 from the gospels, but note the assimilation/elaboration of the first Hosannah of Matt 21:9 and Mark 11:9 to create a refrain. The chant is bound together by the homoeoptoton of lines 2 and 4 and by the verbatim repetition of 3 and 5.

IV POST-SANCTUS

Μετὰ τούτων καὶ ἡμεῖς τῶν δυνάμεων (12)
δέσποτα φιλάνθρωπε (7)
boωmen kaî lęgomen (7)

᾽Άγιος εἶ καὶ πανάγιος (9)
5   καὶ ὁ μονογενής σου Υἱὸς (9)
    καὶ τὸ Πνεῦμά σου τὸ ἅγιον (9)
ἅγιος εἶ καὶ πανάγιος (9)
καὶ μεγαλοπρεπὴς ἡ δόξα σου (10)

ὅς τὸν κόσμον σου οὕτως ἠγάπησας (11)
10   ὥστε τὸν Υἱὸν σου τὸν μονογενῆ δοῦναι (13)
ἵνα πᾶς ὁ πιστεύων εἰς αὐτόν (10)
    μὴ ἀπόληται (5)
    ἀλλ᾽ ἔχῃ ζωὴν αἰώνιον (9)

IV POST-SANCTUS

With these powers
O Lord, lover of man,
we also cry and say:

Holy are you and all-holy
5   and your only-begotten Son
   and your Holy Spirit.
Holy are you and all-Holy,
   and magnificent is your glory;

for you so loved the world
10 that you gave your only-begotten Son
that all who believe in him
   should not perish
   but have eternal life.

IV THE POST-SANCTUS

1: Line 1, with its reference to the angels, bridges the Sanctus to form a connection with the angelic choirs mentioned in the Intro-

The Anaphora of St John Chrysostom   57

ductio ad Sanctus. The Post-Sanctus of BAS begins in the same
way. These words present as accomplished what is presented as a
request towards the end of the Introductio ad Sanctus in SER (μεθ
ὧν δέξαι καὶ τὸν ἡμέτερον ἁγιασμὸν) and GREG (δέξαι μετὰ τῶν
ἀοράτων καὶ τὴν ἡμετέραν φωνήν). The hyperbaton whereby καὶ
ἡμεῖς, the bond to the preceding section, is enclosed reinforces the
association of men with angels.

1–3: These lines are the introduction to the Post-Sanctus, connecting it with the preceding, renewing the vocative in line 2 and
introducing the hymn of 4–13 in line 3. The longer opening line is
followed by a balanced pair. Lines 1–3 are, roughly speaking,
periodic: the prepositional phrase encloses the subject in line 1,
and the double verbs of line 3 embrace the double vocative of line 2.
The verbs in line 3 recall ᾄδοντα of IIIA.11, and like it introduce a
short hymn of praise (lines 4–8). The whole is managed with
economy and compression, as a comparison with the similarly
balanced but more ample parallel passage in BAS will show:

Μετὰ τούτων τῶν μακαρίων δυνάμεων   (13)
δέσποτα φιλάνθρωπε   (7)
καὶ ἡμεῖς οἱ ἁμαρτωλοί   (8)
βοῶμεν καὶ λέγομεν   (7)

4–6: These are a triplet of isocolonic lines. The figure kuklos
(repetition of the initial word of a sentence or period as the
concluding word of the succeeding clause or sentence) is apparent
in the triplet's opening and closing with the same word. It is not
clear whether the repetition ῞Αγιος . . . πανάγιος . . . ἅγιον should
be regarded as simple anadiplosis-plus, or as a kind of paronomasia.

7–8: Line 7 repeats line 4 verbatim and thus, as always in such
cases, we have, arching over lines 5–6, epanaphora and antistrophe
combined. The juxtaposition of ἅγιον of 6 and ἅγιος of 7 suggests
the figure anastrophe as well. Line 7, through this repetition,
provides a hypostrophe after the trinitarian parenthesis in 5–6, a
phenomenon already observed (II.14,23). Line 8 concludes the
acclamatory series of 4–8 with a shift to the third person (from
acclaim of the person of God to acclaim of an attribute), thereby
substituting a new closing member in the parallel construction
suggested by lines 4 and 7. Lines 4–8 are the human echo and
amplification of the angelic Sanctus. The economy and austerity of

CHR in this section can be seen by comparison to corresponding passages of JAS and BAS. To the compact, almost elliptical acclamation and trinitarian formula of lines 4–6 compare the extended acclamation of the persons of the Trinity in JAS; to 4 and 7–8 compare BAS's ample opening of the Post-Sanctus.[11]

9–13: These few lines adapted from John 3:16 (see Wagner, pp. 102–6) are the summary equivalent, unique to CHR, of the ample *oratio oeconomiae* found in other anaphoras. Lines 9–12 are a propulsive series of subordinate clauses, connected to the preceding by the initial relative pronoun, and internally by the succession of conjunctions. Lines 9–10 are nearly balanced. Both end with a verb, but a chiasmus has been effected through the arrangement κόσμον . . . οὕτως (AB)/ὥστε . . . Υἱὸν (BA; cf. the alternative chiasmus in John 3:16). Line 11, only slightly reduced in length, introduces the purpose clause with conjunction and complex subject. Lines 12 and 13 have been set apart to bring out their arsis and thesis (presentation of an idea first negatively and then positively, the positive idea being introduced by ἀλλὰ). In this arrangement, the short line 12 is an abrupt truncation, partly to give point to the antithesis, partly to prepare for the long concluding line 13.

The Post-Sanctus can be divided into an introduction (1–3) and a hymn-like prayer of praise (4–13). The hymn falls into two parts anticipated by the vocatives of line 2, lines 4–8 answering to δέσποτα, lines 9–13 to φιλάνθρωπε. It also shows correspondences to the praise of section II, IV.4–8 corresponding to II.6–13 and IV.9–13 to II.14–19. At the same time, IV.4–8 link the Introductio ad Sanctus and Sanctus through IV.9–13 to the following Institution Narrative.

V   NARRATIO INSTITUTIONIS

Ὃς ἐλθὼν		(3)
καὶ πᾶσαν τὴν ὑπὲρ ἡμῶν οἰκονομίαν πληρώσας		(16)
τῇ νυκτὶ ᾗ παρεδίδου ἑαυτόν		(11)
λαβὼν ἄρτον ἐν ταις ἁγίαις αὐτοῦ		(4+7)
5	καὶ ἀχράντοις	(4)
	καὶ ἀμωμήτοις χερσίν	(7)
εὐχαριστήσας	καὶ εὐλογήσας	(10)
ἔκλασεν	καὶ ἔδωκεν	(7)

	τοῖς ἁγίοις αὐτοῦ μαθηταῖς	(9)
10	καὶ ἀποστόλοις εἰπών	(7)
	Λάβετε	(3)
	φάγετε	(3)
	τοῦτ᾽ ἐστὶν τὸ σῶμά μου	(7)
	τὸ ὑπὲρ ὑμῶν	(5)
15	Ὁμοίως καὶ τὸ ποτήριον	(9)
	μετὰ τὸ δειπνῆσαι λέγων	(8)
	Πίετε ἐξ αὐτοῦ πάντες	(8)
	τοῦτ᾽ ἐστὶν τὸ αἷμά μου	(7)
	τὸ τῆς καινῆς διαθήκης	(8)
20	τὸ ὑπὲρ ὑμῶν	(5)
	καὶ πολλῶν ἐκχυνόμενον	(8)
	εἰς ἄφεσιν ἁμαρτιῶν	(8)
	Ἀμήν	

V NARRATIVE OF THE INSTITUTION

When he had come
  and fulfilled all that he was meant to do for us
on the night when he gave himself up
he took bread in his holy
5   and undefiled
        and blameless hands,

gave thanks and blessed it,
broke it and gave it
to his holy disciples
10   and apostles, saying,

'Take
Eat
this is my body
   which is for you.'

15 Likewise also the cup
  after supper, saying,
  'Drink from this, all of you;

this is my blood
of the new covenant
20 which is shed for you
and for many
for the forgiveness of sins.'
Amen.

V   THE INSTITUTION NARRATIVE

1–2: A connection with IV is created through the initial relative pronoun. The paired participles allude to the Incarnation and Life of Christ and epitomise the ample handling of the *oratio oeconomiae* in the Post-Sanctus in other anaphoras (BAS, JAS, MARK, BAS-Alex, GREG) in the position parallel to IV.9–13. These lines are dramatically asymmetrical, Ὃς ἐλθὼν pregnant in its brevity compared, for example, to the lengthy account of the Incarnation in BAS. Line 2, with its greater length, enclosure and alliteration (πᾶσαν . . . πληρώσας) suggests a completeness, however summary (cf. the conclusion of the summary account of the Life of Christ in JAS: πάντα ᾠκονόμησε πρὸς σωτηρίαν τοῦ γένους ἡμῶν).

3: Line 3 provides the temporal setting (based on 1 Cor 11:23) for the Institution Narrative. CHR, with GREG and MARK, begins this abruptly; contrast the prologue-like μέλλων γὰρ etc. in BAS and BASAlex after allusion to the Command-to-repeat, and μέλλων δὲ etc. in JAS. Lietzmann (23) remarks on the substitution in BAS and CHR of παρεδίδου ἑαυτόν for the scriptural παρεδίδετο (see also MARK and GREG). JAS offers the interesting elaboration of an epidiorthosis (correcting or restricting of a previous assertion) in ἐν τῇ νυκτὶ ᾗ παρεδίδετο μᾶλλον δὲ ἑαυτὸν παρεδίδου.

4–6: The notable feature here is the parascriptural mention of Christ's hands. This takes the form of a prepositional phrase marked by extension and polysyndeton in a pleonastic adjectival congeries. The adjectives of the series are given particular coherence by the alliteration of their common initial alphas and proparoxytone accentual patterns; the second and third adjectives are joined more closely still by homoeoteleuton. A crescendo pattern is also apparent. The progression in length of the adjectives by syllable count is 3,3,4, but the double consonants of ἀχράντοις may be viewed as having a lengthening effect. The three components of the propositional phrase are balanced (7,4,7 syll).

This symmetry is achieved by placing αὐτοῦ in the first member of the series. The balance and relative sobriety of CHR here is apparent in comparison to the longer series of adjectives and ample final line of the corresponding text of JAS:

ἐπὶ τῶν ἁγίων (6)
καὶ ἀχράντων (4)
καὶ ἀμώμων (4)
καὶ ἀθανάτων αὐτοῦ χειρῶν (9)

7–8: The paired participles and paired finite verbs of 7–8 exhibit internal assonance and homoeoteleuton. Line 7 has the last of a long series of participles which runs through lines 1, 2, 4 and 7 and culminates in the finite verbs of line 8. In other anaphoras (BAS, JAS, MARK) this point is the locus for even greater elaboration in the number of participles and the greater periodicity of ending in a single finite verb. CHR mitigates the propulsiveness and pleonastic accumulation encountered elsewhere through the symmetry of 7–8.

9–10: Here CHR, in common with other anaphoras (BAS, GREG, BASAlex), amplifies the simple τοῖς μαθηταῖς of Matt 26:26 through the insertion of the adjective and the doubling of μαθηταῖς with ἀποστόλοις. Further amplification is found in JAS and MARK, where the doublet 'disciples and apostles' is preceded by the adjectival doublet ἁγίοις καὶ μακαρίοις. The oxytone εἰπών ends the line on a downbeat in preparation for the quote to follow (as in many other anaphoras; contrast εἶπεν of Matt and Mark).

11–14: These stark words from Matt 26:26 (and 1 Cor 11:24) are powerful in their concision and abruptness, the result of the isocolon of 11 and 12 and the asyndeton throughout. In line 14 CHR retains the simplicity of 1 Cor 11:24. Contrast the various degrees of elaboration found elsewhere (see Lietzmann, pp. 20–40).

14–15: These are taken verbatim from 2 Cor 11:25 save for the substitution of ὁμοίως for ὡσαύτως. The elaborations of this component in other anaphoras are many (see Lietzmann, pp. 20–40). Suffice it to say that here CHR eschews radically any amplification, even those with biblical warrant. Note that CHR (with JAS, MARK and GREG) retains the chiastic arrangement of First Corinthians whereby the order of the opening of the Bread and Cup Narratives is inverted.

15–21: These lines are a stark cento of scriptural material. Note the elaboration in the triplet of phrases introduced by articles in 18–20. Lines 20–1 might, of course, be combined. I have divided them to point up the doubling of πολλῶν of Matt and Mark with ὑμῶν of Luke, which recalls the earlier τὸ ὑπὲρ ὑμῶν of line 14. Contrast the additional doubling of the participle in JAS and MARK: ὑπὲρ ὑμῶν καὶ πολλῶν ἐκχυνόμενον καὶ διαδόμενον.

The overall impression of the Institution Narrative in CHR is one of restraint, compression and symmetry, especially by contrast to the parallel sections in most other anaphoras. The bread and wine portions in CHR are asymmetrical, the wine portion being compressed and summary. There is no attempt to balance the two as in other anaphoras, though the congeries of phrases in 18–22 balances, to a degree, the congeries and doublets of 4–8.

VI ANAMNESIS

	Μεμνημένοι τοίνυν τῆς σωτηρίου ταύτης ἐντολῆς	(16)
	καὶ πάντων ὑπὲρ ἡμῶν γεγενημένων	(12)
	τοῦ σταυροῦ	(3)
	τοῦ ταφοῦ	(3)
5	τῆς τριημέρου ἀναστάσεως	(10)
	τῆς εἰς οὐρανοὺς ἀναβάσεως	(10)
	τῆς ἐκ δεξιῶν καθέδρας	(8)
	τῆς δευτέρας καὶ ἐνδόξου πάλιν παρουσίας	(14)
	τὰ σὰ	(2)
10	ἐκ τῶν σῶν	(3)
	σοὶ προσφέροντες	(5)
	κατὰ πάντα	(4)
	καὶ διὰ πάντα	(5)
	σὲ ὑμνοῦμεν	(4)
15	σὲ εὐλογοῦμεν	(5)
	σοὶ εὐχαριστοῦμεν	(6)
	Κύριε	(3)
	καὶ δεόμεθά σου	(6)
	ὁ Θεὸς ἡμῶν	(5)

VI ANAMNESIS

We, therefore, remembering this saving commandment
and all the things done for us:

             the cross
             the tomb
5   the resurrection on the third day
             the ascension into heaven
             the session at the right hand
             the second and glorious coming again
             offering you
10   your own
                   from your own
                   in all
                   and through all,
             we hymn you
15   we bless you
             we thank you
             O Lord
             and we pray to you
             Our God.

VI THE ANAMNESIS[12]

1–2: Line 1 is enigmatic because of the notorious absence from
CHR of the Command-to-Repeat. Why ταύτης? What is the command so emphatically recalled? Various hypotheses have and can
be put forward to explain this anomaly, but the question is beyond
the scope of this study. Line 2 provides the transition into the
following catalogue and points up the equivocal use of
Μεμνημένοι, that is, that remembering involves both obedience to
command and grateful recall of past events made present. The
summary, inclusive character of this line is reinforced by the
extension πάντων . . . γεγενημένων enclosing the prepositional
phrase (cf. II.23–6, V.2). The vague, summary character of this line
contrasts with the specific reference to the Passion in its parallels at
the opening of the anamnesis catalogue in BAS, JAS, CA and
BASAlex. The question arises whether line 2 is an introduction,
embracing specifically what follows, or refers to other saving
actions as well. Recall in this connection II.23–6 and V.2 just cited,
and compare the opening of the catalogue in GREG (μεμνημένοι
τῆς ἐπὶ γῆς συγκαταβάσεως etc.) and in the *Anaphora Ignatii Antio-
cheni* ('*Mente igitur recolentes ea omnia, quae pro nobis, et propter nos
dispensatorie a te perfecta fuerunt, nativitatem*' etc.) and other Syro-
Antiochene anaphoras (see *Prex Eucharistica*, pp. 300, 304, 314).

3–8: This catalogue is a congeries marked by asyndeton (contrast the polysyndeton of this catalogue in JAS, CA, BASAlex and GREG, and in a similar catalogue by Gregory the Theologian in Or XVII.12 [PG 35.980AB]), by epanaphora in the repeated articles, homoeoptoton in the repeated genitive endings and homoeoteleuton in lines 3–4, 5–6 and 7–8. There is lengthening of the paired phrases through lines 3–6 (3,3 and 10,10 syll) and a cutback in line 7 preparatory to the longer line 8. A similar crescendo is evident in the insertions of 5–8: 5 inserts a single adjective between article and noun, 6 and 7 a prepositional phrase and 8 a pair of adjectives plus an adverb. The final words of line 8 close the catalogue with an alliterative pleonasm.

The parallel passage in BAS is worth quoting for the differences it displays in the treatment of the same material:

τῶν σωτηρὶ ων αὐτοῦ παθημάτων   (11)
τοῦ ζωοποιοῦ σταυροῦ   (7)
τῆς τριημέρου ταφῆς   (7)
τῆς ἐκ νεκρῶν ἀναστάσεως   (9)
τῆς εἰς οὐρανοὺς ἀνόδου   (8)
τῆς ἐκ δεξιῶν σοῦ τοῦ Θεοῦ καὶ
                    Πατρὸς καθέδρας   (15)
καὶ τῆς ἐνδόξου καὶ φοβερᾶς δευτέρας
                    αὐτοῦ παρουσίας   (18)

Here the ansyndeton is not thoroughgoing, the epanaphora is a little varied, and a diminished homoeoteleuton is evident only between the sixth and seventh lines. The amplitude characteristic of BAS is apparent in the insertion of adjectives in the first two lines and of additional words in the fifth and sixth lines.

9–11: The artifice of these lines can be seen by comparison to the passage in Irenaeus, *Adversus haereses* 4.31.4, quoted by Ledogar (p. 38): προσφέρομεν δὲ αὐτῷ τὰ ἴδια. Their slightly cryptic character is suggested by the fact that in BASAlex and GREG the equivalent of line 10 reads ἐκ τῶν σῶν δώρων. The alliterative congeries of σὰ/σῶν/σοὶ, with their polyptoton at the auditory level at least (the three are not literally the same word), heighten the compressed, staccato character of 9–11 which finds relief in the expansive participle προσφέροντες. This participle closes the series of phrases of 10–12 but, being a participle, it also creates an expectation of something to follow (note the later substitution in CHR and BAS of προσφέρομεν).

12–13: This balanced pair of prepositional phrases with anti-strophe has given rise to confusion and speculation. Whatever the origin or original significance of the lines, we may point out that they recall πάντων of line 2, and that their meaning is something like 'on account of all these things distributively (κατά) and collectively (διά)'. They insert a retardative element between προσφέροντες and the finite verb of the people's chant σὲ ὑμνοῦμεν towards which it points. They may be viewed as balancing τὰ σὰ/ἐκ τῶν σῶν of lines 9–10, as σὲ ὑμνοῦμεν balances σοὶ προσφέροντες. An alternative way of balancing the phrases in lines 14–16 is found in BASAlex and GREG in the triplet: κατὰ πάντα καὶ διὰ πάντα καὶ ἐν πᾶσιν.

14–19: This is the people's acclamation, but it is treated here as a part of what goes before, because it is required to complete the sentence whose only verbal elements so far have been participles. Lines 14–16 are a congeries of verb phrases of considerable compressed energy due to asyndeton, epanaphora with polyptoton, and homoeoteleuton. Their energy is heightened by their crescendo due to the lengthening verbs of the series. Κύριε concludes the crescendo while breaking its movement and prepares for the following phrases, which are both a coda to 14–16 (as well as to the entire anamnesis) and an anticipation of VII.4. Line 18 reverses the order of pronoun/verb of 14–16, creating a chiasmus. The final phrase in line 19 amplifies the breathless Κύριε of line 17 and gives the anamnesis an appropriately sonorous ending.

However one might choose to view this anamnesis from the point of view of conceptual integrity, it does form a neat literary period consisting of
1)   two participial phrases in chiastic relationship: Μεμνημένοι plus genitive phrases (AB), τὰ σὰ etc. plus προσφέροντες;
2)   adverbial prepositional phrases in 12–13;
3)   object/verb triplet in 14–16;
4)   pause, and coda in 17–19.
Looking at it in another way, the relaxation of the long lines of 1–2 is followed by a set of tension-building congeries, each equipped with a concluding feature which partially relaxes the tension: 3–7 followed by the long line 8, 9–11 with προσφέροντες, 12–13 with the verb of 14. Lines 14–16 bring the grammatical tension to a close, but by their congeries, asyndeton and crescendo they maintain a tension which, after the pause on Κύριε, is resolved finally by the coda of lines 18–19.

VII EPICLESIS

Ἔτι προσφέρομέν σοι   τὴν λογικὴν ταύτην   (7+6)
             καὶ ἀναίμακτον λατρείαν   (8)
  καὶ παρακαλοῦμεν   (6)
  καὶ δεόμεθα   (5)
5 καὶ ἱκετεύομεν   (6)
κατάπεμψον τὸ Πνεῦμά σου τὸ ἅγιον   (12)
ἐφ᾽ ἡμᾶς καὶ ἐπὶ τὰ προκείμενα δῶρα ταῦτα   (15)
καὶ ποίησον   τὸν μὲν ἄρτον τοῦτον   (10)
       τίμιον σῶμα τοῦ Χριστοῦ σου   (9)
10   μεταβαλὼν τῷ Πνεύματί σου τῷ ἁγίῳ ῾Αμήν   (15)
    τὸ δὲ ἐν τῷ ποτηρίῳ τούτῳ   (10)
    τίπιον αἷμα τοῦ Χριστοῦ σου   (9)
    μεταβαλὼν τῷ Πνεύματί σου τῷ ἁγίῳ Ἀμήν   (15)
ὥστε γενέσθαι τοῖς μεταλαμβάνουσιν   (12)
15   εἰς νῆψιν ψυχῆς   (5)
    εἰς ἄφεσιν ἁμαρτιῶν   (8)
    εἰς κοινωνίαν τοῦ ἁγίου σου Πνεύματος   (13)
    εἰς βασιλείας πλήρωμα   (8)
    εἰς παρρησίαν τὴν πρὸς σέ   (8)
20   μὴ εἰς κρίμα   (4)
    ἢ εἰς κατάκριμα   (6)

VII EPICLESIS

We offer you too this reasonable
          and bloodless service
We beseech
and pray
5 and entreat you,
Send down your Holy Spirit
    upon us and upon these gifts set forth
and make this bread
    the precious body of your Christ,
10 changing it by your Holy Spirit, Amen.
and what is in this cup
    the precious blood of your Christ,
changing it by your Holy Spirit, Amen.
so that they may become to those who partake

15   for purity of soul
            for forgiveness of sins
            for fellowship with the Holy Spirit
            for the fullness of the Kingdom
            for boldness towards you
20   not for judgement
            nor for condemnation.

VII   THE EPICLESIS

1–2: These lines are the prologue to the Epiclesis. The opening words of line 1 are a hypostrophe recalling VI.9–11 after the intervening acclamations of the people in VI.14–19; comapre BAS Διὰ τοῦτο καὶ ἡμεῖς etc. and contrast BASAlex, which springs from δεόμεθα of the acclamation directly into Καὶ δεόμεθα καὶ παρακαλοῦμέθ σε etc. The following words of 1–2, an amplification of τὴν λογικὴν λατρείαν of Rom 12:1, announce a theme which will be returned to subsequently.

3–5: This balanced triplet of verbs frames δεόμεθα, recalled from VI.18, in the middle of a pleonastic congeries with polysyndeton to give its request greater intensity.

6–7: The request for the sending of the Holy Spirit is handled with a simple imperative as elsewhere (JAS, MARK, GREG) and an unelaborated reference to the Spirit (contrast JAS, MARK). The prolongation of the second prepositional phrase in 7 brings some closure to the κατάπεμψον request.

8–13: Thus the request is renewed in καὶ ποίησον in line 10. The simplicity of this single imperative is in stark contrast to the congeries of verbs in BAS: καὶ εὐλογῆσαι αὐτὰ καὶ ἁγιάσαι καὶ ἀναδεῖξαι. Note the balance of these lines: 8–10 which concern the bread have lengths of 10, 9 and 15 syllables; 11–13 which concern the wine also have 10, 9 and 15 syllables. Isocolon between lines 8 and 11 is achieved by the lengthening of the reference to the wine through the periphrasis in 11 (cf. CA τὸ ποτήριον τοῦτο; BAS, MARK, BASAlex, GREG τὸ δὲ ποτήριον) and between 9 and 12 by the substitution of one bisyllabic word for another. The refrain-like lines 10 and 13 are identical. This interlocked series is further connected: 8 and 11 by the particles μὲν and δὲ and antistrophe; 9 and 12 by epanaphora, antistrophe and parison; 10 and 13 by verbatim repetition. The paired triple lines of this series are joined, in addition, by the contrasting particles.

14–21: After the introductory line 14 this prayer for the communicants is a congeries of prepositional phrases with asyndeton, epanaphora and parison, save in line 18 which, with its genitive/ accusative word order, forms a chiasmus with the order of words prevailing in 15–17. The 'normal' word order is restored in 19 preparatory to the departure from the pattern in 20–1. In 20–1 the series of prepositional phrases continues, but the assonant μὴ ἢ anticipate the prepositions, and the homoeteleuton and paranomasia of κρίμα/κατάκριμα bring the series to a conclusion with a terse, elliptical word play (contrast BAS καὶ μηδένα ἡμῶν εἰς κρίμα ἢ εἰς κατάκριμα ποιῆσαι μετασχεῖν). Contrast this series in CHR with the same series' crescendo in JAS, its amplitude in CA and its length in MARK.

The Epiclesis is readily divided, after the introductory lines 1–2, into two parts: I The Prayer for the Elements (3–13), and II the Prayer for the Communicants (14–21), which had been anticipated by ἐφ᾽ ἡμᾶς of line 7. The two sections are contrasted by the presence of multiple verbal elements in the first part (lines 3–6, 7, 10, 13) and the single γενέσθαι in the second. If we view Section VII as a whole we find a pattern of a long introductory line (1 and 2), a congeries of verbal phrases (3–5), a long supplication (6 and 7), an interlocked congeries of longer phrases (8–13), a transitional line of moderate length in line 14 and a congeries of prepositional phrases in lines 15–21. If we exclude lines 1–2 as introductory, then the Epiclesis is composed of two congeries of short phrases (3–5, 15–21) balanced on either side of the central portion by the longer lines 6 and 14.

VIIIA–H   THE INTERCESSIONS

The intercessions are lengthy. We shall deal with them by groups of sub-sections, and only selectively (see the comparative study by Engberding in *Oriens Christianus* 46 [1962] 33–60).

VIII   INTERCESSIONES

A. Ἔτι προσφέρομέν σοι τὴν λογικὴν ταύτην λατρείαν   (16)
    ὑπὲρ τῶν ἐν πίστει ἀναπαυσαμένων   (12)
    πατέρων   (3)

	πατριαρχῶν	(4)
5	προφητῶν	(3)
	ἀποστόλων	(4)
	κηρύκων	(3)
	εὐαγγελιστῶν	(5)
	μαρτύρων	(3)
10	ὁμολογητῶν	(5)
	ἐγκρατευτῶν	(4)
	καὶ παντὸς δικαίου ἐν πίστει τετελειωμένου	(15)
	ἐξαιρέτως τῆς παναγίας	(9)
	ἀχράντου	(3)
15	ὑπερενδόξου	(6)
	εὐλογημένης δεσποίνης ἡμῶν	(10)
	θεοτόκου καὶ ἀειπαρθένου Μαρίας	(13)
	τοῦ ἁγίου Ἰωάννου	(7)
	τοῦ προδρόμου καὶ βαπτιστοῦ	(8)
20	καὶ τῶν ἁγίων καὶ πανευφήμων ἀποστόλων	(14)
	καὶ τοῦ ἁγίου τοῦδε	(?)
	οὗ καὶ τὴν μνήμην ἐπιτελοῦμεν	(10)
	καὶ πάντων τῶν ἁγίων σου	(8)
	ὧν ταῖς ἱκεσίαις ἐπίσκεψαι ἡμᾶς ὁ Θεός	(15)
B.	καὶ μνήσθητι πάντων τῶν κεκοιμημένων	(12)
	ἐν ἐλπίδι ἀναστάσεως ζωῆς αἰωνίου	(15)
	καὶ ἀνάπαυσον αὐτούς	(7)
	ὅπου ἐπισκοπεῖ τὸ φῶς τοῦ προσώπου σου	(13)

VIII INTERCESSIONS

A. We offer you also this reasonable service
   for those who rest in faith
   fathers
   patriarchs
5 prophets
   apostles
   preachers
   evangelists
   martyrs
10 confessors
   ascetics
   and all the righteous perfected in faith;

```
          especially our all-holy
                immaculate
15              highly glorious
                blessed Mother of God
                and ever-virgin Mary;
                Saint John
                forerunner and Baptist
20              and the holy and honoured apostles
                and this saint
                    whose memorial we are keeping
                and all your saints.
          At their prayers look upon us, O God.
```

B.   And remember all those who have fallen asleep
            in hope of resurrection to eternal life
      and grant them rest
            where the light of your countenance shines.

AB   THE MEMENTO OF THE SAINTS AND OF THE DEPARTED

A1–2: Line one is a virtual hypostrophe after the catalogue-like congeries of VII.15–21. It is a prologue-like reprise, with slight reduction, of VII.1–2, and recalls σοὶ προσφέροντες of VI.11. Once focus and momentum are regained, line 2 states the subject of VIII.A. The preposition ὑπὲρ governs the long homoeoptoton of genitive cases through line 23. The enclosed word order of line 2 is matched by that of line 12, with the identical prepositional phrase enclosed, thus framing the catalogue of lines 3–11.

3–12: This catalogue of categories of saints is a long congeries with an almost thoroughgoing asyndeton and homoeoteleuton. Line 12 closes the series with the all-inclusive παντὸς, its length and its correspondence to line 2.

13–17: The opening ἐξαιρέτως shifts the focus from saints in general, and saints in particular categories, to particular saints. The adjectives of 13–16 are another congeries with asyndeton, also assimilated by their shared paroxytone accents. Note the crescendo effect through the shorter adjectives of lines 13–15 to the longer lines 16–17, culminating in the unique titles and proper noun of 17.

18–19: There is no connective to the commemoration of the Baptist. Unlike the commemoration of the Theotokos, the saint's name comes first and his epithets later. Contrast the more elaborate treatment of the Baptist in JAS, and even more in BASAlex and MARK. 20–3: From asyndeton between 13–17 and 18–19 we move to polysyndeton in lines 20, 21 and 23. The pair of adjectives modifying the apostles in line 20 balance the two nouns of line 19. Lines 21–2 have the rather rubrical sound of all such fill-in-the-blank commemorations. Line 23 completes the genitive series at last. It is truncated preparatory to the longer relative clause of line 24, which extends the conclusion of this long sub-section with an imperative request on behalf of the congregation, ἡμᾶς ὁ Θεός, answering to προσφέρομέν σοι of line 1.

This sub-section shows an ABABA+ movement from general (line 2) to specific (3–11) to general (12) to specific (13–22) and back to general plus concluding prayer at the close (23–4). Congeries of nouns and adjectives in 3–11 and 13–19 are balanced by the longer lines 1–2 and 20–4.

B: Initial καὶ links the imperative μνήσθητι back to ἐπίσκεψαι of A24, but with an abrupt shift from ἡμᾶς to those fallen asleep. καὶ ἀνάπαυσον of line 3 continues in the imperative series and gives specificity to μνήσθητι. Lines 2 and 4 gloss and give amplitude to lines 1 and 3, thus adding weight to this otherwise summary section. Note the curious (coincidental) series of ἐπίσκεψαι of A25, ἐπισκοπεῖ of B4 and ἐπισκοπῆς of C2.

C. Ἔτι παρακαλοῦμέν σε (8)
μνήσθητι Κύριε πάσης ἐπισκοπῆς ὀρθοδόξων (16)
τῶν ὀρθοτομούντων τὸν λόγον τῆς σῆς ἀληθείας (15)
παντὸς τοῦ πρεσβυτερίου (8)
5 τῆς ἐν Χριστῷ διακονίας (9)
καὶ παντὸς ἱερατικοῦ τάγματος (11)

D. Ἔτι προσφέρομέν σοι τὴν λογικὴν ταύτην λατρείαν (16)
ὑπὲρ τῆς οἰκουμένης (7)
ὑπὲρ τῆς ἁγίας καθολικῆς καὶ ἀποστολικῆς ἐκκλησίας (20)
ὑπὲρ τῶν ἐν ἁγνείᾳ καὶ σεμνῇ πολιτείᾳ διαγόντων (18)
5 ὑπὲρ τῶν ἐν ὄρεσιν (7)

```
        καὶ σπηλαίοις                                    (4)
        καὶ ταῖς ὀπαῖς τῆς γῆς                           (7)

        ὑπὲρ τῶν πιστοτάτων βασιλέων                     (11)
        τῆς φιλοχρίστου βασιλίσσης                       (9)
10      παντὸς τοῦ παλατίου καὶ τοῦ στρατοπέδου αὐτῶν    (14)
        δός αὐτοῖς Κύριε εἰρηνικὸν τὸ βασίλειον          (15)
        ἵνα καὶ ἡμεῖς                                    (5)
        ἐν τῇ γαλήνῃ αὐτῶν                               (7)
        ἤρεμον καὶ ἡσύχιον βίον διάγωμεν                 (14)
        ἐν πάσῃ εὐσεβείᾳ καὶ σεμνότητι                   (12)
```

```
E.  Μνήσθητι Κύριε τῆς πόλεως                             (6+4)
        ἐν ᾗ παροικοῦμεν                                 (6)
        καὶ πάσης πόλεως                                 (6)
        καὶ χώρας                                        (3)
5       καὶ τῶν πίστει κατοικούντων ἐν αὐτοῖς            (11)
```

```
F.  Ἐν πρώτοις μνήσθητι Κύριε τοῦ ἀρχιεπισκόπου ἡμῶν
                                               τοῦδε    (18+)
```

```
G.  Μνήσθητι Κύριε   πλεόντων                            (6+3)
                     ὁδοιπορούντων                       (5)
                     νοσούντων                           (3)
                     καμνόντων                           (3)
5                    αἰχμαλώτων                          (4)
        καὶ τῆς σωτηρίας αὐτῶν                           (8)
```

```
H.  Μνήσθητι Κύριε τῶν καρποφορούντων                    (12)
        καὶ καλλιεργούντων                               (6)
        ἐν ταῖς ἁγίαις σου ἐκκλησίαις                    (10)
        καὶ μεμνημένων τῶν πενήτων                       (8)
5   καὶ ἐπὶ πάντας ἡμᾶς τὰ ἐλέη σου ἐξαπόστειλον         (17)
```

C. Again we pray you,
    remember, Lord, the whole orthodox episcopate
    who rightly teach the word of your truth
    all the priesthood

the diaconate in Christ
and every order of the clergy.

D. We offer you too this reasonable service
    for the world
    for the holy, catholic and apostolic Church
    for those who live in a chaste and reverent state
    for those in mountains
        and in dens
        and in caves of the earth.

For the most faithful sovereign
    the Christ-loving queen
    for all their household and army:
grant them, Lord, a peaceful reign
    that we too
    in their peace
may lead a quiet and peaceful life
in all godliness and honesty.

E. Remember, Lord, the city
    in which we dwell
    and all cities
    and lands
    and all who dwell in them in faith.

F. Above all remember, Lord, our archbishop N.

G. Remember, Lord, those at sea
    those travelling
    the sick
    those in adversity
5   those in captivity
    and their salvation.

H. Remember, Lord, those who bring forth fruit
    and do good works
        in your holy churches
    and remember the poor
    and send out your mercies upon us all.

VIIIC–H   INTERCESSIONS FOR THE LIVING

C   The Prayer for the Hierarchy: In contrast to the gliding transition from sub-section A to B, line C1 which opens the intercessions for the living has a hypostrophic quality. It renews the presence of the first person plural after A1 and A24, and gives an intensity to the following imperative. Note the play on ὀρθο- , the anadiplosis with interval πάσης . . . παντὸς . . . παντὸς and the variety created in the catalogue of objects for intercession by the alternative patterns of lines 3 and 5. Contrast the ampler treatment of the parallel to this passage in JAS and the long, stark catalogue in MARK.

D: Line 1 is a repetition of A1 and functions in the same way. As in sub-section A, the imperative is postponed until towards the end of this sub-section, though here it has a more specific point of departure and focus. Unlike sub-section A, D repeats ὑπὲρ, creating epanaphora, in each case introducing a new category, with an ever-increasing number of words in the prepositional phrase. The request in 11–15 reintroduces the first person plural, reciprocating with the third person δὸς αὐτοῖς . . . ἵνα καὶ ἡμεῖς . . . αὐτῶν . . . διάγωμεν (ABAB).

E: Through the remainder of the intercessions for the living each section begins with the imperative Μνήσθητι without preliminary, save in a limited way in sub-section F, thus creating a propulsive, catalogue-like series with epanaphora from sub-section to sub-section. Note the linkages in sub-section E created by polysyndeton, the repetition of πόλεως and the paronomasia παροικοῦμεν . . . κατοικούντων, and the concluding zeugma of persons (5) with places (1–4). To the simplicity of this section contrast the multiplication of cities in JAS and MARK, and the request in BAS for this city etc. to be delivered ἀπὸ λιμοῦ λοιμοῦ σεισμοῦ etc.

G: This prayer for those in need is a congeries with asyndeton and homoeoteleuton. Note here too a concluding zeugma joining persons and their salvation. Contrast the crescendo effect of the parallel series in JAS and its presentation with suitable requests for specific needs in BAS: τοῖς πλέουσι σύπλευσον τοῖς ὁδοιποροῦσι συνόδευσον etc.

H: This prayer for those active in the Church corresponds to sub-section C, the prayer for the hierarchy, and thus these prayers frame the intercessions for the living. In addition to their correspondence in position, their internal structure of a triplet of categories plus an all-embracing conclusion also corresponds. Line 5, with the imperative postponed until the end, stands in a quasi-chiastic relationship to line 1. It brings the intercessions for the living to a suitable close, with a return to the first person plural after the series of prayers for third parties and a generalised entreaty after intercessions for specific needs and ministries.

IX DOXOLOGIA

	Καὶ δὸς ἡμῖν	(4)
	ἐν ἑνὶ στόματι καὶ μιᾷ καρδίᾳ	(7)
	δοξάζειν καὶ ἀνυμνεῖν	(7)
	τὸν πάντιμον καὶ μεγαλοπρεπὲς ὄνομά σου	(14)
5	τοῦ Πατρός	(3)
	καὶ τοῦ Υἱοῦ	(4)
	καὶ τοῦ ἁγίου Πνεύματος	(8)
	νῦν	
	καὶ ἀεὶ	
	καὶ εἰς τοὺς αἰώνας τῶν αἰώνων	
	'Αμήν	

IX DOXOLOGY[13]

And grant us
  with one voice and heart
  to glorify and hymn
  your all-honourable and magnificent name
5   the Father
      and the Son
      and the Holy Spirit
        now
      and always
10   and to the ages of ages.
            Amen.

IX THE DOXOLOGY[12]

1–4: The final line of VIIIH recalled the focus to the first person plural after the intercessions for third parties. The opening of the

Doxology takes its departure from that, providing a seamless connection with the connecting Καὶ, the imperative and the repetition of the first person plural pronoun. The opening line of the Doxology is in a chiastic relationship to the final line of VIIIH: ἐπὶ πάντας ἡμᾶς . . . ἐξαπόστειλον (AB)/ δὸς ἡμῖν (BA).

Lines 2–4 consist of a long infinitive clause dependent on δὸς. They are triplet of balanced pairs: line 2 is a prepositional phrase with paired objects of equal length; line 3 has a pair of infinitives of equal length; line 4 has two compound adjectives, the second of them longer, leading up to ὄνομά σου which responds to δὸς ἡμῖν of line 1. The pairs are somewhat pleonastic. Of course, mouth and heart in line 2 are not the same thing, but the repetition of the irregular numerical adjective in its two different stems brings home the idea of oneness in repeated, almost painstaking detail. Nor are δοξάζειν and ἀνυμθεῖν identical in meaning, but they are close enough to give the line a cumulative, quasi pleonastic quality. This would apply to the compound adjectives of line 4 as well.

5–10: From three doublets in lines 2–4 we move on to two triplets in the formulae of lines 5–7 and 8–10. The polysyndeton slows the movement of the triplets and provides some relaxation after the tension of the congeries in 1–4, a relaxation enhanced by the familiar concluding formula of 9–10.

Lines 1–4 form a period in the sense that meaning is not complete until the conclusion of line 4. In a larger sense, however, the period continues through 5–10, for the genitives of 5–7 are in apposition to σου of line 4, and the adverbs and prepositional phrases of 8–10 modify the infinitives of line 3. Thus the whole of the Doxology is a single, balanced, tripartite sentence developing after its introductory words in line 1, which bond it to Section VII, through the triplet of doublets in 2–4, through the second, trinitarian triplet of 5–7, down through the swelling cadential formula of 8–10.

CONCLUDING OBSERVATIONS

Considerations of space allow only a brief conclusion. That CHR exhibits many of the features of artistic prose, especially those associated with but not, of course, peculiar to the so-called Second Sophistic,[14] is fairly obvious, as is, I hope, the fact that it employs these with considerably greater economy than other Greek anaphoras with which it might be compared. I do, however, wish to offer a few observations in a summary way on certain stylistic features remarked upon in the course of the commentary.

1 Thematic words

CHR can be divided into two parts according to the use of two themes: (I) the *eucharistia* theme, and (II) the προσφέρομέν σοι . . . λατρείαν theme. They overlap slightly, but theme I dominates through sections I–VI and theme II in sections VII–VIII, though it is adumbrated in section VI. This can be presented in a schema as follows:

Theme I	Theme II
I.7	
II.3,20	
III.1	
V.7	
VI.16	VI.11 (σοὶ προσφέροντες)
	VII.1
	VIIIA.1
	VIIID.1

The distribution of words of praise seems also to fit into this pattern, for they are concentrated in the part of the anaphora where the *eucharistia* theme dominates (II.2–4, III.11 and B, IV.3 and 4–9, and VI.14–16) and are not given a reprise until IX. Praise is, of course, implied in Theme II, for the λατρεία is the θυσία αἰνέσεως of the people's pre-anaphoral acclamation, but we are speaking here of the explicit, verbal level.

2 Linkage between sections

The division of CHR into sections is, of course, artificial, but it is well supported by the observation of basic, common patterns in anaphoras and by a certain logic, and it is not unreasonable to suppose that CHR was put together with some such structure explicitly or implicitly in mind. Linkages between sections seem to be of two basic kinds: the bond link, an immediate connection between the final line of one section and the first line of the next, and the bridge link which bonds two sections together over their join. These can, of course, be used in combination. Bond links occur at the joins of I and II (repetition of words), III and II (καὶ), III and IV (καὶ), IV and V ῞Ος), V and VI (ταύτης?), VIIIA and B (καὶ) and VIIIH and IX (καὶ). Bridge links, which often occur in association with a prologue-like opening of a section, are more complex and are too various to describe here. I shall merely cite them and allow the curious reader to review the descriptions of them in the commentary: II.3,20 to I.7, III.1 to II.20, IV.1 to IIIA.3–6, IV.3 to IIIA.11, IV.4 to IIIB.1, V.1 to IV.10, VII.4 to VI.18, VIIIA.1 to VII.1 and internal connections in VIII.

3 Sentence structure

CHR employs both paratactic (parallel clauses, non-periodic) and hypotactic (subordinate clauses, perhaps periodic) styles. Paratactic modules occur mostly in the earlier sections (I, II.6–13, 14–19, IV.3–6, 7–8) but are found later as well (VII.1–13, VIIIB, VIIIH). Of the hypotactic patterns only three form a period in the popular sense: section IV.1–3, section VI and section V.1–8. The dominant hypotactic pattern is of a leading main verb followed by one or more subordinate or dependent constructions, in one case periodic in that statement of complete thought is postponed or protracted (IX), in the remaining cases simply the addition of subordinate elements for gradual elaboration or precision of meaning (II.1–5, 20–27, IIIAB, IV.9–13, VIIIA, VIIID.11–15). All in all the tendency in CHR is to have long sentences, however stitched together, some of them extensive (IIIAB, V.1–14, VI, VII, VIIIA, IX).

4 Hypostrophe

An interesting feature of CHR is the various use of hypostrophe, the restating of a theme, redirecting of focus, after even short parenthesis or digression (see II.12, 14, 20, 23, III.1, IV.1, VII.1, VIIIA.1, VIIIC.1, VIIID.1, VIIIE.1 and the comments on them).

5 Refrains

We have noted the use of refrain-like repetitions, as in responsorial psalmody, in II.12–13, 21–22, IIIB.3,5, IV.4,7, VII.10, 13 and, with greater extension, in VII.1–2, VIIIA.1, D.1. This is a rich stylistic device, with musical and incantatory quality and, as in the last case, a powerful unifying effect.

6 Tension and relaxation

The creation of tension and its relaxation through the use of congeries followed by a concluding line is a common trait (see II.5, 12 & 13, 37, IIIA. 10 & 11, VI passim, VIIIA.12, 24, E.5, G.6, H.5). Another related phenomenon is the shortening (truncation) of a line relative to the length of line(s) in the preceding series preliminary to a longer concluding line (see I.4, 9, II.4, III.10, VI.7, VII.20, VIIIA.23).

Finally, something should be said about the relative sobriety of CHR. Comparisons with other Greek anaphoras have been made throughout the commentary, as far as space allowed. Further comparisons will bear out the tendency of these to show that, though CHR exploits the same resources of late-antique *Kunstprosa* and shows the same tendencies towards pleonasm, elaboration and amplification as the other developed anaphoras, in most instances these resources are used in CHR more sparingly and these tendencies are mitigated and controlled. This is not to say that CHR is a BAS *manqué*, that its economies are the result of some process of reduction or epitomisation. The stylistic difference between CHR and its more exuberant fellows arises from the imposition of a particular taste on the common structure, materials, texts and compositional and/or editorial resources of the anaphora tradition. The precise description of the character of this taste, beyond the primitive notions suggested here, awaits the refinement of the stylistic analysis of CHR and the other anaphoras, and the determination of their precise situation in the spectrum of late-antique *Kunstprosa*. Whether this essay will serve as a modest contribution to this process or no, it is hoped that it will have called attention to the fact that CHR and other Greek anaphoras are works of Christian literary art, and that it may provide those in whose lives CHR is a living presence with a heightened appreciation of it.

80 *Language and the Worship of the Church*

Notes

1. I wish at the outset to thank Roger Brooks, James Ely, Jeannette Sheerin, Phillip Sloane and Robert Taft, SJ for their encouragement and help with this essay.
2. Sophie Antoniades, *Place de la liturgie dans la tradition des lettres grecques* (Leiden, 1939) pp. 118–37; Hieronymus Engberding, 'Die Kunstprosa des eucharistischen Hochgebets der griechischen Gregoriusliturgie', in A. Stuiber and A. Hermann (eds), *Mullus: Festschrift Theodor Klauser* (Münster/W, 1964) pp. 100–10.
3. The text of CHR is taken from A. Hänggi and I. Pahl (eds), *Prex Eucharistica: Textus e variis liturgiis antiquis selecti (Spicilegium Friburgense* 12, Fribourg, 1968) pp. 224–8.
4. All texts are quoted and referred to from *Prex Eucharistica*, with the following abbreviations: CA = the Anaphora from the Apostolic Constitutions (pp. 82–94), MARK = the Anaphora of St Mark (pp. 102–15), SER = the Anaphora from the *Euchologion* of Serapion (pp. 128–33), BAS = the Byzantine Anaphora of St Basil (pp. 230–42), JAS = the Greek Anaphora of St James (pp. 244–60), BASAlex = the Alexandrian Anaphora of St Basil (pp. 348–56) and GREG = the Anaphora of St Gregory of Nazianzus (pp. 358–72).
5. Colometry has proven a sore subject; see the discussion of its fortunes and a fresh approach to it in Thomas N. Habinek, *The Colometry of Latin Prose* (Berkeley, 1985).
6. The definitions are adapted from James M. Campbell, *The Influence of the Second Sophistic on the Style of the Sermons of St Basil the Great* (Catholic University of America Patristic Studies 2, Washington, 1928). For a more sophisticated and detailed account of the figures see H. Lausberg, *Handbuch der literarischen Rhetorik*, 2 vols (Munich, 1960).
7. Works frequently cited: R.J. Ledogar, *Acknowledgement: Praise-Verbs in the Early Greek Anaphora* (Rome, 1968); H. Lietzmann, *Mass and Lord's Supper: A Study in the History of the Liturgy*, trans. D.H.G. Reeve (Leiden, 1979); G. Wagner, *Der Ursprung der Chrysostomusliturgie (Liturgiewissenschaftliche Quellen und Forschungen* 59, Münster, 1973). An excellent bibliography of materials pertinent to some of the matters discussed here has been provided by A. Gerhards, *Die griechische Gregoriusanaphora: Ein Beitrag zur Geschichte des Eucharistischen Hochgebets* (LQF 65, Münster, 1984) XV–XXIV.
8. This is the subject of the first instalment of an extensive study by Robert Taft, SJ, 'The Dialogue before the Anaphora in the Byzantine Divine Liturgy. I: The Opening Greeting', *Orientalia Christiana Periodica* 52 (1986) 299–324.
9. Note that σχῶμεν is an interpolation into an earlier Ἄνω τὰς καρδίας (See Taft, 'The Dialogue . . . II: The Sursum Corda', forthcoming in *OCP*). The insertion of σχῶμεν clarifies meaning, provides a more hortatory tone (see Taft, ibid., on the peremptory character of the line without it) and fills out the line to maintain the isocolon prevailing through lines 4–7.

10. See Ledogar, pp. 13–28.
11. Cf. the triplet in John Chrysostom's *De angusta porta* . . . (PG 51.415): ἅγιος γάρ ἐστι, καὶ πανάγιος, καὶ ἁγίων ἁγιώτατος.
12. See Ledogar, pp. 29–42.
13. See Ledogar, pp. 43–54.
14. See, for example, R.R. Ruether, *Gregory of Nazianzus: Rhetor and Philosopher* (Oxford, 1969) pp. 55–128.

4

Rhetoric and Liturgy

Peter Mack

I INTRODUCTION

I begin with an outline of the subject matter and thought of rhetoric. The three sections following will consider ways in which ideas about rhetoric can be applied to liturgy: general issues, structure and content, and style. I have decided to use the *Book of Common Prayer* of 1552 as an example throughout, to illustrate the ways in which ideas about rhetoric might be used to analyse a particular liturgy. For the sake of simplicity Cranmer is treated as its author. Some of the problems involved in taking this view are considered later.

Rhetoric originated in Sicily in the fifth century BC, as a training in speech-making and more generally as a preparation for active participation in the political life of the city state.[1] Its principles and its techniques for producing speeches were soon applied to composition in general. Alongside its role as a training for politics, rhetoric became a training in the use of language. It was the principal subject of advanced education in antiquity, it played an important though variable role in the Arts course of medieval universities and it underwent an immense revival in the fifteenth and sixteenth centuries. The best definitions are those of Aristotle ('The science of finding the available means of persuasion in any subject whatever') and Quintilian ('The art of speaking well').[2] In trying to understand rhetoric it is important to give attention both to the general principles and to the detailed methods of work and techniques of presentation set out in handbooks of rhetoric.[3]

The central principle underlying rhetoric is that the speech writer must continually reflect on who the audience are and on what he wants them to think. The available means of persuasion, according to Aristotle, are reason, emotion and character.[4] In other words rhetoric aims to teach speakers to handle the subject matter of the speech, the techniques of reasoning, speaking and creating emotion, the character of the audience, and their own projected characters, in such a way as to make the audience assent to the point of view they are presenting. The repertory of techniques described in the manuals is supposed to make it possible to keep all these elements in mind by organising a sequence of thought operations. The risk is that the sequence of operations will become such a preoccupation in itself that awareness of its underlying rationale will be weakened.

According to the manuals there are three kinds of speech, corresponding to three kinds of audience: the judicial speech, presented for the prosecution or the defence in a lawsuit, which is always treated as the basic type; the political or deliberative speech; and the epideictic or demonstrative speech, concerned with praise and blame.[5] The techniques set out for writing these three types of speech were easily generalised or adapted to fit other types of composition. In the Middle Ages specialised rhetorics were composed, adapted to particular types of writing: for instance, the preaching manual and the letter-writing manual.[6]

The handbooks of rhetoric identify five tasks for the orator: invention, finding the subject matter to be used in the speech; disposition, putting it in order; style; memory; and delivery. Most rhetoric textbooks describe ways of going about all five tasks, but some are restricted to one (for example, invention or style) or to one group of techniques.

In the principal general handbooks most space is devoted to invention. The section on invention is organised according to the divisions of the speech. The judicial speech has four main parts (though several authors find more by sub-division): introduction (*exordium*), narration (giving an account of the events in a case), proof and refutation, and conclusion. Under each part the section on invention describes the possible contents and the way to find the contents likely to be most effective in a given situation. Thus the introduction aims to make the audience attentive, eager and well disposed, and to set out the plan of the speech. The ways of doing this vary according to the type of audience and its perceived mood. Under narration, instruction is offered in choosing and handling material so that it will be brief, plausible and favourable. Under proof and refutation are described ways of looking into the circumstances of a case and methods for discovering and presenting proofs and arguments of rebuttal. Quite a lot of general logical training is often set out here. The conclusion involves summary and the preparation of an emotional appeal to the audience.

The organisation of invention according to the structure of the speech rather pre-empts disposition, which is accordingly restricted to a discussion of the circumstances under which normal order may be varied or one of the usual sections omitted.

Under style, the three levels (grand, middle and plain) are described and illustrated. The level of a style depends in part on the vocabulary used, in part on the way the figures are employed. Then the qualities of a polished style (at all levels) are set out: taste (that is, correctness and clarity), artistic composition and distinction. To some extent this is done negatively by considering faults of diction and composition. Under distinction the figures are described, divided into figures of diction, including the tropes, and figures of thought. In *Rhetorica ad Herennium* sixty-four figures, some of them with several sub-types, are listed, involving such things as metaphor, clauses of matching length, patterns of sounds, words and constructions, description, understatement and comparison. The section on memory outlines the system of artificial memory, while that on delivery considers practice, tone of voice and gestures.

Some more specialised Latin rhetorics, such as Cicero's *Orator*, also set out rules for writing artistic prose involving set rhythmic patterns at phrase endings.[7] This sytem was further systematised and adapted to an accentual approach to rhythm in the treatises on letter-writing. In this form it is known as the *cursus*, and is undoubtedly an important feature of medieval Latin prose composition. Some people have tried to extend the theory to English prose, but their success is in dispute.[8] Other approaches to style are embodied in the medieval arts of poetry, which teach ways of rewriting existing material through amplification and diminution of particular sections, and in Erasmus's *De copia*, which describes a number of ways of achieving variety of expression and a full style.

Although the manuals are detailed and precise in their instructions, three considerations make their influence on writing harder to detect. First, although rhetoric was notionally focused on producing three types of speech, the idea that its precepts could be applied to many other kinds of writing with appropriate (but unspecified) adjustments was established at a very early stage. From later antiquity onwards, when the political incentive for learning how to make speeches had disappeared, that idea is implicit in using it as a training. It is often a matter of judgement and taste to detect the rhetorical principle beneath the adaptation to a different genre of writing. In many cases, elements which one critic might ascribe to rhetoric might be regarded by another as a consequence of genre, of imitation or of independent thought. The second consideration is that on one view rhetoric aims to do no more than systematise precepts for good writing. The good writing which rhetoric seeks to analyse and reproduce necessarily preceded the systematisation. Hence many examples of, for example, rhetorical figures are taken from writings such as the Homeric epics and the Old Testament, whose authors were not trained in rhetoric. Since this is so, it must be possible for a later writer without any direct recourse to rhetoric to produce a form which rhetoric advocates. Finally, one of the key precepts of the art of rhetoric concerns the need to conceal the art, lest the speaker is suspected of being too sophisticated in argument.

Thus there is a certain difficulty in defining rhetorical writing. On one view any writing which continually keeps in mind the task of persuading an audience is rhetorical. This would make the class of rhetorical writing very broad indeed, excluding only those parts of writing in which the writer expresses a message without any thought of the impression made on a reader. On another view any writing which uses any specifically rhetorical technique (such as the figures, or the attributes of person or place) for any purpose might qualify. The student of the history of rhetoric tends to take a more restricted view, concentrating on writing which manifests substantial use of the principles or the specific precepts found in the textbooks of rhetoric. This will not necessarily include all the writings of someone trained in rhetoric, since the best student of rhetoric is precisely the one who understands how and when to use the techniques in such a way as to make the writing appear artless.

It would be possible to take the opposite view, stating boldly that all writing is rhetorical and pronouncing whatever is found in all writing to be an aspect of rhetoric. In effect this would only transpose the argument. The historian of rhetoric would then end up trying to estimate degrees of rhetoric, or degrees of traditional rhetoric, within particular works. Rhetorical analysis of either kind will look at aims, at structures and at techniques.

That Cranmer was familiar with the precepts of rhetoric can be inferred from his education, from his library[9] (which included a manuscript of Cicero's *De inventione* and printed copies of Aristotle's *Rhetoric*, Cicero's *Topica*, Quintilian, Erasmus' *De conscribendis epistolis* and Ravisius Textor's *Officina*) and from the construction of his sermons. How he might have made use of this knowledge in translating, adapting and composing liturgy in English is a matter for speculation.

After outlining some general issues involved in applying rhetoric to liturgy, I shall consider from a rhetorical point of view some of the structures incorporated in the *Book of Common Prayer* of 1552[10] and some of the styles employed. I have chosen to use the 1552 version because it contains Cranmer's later and less constrained thoughts, and because so much of its language endures through the revisions of 1559 and 1662 to become the substance of the Prayer Book of the Anglican Church.

II GENERAL ISSUES

Any rhetorical analysis which is not concerned purely with identifying verbal forms depends on considering the relations between author, aim, subject matter and audience. In the case of liturgy the concepts of author and audience are to some degree problematic, while any idea of an aim is both complex and variable over time.

In a speech the author is (at least fictionally)[11] identical with the person who will deliver the speech on some particular occasion to a known audience whose likely feelings at the time of delivery can be estimated. In composing a liturgy the writer is producing material which other people of widely differing character (both priests and people) will have to say many times over in many different situations with some degree of assent and belief.

In the Prayer Book Cranmer had to produce, as far as possible from traditional materials, an English text which would conform to people's ideas of what worship should be while satisfying at least to some degree a broad range of theological opinion.

His choice (perhaps enforced or inevitable) of the Sarum rite as a basic text provided him with elements and an outline which would have been familiar. His ideals of writing come out in his clarity and in his desire for simplification. These points are made explicit in his Preface. The other emphasis there is on instruction, in particular on the need for the whole Bible to be read frequently.

This impulse to instruction is reflected also in the Exhortations first composed for the *Order of the Communion* of 1548.[12] If these are the aims of his adaptation, Cranmer is not so explicit in the Preface about what he takes the general purpose of liturgy to be. He is more forthcoming in two of his controversial works, defending 1549 and attacking Gardiner's response. Christ ordained the sacraments

> that every man should receive them for himself, to ratify, confirm and stablish his own faith and everlasting salvation.

> His holy supper was ordained for this purpose, that every man eating and drinking thereof should remember that Christ died for him, and so should exercise his faith, and comfort himself by the remembrance of Christ's benefits; and so give himself also clearly unto Him.[13]

The main purposes of the sacrament mentioned here are confirming one's belief and one's salvation, remembering and believing in what Christ did, receiving comfort and giving thanks. To these Cranmer adds an element of declaration and testimony of belief, and a strong feeling of comfort in relation to the tribulations of the world.[14] Although these excerpts express his opinions about the positive value of the Eucharist (in spite of his rejection of any element of sacrifice and of any real presence), these opinions do not dictate the contents of his service. The chief elements are traditional. The issue is what meaning Cranmer emphasises in selecting and simplifying.

It is also worth bearing it in mind that, although 1552 by and large became the liturgy of the Church of England, when it was being composed it must have seemed a more temporary measure. Between 1549 and 1552 Cranmer moved further in the direction of Protestant theology, while the Marian exiles who agreed to the Church settlement of 1559 seem to have expected yet further reform in due course. To take the case of one of Cranmer's more substantial omissions, the hymns, it seems clear that Cranmer wanted hymns in the services but realised that he did not have a gift for writing them. If suitable hymns had subsequently been written he would probably have included them.[15]

Just as one kind of rhetorical analysis can be directed at Cranmer's perception of his task and his performance of it, another can centre on the priest's role as speaker and the relationship between priest and congregation assigned by the liturgy.

At some points of the service the priest is the leader of the congregation and their chief spokesman to God, as when he leads them in prayer. At other times he is their instructor, reminding them of their duties, requiring them to absent themselves if their state of conscience is inappropriate. At other times he is God's representative, breaking the bread or pronouncing the blessing. Sometimes the congregation is envisaged as praying directly to God, sometimes as receiving instruction from the priest. Sometimes these functions can overlap a little. For example, it seems likely that the address of the Prayer of Humble Access said by the priest on behalf of the congregation – 'We doe not presume to come to this thy table (O mercyfull Lorde) trusting in our owne righteousnesse . . . we bee not worthye, so much as to gather up the crommes under thy table' – might be considered more apt as instruction to the people concerning their status (which fictionally they are held to assent to, since the form indicates that the priest says the prayer for them) than as an address to God, at whose table they are kneeling. In other words I am suggesting that the double role of the priest as the people's instructor and representative is being exploited here, as the content is addressed to the people, reminding them about their unworthiness, even though the form is addressed to God, as a prayer protesting their unworthiness.

One can also analyse a service from the point of view of the congregation. In the Holy Communion the words of the prayers and exhortations indicate a series of preparatory attitudes that the people are supposed to go through: penitence, comfort, supplication and thanksgiving. At the climax of the service, when the bread and wine are administered, the priest prays with each communicant individually, explaining that the actions of eating and drinking are performed in remembrance of Christ's sacrifice, as an encouragement to faith, and should be accompanied with thanksgiving. In a way these words which speak of the people's thoughts and purposes are silent about their feelings and attitudes. This silence may reflect a reluctance to engage in expressions which require mystery and poetry rather than plainness and didacticism. The final section of the service involves the congregation in rededication, thanksgiving, praise and blessing.

It seems clear that the model of persuasion which rhetoric (judicial and deliberative rhetoric at least) proposes for the relation of speaker and audience is inadequate here. With the exception of the first Exhortation, the priest does not persuade the people (although it is interesting to note that Morning and Evening Prayer have a similar persuasive element in their opening Exhortations). There is no question of persuading, or indeed of informing, an omniscient God of anything. In epideictic rhetoric persuasion is mixed with celebration and exhortation. This suggests a slightly better model, but one which is still inadequate. Nor does rhetoric offer any suggestion for a way to consider the bonding or solidarity brought about among the worshippers through liturgy.

These considerations lead us to rehearse one of the central features of liturgy: the language is human, but the kinds of communication aimed at transcend ordinary human notions of how language is to be used purposefully. They also emphasise the degree to which applied rhetoric is a verbal art, and even one concerned with the written word. Any full analysis of liturgy has to give attention to the place of the liturgical action, and to the ways in which the symbolic meanings of the actions (giving, eating, washing) affect the language formulations and are reflected in them. The textbooks of rhetoric deal with action only in a very restricted way: the kinds of gesture a speaker might employ in relation to the different styles of delivery.[16]

III STRUCTURES AND CONTENT

I am going to consider structure and content at three levels: the service as a whole, particular sections of a service and individual elements. Apart from admonitions and sermons, which are types of oration, the other individual elements have to be considered not as variants of the four-part oration but as separate genres. Since no specialised rhetoric for the production of liturgy has been composed, the issue will be the extent to which the organisation of each form I have identified within Cranmer's text reflects rhetorical principles in its structure. The analysis will tend to favour structure over content at the higher levels because, for the most part, Cranmer reduced and reorganised existing material.

That Cranmer simplified the services he inherited to a considerable degree has often been commented on.[17] The kinds of sectional analysis which Evan Daniel performed on the services of the *Book of Common Prayer*, and which I shall follow, would be much harder to do and would produce much more complex results with, say, the Sarum services.

Daniel divides Morning Prayer into four parts:

1   Penitential Introduction (up to the absolution)
2   Service of Praise and Thanks (to the end of the psalm)
3   Reading Scriptures and Profession of Faith (from the lessons to the creed)
4   Prayers and Thanksgivings (from the mutual salutation to the collects).[18]

A rhetorician might seek to analyse this structure in different ways. If the whole service is an address by the congregation to God, then the first two sections can be regarded as an introduction, preparing the speakers and inducing a favourable disposition in God. The scripture reading and profession of faith can be seen as a persuasion to God indicating the obedience and belief of the congregation, the prayers as the congregation's appeal to God and the Thanksgiving as the conclusion. Alternatively, if the service is regarded as a message to the congregation, the first section is preparatory, putting the congregation in the right frame of mind to begin, the second section is narrative, setting out what is expected of them, the third is argumentative and the fourth is a conclusion. Neither of these is exactly equivalent to Daniel's own view, expressed in his introduction to the fourth section.

> Having prepared ourselves, by confession and absolution, to engage in the worship of God, having had our hearts stirred up to devotion by the singing of the psalms and canticles, and having declared our own personal belief in the great truths which the holy scriptures set forth, we now enter upon that part of the service which is devoted more especially to prayer.[19]

Yet a further alternative would be a more radical disassembly of the main positions taken and stories told, relating them all to some umbrella question such as 'ought God to be praised and worshipped by us?'.

In all these examples, however, the rhetorical precept has to be adapted a good deal to fit the form of the service. It is also true that within each section there is a great deal of diversity, leading to a far more complex overall structure than rhetoric envisages. It would be much easier to argue that the tendency of Cranmer's revision was to articulate structures like those Daniel suggests, but apart from the danger of circularity this would also mean much less as far as the influence of rhetoric is concerned.

The Holy Communion is a longer and more complex service than Morning Prayer, but Daniel divides it fairly clearly into three large sections:

1 Antecommunion (up to the prayer for the church militant)
2 Communion (up to the administration of the sacrament)
3 Post-communion.[20]

It can further be suggested that the first and third sections form a single service, beginning with a preparation focused on repentance, continuing with instruction (epistle and gospel), profession of faith (creed) and exhortation (sermon) and ending with prayer, thanksgiving and blessing. The Communion itself, while remaining the climax, is then seen as being inserted within a self-sufficient structure, a service within a service. Both the Antecommunion and the first part (the majority) of the Communion section can be seen as preparatory, first of the congregation as a whole, and later of the group within the congregation choosing to communicate. Both preparations emphasise repentance and the forgiveness of sins (the former by its use of the ten commandments).

The second preparation in 1552 puts greater emphasis than in other versions of the Eucharist on conscience and the attitude of the communicant, before moving to a much briefer preparation of the elements. No doubt this reflects Cranmer's wish to increase the importance of the state of the communicant's soul and to diminish any sense that the elements of the rite are imbued with magical powers. It may also reflect, as the Exhortations perhaps do, anxiety about how the congregation would react to the change by which communion was to become a more regular occurrence and more a part of ordinary life.

The purposes of the sacrament which Cranmer mentions are embodied in the service in different ways. Belief is confirmed through the creed. Christ's sacrifice is remembered in the third exhortation, the prayer of consecration, the words of administration, the Lord's prayer, the prayer of oblation and the gloria. Comfort is received in the third exhortation, the absolution, the comfortable words and the blessing. The whole last section of the service is devoted to thanksgiving. However much these ideas, and ideas about preparation, are brought out in Cranmer's simplification of the service, the basic structure comes from previous versions of the Eucharist.

On the basis of 1552 it would appear that rhetoric does not have much to contribute to the analysis of whole services. Some rhetorical ideas about introductions and conclusions may correspond with elements of services, and rhetoric will encourage the reader to look at the intentions of the author and the roles of the priest, but on the whole the services have their own basic structures and their own histories of development. Possibly for the early Christian period the historian of liturgy might use rhetoric to analyse the shape of the services; after that the historical development of each service has its own overriding logic.

Sections within services which might invite rhetorical analysis include the penitential preparation for Morning Prayer, the communion proper from exhortations to administration, and the first section of the marriage service (up to the blessing). Here I shall give some attention to the first of these.

The section begins with one or more sentences from scripture chosen by the priest from eleven provided. All the sentences are concerned with repentance, some giving more emphasis to the wickedness of mankind, others more to God's mercy and the forgiveness of sins. The exhortation which follows picks up from the sentence by recalling the frequency with which scripture exhorts us to confess our sins. The idea of confession is linked forward into the service proper by the observation that the most important time of all to confess is at worship,

> when we assemble and mete together, to rendre thanks for the great benefytes that we have receyved at his hands, to set foorth hys moste worthy prayse, to hear hys most holy word, and to aske those things which be requisite and necessarye, as well for the body as the soule.

As Daniel has pointed out, this passage may stand as a statement of the duties of worship (the practice rather than the theory).[21] The elements he lists – thanksgiving, praise, reading scripture and prayer – form the contents of the service which follows. The exhortation introduces the whole service by listing its contents, as an introduction should, as well as propelling the congregation into the first action. The sentence draws attention to the need for confession, the exhortation argues and urges that the congregation should confess immediately.

The confession takes the form of a prayer. After addressing God, the people set out their failings in a series of patterned statements emphasising that they have followed their own desires and have failed to obey God's law. This part of the prayer concludes with the recollection of God's mercy. This leads to the petition for mercy and, in Christ's name, for the improvement of life.

The priest replies with an absolution cast in a middle mode between prayer and address to the congregation. It is not a prayer, but it begins and ends like one, and it makes requests of God. On the other hand it refers to God in the third person throughout. This absolution emphasises God's mercy and the power given to priests to absolve the penitent.

> Wherefore we beseche him to graunt us true repentance and his holy spirite, that those thinges may please him, which we do at this present, and that the rest of our life hereafter may be pure and holy: so that at the last we may come to hys eternall joye, through Jesus Christ our Lord.

Because God is habitually merciful, He is asked to be merciful again. Further the priest requests (and here he seems to be speaking to God as much as to the congregation) that the service will be pleasing to God and that the subsequent lives of the people will be pure and holy so that they will reach heaven. Once more then the introductory function of this section is emphasised, leading into a good service and beyond that to a pure life and ultimately to heaven. The orator too is advised to emphasise in the *exordium* the importance of what he will say for the lives of his audience and the greatness of the benefits they can obtain from it.

The whole section both embodies a typical Christian cycle of penitence for past sin, confession, forgiveness and hope for the future, and at the same time introduces the elements of the service and emphasises the benefits to life they offer. It is possible to discern quite a strong presence of rhetorical ideas about introductions here, perhaps particularly here since this is a section which does not follow a clear model from previous liturgy. It is only fair to add that Cranmer's authorship of this introduction has been questioned.[22]

Next I should like to look at some particular elements within the service. A simple example is the collect. All collects have the same shape: (i) an address to God, with (ii) the addition of some attribute or the recollection of some divine or saintly action, (iii) the petition (sometimes (iv) the purpose of the request) and (v) the conclusion (some variant of 'through Jesus Christ our Lord'). Cranmer understood this very pithy form of prayer perfectly, and his collects follow this pattern, as:

> Blessed lord, which hast caused all holy Scriptures to bee written for our learnyng; graunte us that we maye in suche wise heare them, read, marke, learne, and inwardly digeste them; that by pacience, and coumfort of thy holy woorde, we may embrace, and ever holde fast the blessed hope of everlasting life, which thou has geven us in our saviour Jesus Christe.   (Advent 2)

or, with a little adjustment:

> Graunt, o mercifull God, that as thyne holy apostle James, leavyng his father and all that he had, without delay was obedient unto the calling of thy sonne Jesus Christ, and folowed hym; so we, forsakyng all wordly and carnal affeccions, may be evermore ready to folowe thy commaundements; thorough Jesus Christ our lorde.   (St James)

or, with even more adaptation, in honour of its subject:

> Mercyful father, geve us grace, that we never presume to synne thorough the example of any creature; but if it shall chaunce us at any tyme to offende thy divine majestie; that then we may truely repent, and lament the same, after the example of Mary Magdelene, and by lyvely fayth obtaine remission of all our sinnes; through the only merites of thy sonne our saviour Christ.[23]

Besides Cranmer's observation of the set form of the collect one might notice his tendency to arrange two of his elements so that they are linked in meaning and balanced in form. Thus, for example, the attribute of St James is in two parts which correspond to the two parts of the petition, in meaning and, approximately, in length and structure. The form itself could be regarded as analogous to some of those described in the letter-writing rhetorics,[24] for example in some of the types of letters involving requests, but the similarity probably results from similarity of function rather than from direct influence.

The exhortations are sometimes organised in similar ways to orations. The third exhortation at Holy Communion ('Derely beloved in the Lord: ye that mynde to come . . .') can be used as an example. This exhortation falls into four sections. At first the priest addresses those members of the congregation who have chosen to communicate and reminds them that St Paul advised everyone to examine themselves carefully before taking Holy Communion, because while the benefits are great if the action is performed in penitence and faith, the dangers are equally great if the circumstances are wrong. This introduction sets out the basic premiss of his argument, which he takes from St Paul, as well as the two points which the exhortation will develop.

The second section enlarges on the dangers of inappropriate communion, leading to the conclusion that anyone in a state of sin should withdraw so as not to put his or her soul in further danger. The third section (from 'Judge therefore yourselves') continues the address to those in a state of sin but also acts as a sort of bridge to the other group and a reminder of the acts of preparation they have already performed by outlining the stages of spiritual reconstruction: self-examination, repentance, faith, amendment, restitution and thanksgiving for God's mercy. In the fourth section the act of communicating is exemplified as an act of remembrance of Christ's sacrifice and as a gift of Christ, giving a pledge of his love. The section concludes with a thanksgiving.

Although the matter of the exhortation combines praise and discussion of the communion with a warning, it is not constructed in the most simple rhetorical form (proof and refutation). However, in the way it moves from introduction with narration through argument to conclusion, and the way the conclusion develops more emotionally persuasive material concerning Christ's sacrifice and his promises, it does seem to correspond to rhetorical ideas.

A more straightforward oration structure is found in the Homily on Bible Reading.[25] In this homily Cranmer begins with an outline of what he is going to prove (dispensing with the introduction because the audience has been prepared by the earlier parts of the service). The remainder of the first part consists of arguments in favour of Bible reading. The second part begins with a summary of what has been said and continues with a refutation of arguments against and a conclusion. Even in this example the introduction is omitted and the narration reduced as far as possible.

The foregoing will have shown that while rhetorical and generic structures can be found in the Prayer Book, they are often in such an applied form that a strong direct contribution from rhetoric would be hard to argue for. Also the structures of the services involve a degree of complexity and repetitiveness which, although it is certainly not unprecedented in ancient oratory, nevertheless would be regarded by the precepts of rhetoric as excessive and as a bar to comprehension and persuasion.

4   STYLE

Curiously the analysis of style is both a strong and a weak point of rhetoric. Rhetorics describe and give examples of a huge range of stylistic devices. Their labelling and discussion of particular figures almost certainly helps writers to reflect on their use. The grouping as a whole, though, is inadequately organised. There are a very large number of figures and they are not properly sorted into groups or differentiated according to their relative importance.[26] Rhetoric's attempt to divide style into three levels also fails: in its method, because the criteria of division (vocabulary choice and the use of the figures) are not kept separate from the qualities which all styles may possess; and in its scope, because three levels cannot do justice to the subtleties of distinction we habitually make in using and analysing language. Finally there is the much broader theoretical difficulty that purely formal (that is, context- and content-free) stylistic analysis is almost impossible. We always judge the style of a piece in relation to its subject and its situation. All our perceptions of style are involved with notions about appropriateness.

The highest praise has traditionally been given to the style of the collects. Here is Cranmer's original collect for St Thomas's day.

Almightie everliving God, which for the more confirmacion of faith; didst suffer thy holy apostle Thomas to bee doubtfull in thy sonnes resurreccyon; graunte us so perfectly; and without all doubt to beleve in thy sonne Jesus Christe; that our fayth in thy syghte never be reproved; here us, O Lorde, through the same Jesus Christe, to whome with thee and the holy goste be all honour.

All the words used in this collect were quite ordinary and familiar. The main feature of the collect is the way in which the attributes given to God are balanced in the petition. Both sections are long, but the sentences are extended through their subordinate clauses in a way natural to English word order. Both main clauses are held up by one qualification near the beginning; both repeat 'faith', 'doubt' and 'thy son'; both are of approximately the same length (just over 30 syllables). The balancing also introduces a difference. God allowed Thomas to doubt so that belief would be confirmed; we pray not to doubt so that we may never be reproved. Thomas's doubt was both permitted and reproved, in order to strengthen faith.

In this collect ordinary linguistic resources are transformed into something memorable, through the way the parallelism of the sentence organisation reflects the development of the prayer's thought. Although one can certainly find rhetorical figures that offer suggestions for the prayer (figures involving word repetition, such as *traductio*, and figures involving balancing length of clauses, such as *isocolon*) there is nothing that offers a close model. This a result of the difference between the languages and of the tendency for good writers not to copy model forms but to adapt them.

Nor is it easy to talk of classical models for the rhythms. A high proportion of the *clausulae* of this prayer end with the strong stresses forbidden by the *cursus*. Here is the original 1549 collect for Tuesday after Easter. In 1662 it was assigned to the Sunday after Easter.

> Almyghty father, whiche haste geven thy only sonne to dye for our synnes, and to ryse agayne for our justificacion; Graunt us so to put awaye the leven of malyce and wyckednes, that we maye alwaye serve thee in purenes of lyvynge and truth; through Jesus Christe oure Lorde.

Here the balance is fourfold; the two clauses of the attribute balance each other and then balance the two clauses of the petition (for our sin/for our justification : : The leven of malyce and wyckedness/pureness of lyvynge and truth). In both cases evil is set against good, in the two together God's goodness is seen as a model for us to adopt a good life in return. The image of the leaven is striking, referring both to the unleavened bread of the passover and to the 'old leaven' of I Cor 5:7.

The rhythm here is easier to analyse, though it is no more classical. It is based on fairly short rhythmic units (compared with the previous collect). The units are at first equal (two stresses) but later lengthen, in ways which suit the pattern.

> whiche háste géven
> thy ónly sónne
> to dýe for our sýnnes,
> and to rýse agáyne for our jústificácion.

Here the syntactic patterning of units three and four maintains the transition to the doubling of stresses.

> Gráunt us
> Só to put awáye
> The léven of mályce and wickédness
> That we may álwaye sérve thée
> In púrenes of lývynge and trúth.

The units gradually lengthen, then the three three-stress units are set against each other. The patterns of units three and five are close enough almost to set up an expectation of a regular (i.e. verse) form. Indeed the stress pattern of alliterative verse (two half-lines with two stresses in each) may lie behind the effect of the collect. Alliteration itself plays only a very small part in the effect of either collect.

Of the collects quoted earlier, the rhythmic effects are probably strongest in Advent 2. The first two clauses of the petition can almost be made into a couplet.[27] Only the three stresses together on 'réad, márk, léarn' prevent it. The way the two-stress units of the remainder of the petition culminate in the three-stressed 'of éverlásting lífe' is equally striking.

In the collects Cranmer's style sticks very closely to the patterns made obligatory either by the material translated or by the form required. It hardly ever involves unusual words or the introduction of metaphors. In the collects, especially, it is very pithy (and appropriately so); it is occasionally made more dense by the introduction of a rhetorical figure of patterning (for example, see Dr Cuming's example of chiasmus in Advent 1).[28] In the translations there is occasional doubling of words, occasional transfer of one word from a very dense construction to the next phrase, occasional filling out of tightly made contrasts into longer contrasting phrases.[29] In the main, however, the collects are both close to the Latin originals and at the same time (which is hard) plain English.

The collects *are* pithier than the exhortations, but the exhortations hardly waste words. The summary of the points they make often requires almost as many words as the texts themselves. The sentences are much longer, too long for congregational speaking. There is more doubling of words and phrases, and more comparison. Both in movement and in diction they are more dignified. In the first exhortation Cranmer employs fable ('Ye knowe how greuouse and unkynde a thing it is, when a man hath prepared a riche feaste, decked his table with al kinde of prouision, so that there lacketh nothing but the geastes to sit down: and yet they which be called, without any cause most unthankefully refuse to come'), personation ('It is an easy matter for a man to saye, I wyll not communicate, because I am otherwyse letted with worldly business . . . If any man saye, I am a greuous sinner, and therefore am afraied to come: wherefore then doe you not repent and amend?') and rhetorical question ('Which of you, in such a case, would not be moued? Who would not thynke a great injury and wrong done unto him? . . . When you shoulde returne to god, wyll you excuse your selfe, and saye that you be not ready?'), and at the end there is repetition of and word play on 'depart' ('Wherefore, rather then you should so doe, depart you hence and geve place to them that be godly disposed. But when you depart, I beseche you, pondre with yourselues from whom you depart: ye depart from the lordes table, ye depart from your brethren, and from the banquete of moste heauenly fode.'). In comparison with much prose these are restrained and pithy, but put beside the collects it is the latter which seem terse, simple, but pointed with a choice and sparing use of figures.

A longer structure which depends on balanced clauses as much as the collects we have examined, but which makes more use of incremental repetition, is the General Confession for Holy Communion, which depends on Hermann von Wied's *Simplex ac pia deliberatio* (1545).[30] Here the lineation is by phrases, not according to stress.

> Almightie God,
> father of our Lorde Jesus Christe,
> Maker of all thyngs,

Judge of all men,
we knowledge and bewayle
oure manyfolde sins and wyckednes,
whiche we from tyme to tyme
   most grievously have committed,
by thoughte, woord and dede,
agaynst they devine Majestie:
provokyng most justly
thy wrathe and indignacion agaynste us:
we doe earnestlye repente
and be hartely sory for these our misdoynges:
the remembraunce of them is grievouse unto us,
the burthen of them is intollerable:
have mercye upon us,
have mercye upon us,
moste merciful father,
for thy sonne oure Lorde Jesus Chrystes sake;
forgeve us all that is past,
and graunt that we maye ever hereafter
   serve and please thee,
in newness of lyfe,
to the honoure and glory of thy name:
Through Jesus Christ our Lord.

The dignity of the language here comes from the trick, no doubt
imitated from Latin originals, of building long grammatical sequences out of shorter self-contained units which repeat verbal and
syntactic patterns from earlier in the passage. Sometimes the
shorter units are employed to frustrate the expected completion of
the sentence or to extend the sentence beyond the point where the
hearer first hears it complete. Although some of the verbal patterns
and the way the sentences are held up can be described in terms of
the figures of rhetoric, the remarkable thing about the composition
is the way the patterns employed seem to grow out of English
structure. Repeated short rhythmic units of the kind we found in
some of the collects are here set against sections where the clauses
are much longer and the rhythms weaker. Here syntactic parallelism seems more important to the effect than rhythm is. A great
deal in this piece, perhaps more than in the collects, depends on
the weight which some of the shorter phrases will be given in
delivery. One can imagine many different ways of reading the double

'have mercy upon us' in the context of the longer phrases preceding it. These variations of delivery will affect their effectiveness.

A discussion of the literary style of Cranmer's Prayer Book ought to include comparisons with the styles of other authors. The difficulty is to make comparisons which are appropriate, that is, with texts which are trying to do similar sorts of thing and texts which were composed at roughly the same period. For this reason it is not really apt to make comparisons with Shakespeare or with Elizabethan prose writers. I have chosen to refer briefly, since a separate article or a book could consider the styles of mid-sixteenth century prose and the place of the Prayer Book among them, to some earlier and later prayers and to two authors who combined humanist and religious interests, John Fisher (1459?–1535), Bishop of Rochester, and Roger Ascham (1515–68), Queen Elizabeth's tutor.[31]

The texts which Geoffrey Cuming has collected in chapter 2 of *The Godly Order* show how much the canticles and prayers of the *Book of Common Prayer* owe to the English Primers of the reign of Henry VIII. In the case of the Lord's Prayer, it seems that Cranmer's chief merit lay in accepting a series of emendations to a translation (by Joye) which already contains memorable phrases.[32] Cranmer's only independent contribution is an omission which strengthens the sequence of two-stress rhythmic units at the beginning of the prayer.[33] Taken as a whole the prayers of the Primers are surprisingly consonant with Cranmer's prayers. It has often been pointed out that the printed prayers of Elizabeth's reign are very different. Bishop Dowden considered some of them to have 'all the faults of long harangues turned into the outward semblance of prayer by being in the form of an address to the almighty', and he quotes some extraordinary examples. Others he finds acceptable for private meditation but not 'for the solemn dignity of public worship'.[34]

Someone who compared the English Primers of Henry VIII's reign with the Elizabethan prayers might perhaps conclude that the 1530s enjoyed a far higher standard of prayer-writing than the 1580s, in which case it would be our good fortune that Cranmer lived in the earlier period. It is more likely, however, that Cranmer's prayers succeed because of their basis in the Latin Primer.[35] Even in his original prayers he seems to have tuned himself to the spirit he found through these translations into English, rather than to one of novelty. The later prayers seem inappropriate precisely because the authors argue views of their own at length.[36]

The style of Cranmer's contributions to the *Book of Common Prayer* is above all a plain style, which uses ornament only sparingly and which models itself where possible on the language of the Sarum rite and its English translations. Although it is a Prayer Book style it has something in common with Cranmer's style elsewhere. Even in his sermons,[37] which are more strictly rhetorical in structure and which include rhetorical questions, examples and parallel cases, ornament and emotional intensity are avoided. Instead the tone is argumentative and logical, full of matter, but driving home its conclusions with the greatest firmness. Even in his letters, where he observes in his style the status of his addressee, the main sense is of unadorned argument, organised to be sure in clauses which balance each other.

Compared with Fisher he is restrained, English rather than Latin, brief in his sentences, unemotional in his effects.[38] Compared with Ascham he avoids the flourishes: no long sentences, no multiplied parallel examples in parallel phrases, no alliteration.[39] C.S. Lewis's remarks about committee man's prose now read more unkindly than they were meant, but they say something valid about the levelness of Cranmer's usual writing styles.[40] In fact his liturgical prose is better than the rest of his writing. Having to be really terse and selective, having to follow a strict model closely, finding the final improvement in a prayer translation that had already been revised often, brought out his sense of his own language to the highest degree.

There is one final point to make about the style of the liturgy. The liturgy is made up of numerous segments exhibiting styles which differ very markedly. Among the fixed elements the joyful poetic style of the canticles contrasts with the patterned brevity of the responses, the pithy style of the collects and the tight reasoning of the admonitions. To these each service will add variable psalms, Bible readings and a sermon, which will further enrich the stylistic variety. The context puts a premium on variety. A service with many different segments needs different styles. Equally, though, the variations of style among the various elements put each particular style in greater relief. The prose of the collects will seem plainer still when it is put beside the poetry of the canticles and the oratory of a sermon.

To summarise, then, Cranmer makes some use of the figures of speech outlined in the rhetoric manuals. On the whole he uses the figures sparingly, but in such a way that they stand out and make a strong impression. There are places, for example the first exhortation of Holy Communion, in which he employs several figures close together, where the effect is more like that of a speech, with the language correspondingly more ornate. The doctrine of the three styles is not much help in discussing Cranmer. Instead one is struck by the variety of styles employed within a service, by the plainness of Cranmer's range of styles in relation to those of other authors, by the way he suits his English style to his Latin models and by the attention he gives to rhythm. In comparison with artistic prose of the early Tudor period, Cranmer's liturgical style is plain and restrained. He writes prose that is both weighty and suited to be spoken. One does not have to be a good actor to bring out at once its sense and its gravity.

A note on Prose Rhythm

It will be clear that I do not accept the claims that were made in the early years of the century by Clark, Elton, Shelly and others[41] that the Latin *cursus* was a basic feature of artistic English prose style and a crucial element in the style of the *Book of Common Prayer.* Lewis found the statistical arguments inconclusive,[42] while others, including Dr Cuming, have pointed out that once you admit varied forms of the classical types and 'native' types the position is very soon reached (and I think this happens to Clark) where every possible clause ending is defined to be acceptable to the *cursus.* At that point the argument defeats itself.

However, I *do* think that prose rhythm is both an important feature of composition and one that has been neglected. I have made some observations about rhythm because the effect of the prayers required it. The way I choose to place stresses and to cut the prose into rhythmic units is subjective. Others might, by cutting the phrases into different units and placing the stresses differently, reach other conclusions. The study of prose rhythm has not yet reached the stage where one can feel that such judgements are reliable. On the other hand the real advances that have recently been made in prosody (I am thinking of Attridge's *The Rhythms of English Poetry* (1982) in particular) offer some hope of progess in this study.

CONCLUSION

I have tried to combine fairly straightforward practical criticism with analysis based on the principles (and the detailed instructions) of the rhetoric textbooks. Neither type of analysis has produced any results which are very surprising. Although Cranmer's education, his library and his humanist connections suggest that he is likely to have had a considerable familiarity with rhetoric, the consequences of this in his liturgical composition seem to be quite small. In whole services he tends to work from older forms, usually from the Sarum rite, simplifying and removing objectionable material. The strongest tendency here is educative. His services aim to institute regular reading of the whole Bible and to instil a proper Protestant attitude in the worshipper. Particular sections of services are still heavily dependent on the models, mixing different types of material (for example, canticles among the lessons) or repeating material (such as the Lord's Prayer) more than the principles of rhetoric would allow. Perhaps the new penitential introduction to Morning Prayer reflects some influence of rhetorical ideas about introductions.

There is certainly room for more work on Cranmer's liturgical prose style, as there is on prose style generally, but the kinds of analysis that seem most likely to be fruitful do not have much connection with the teachings of rhetoric. The doctrine of the three styles is too inflexible. Cranmer uses the figures only sparingly. Latin rhythm and the rhythms of Latin prose seem to be rather different from their English equivalents. In all these areas, liturgical traditions, Protestant ideas and the prose styles of his near contemporaries seem to offer better help in understanding and estimating Cranmer's achievement than rhetoric can.[43]

Where rhetoric might well have more to offer is in the study of the formation of the Christian liturgy, in as far as it was not based on Jewish services. Some of the oldest elements which Cranmer translates, such as the kyrie, or the versicle and response ('O Lord make haste to help us') suggest, through their use of word and phrase patterning, the possibility of rhetorical influence on style at a much earlier stage. Even if this is right, I would expect that the rhetorical influence on the liturgy would probably be smaller than that on the early Christian apologists, or even on the creation of the gospel narratives. It may also be that one should look, not as I have at the Latin textbooks of rhetoric, but at Greek traditions, which are in some ways richer in their handling of style. The corpus of works attributed to Hermogenes,[44] for example, includes a treatise on the method of awesomeness. One can easily imagine that the authors of early Christian liturgies might have been interested in techniques for producing language likely to be impressive both to ordinary people and to the cultivated elite.[45]

If rhetoric could be shown to have played an important part in the formation of Christian services, a further question would arise: what is the moral propriety of Christian authors using a pagan technique so often associated with deception (or with swaying people's emotions against the promptings of their reason) for such a central religious purpose? Plato's objections to rhetoric are well known,[46] and they are echoed in essential Christian ideas about the importance of inward virtue over virtuous seeming. St Augustine argued that one ought to make responsible use of rhetorical techniques in preaching, in order better to serve the word of God in argument.[47] It seems rather doubtful that this line of argument could be extended to the liturgy. If one employs rhetoric in writing prayers, is one attempting to influence God in ways that might be misleading? Is it any less serious to seek to give members of one's congregation misleading feelings about their relations with God? Set beside this sort of alarming possibility the plainness and didacticism of Cranmer, which is so often accused of being spiritually and emotionally impoverished, begins to seem a positive virtue.[48]

Notes

1. Basic works on the history of rhetoric are: G. Kennedy, *Classical Rhetoric and its Christian and Secular Tradition* (London, 1980), *The Art of Persuasion in Greece* (Princeton, 1963), *The Art of Rhetoric in the Roman World* (Princeton, 1972); A. Michel, *Rhétorique et philosophie chez Cicéron* (Paris, 1960).
2. Aristotle, *Rhetoric*, 1355b27; Quintilian, *Institutio oratoriae*, 2.15.38.
3. One may make a rough distinction between more theoretical treatments, such as Aristotle's *Rhetoric* and Cicero's *De oratore*, and works which are closer to being teaching manuals, such as Cicero's *De inventione*, the anonymous *Rhetorica ad Herennium* (these two are the handbooks most frequently used in the Middle Ages and the Renaissance) and Cicero's *Partitiones oratoriae*. Quintilian's *Institutio oratoriae* combines elements of both types. Some more philosophical modern discussions, including that in Paul Ricoeur's excellent *The Rule of Metaphor* (London, 1978), chapter 1, tend to concentrate on the theory, ignoring the implications of what was actually taught.

4. Aristotle, *Rhetoric*, 135a2–4.
5. It is impractical to provide references for this general account of rhetoric. Justification for what I say will be found in *Rhetorica ad Herennium*, trans. H. Caplan (London: Loeb Classical Library, 1954), which has a very helpful analysis, pp. xlv–xlviii, or in *De inventione*. The following systematic guides may be helpful: R. Volkmann, *Rhetorik* (Munich, 1901); H. Lausberg, *Handbuch der literarischen Rhetorik*, 2 vols (Munich, 1960).
6. On medieval rhetoric see: J.J. Murphy, *Rhetoric in the Middle Ages* (Berkeley, 1974); J.J. Murphy (ed.), *Medieval Eloquence* (Berkeley, 1978).
7. The chief ancient treatments of prose rhythm are: Cicero, *Orator*, 43.147–71.236; Quintilian, *Institutio oratoriae*, 9.4. Latin prose rhythm is studied in: A.C. Clark, *Fontes Prosae Numerosae* (Oxford, 1909), *The Cursus in Medieval and Vulgar Latin* (Oxford, 1910).
8. See the note on Prose Rhythm at the end of Section IV below.
9. Cranmer was at Cambridge between 1503 and 1529, first as a student studying the Arts course, which included rhetoric, and later as a fellow of Jesus College studying divinity, at the time when Erasmus was teaching Greek there. There are biographies by A.W. Pollard (London, 1905) and J. Ridley (Oxford, 1962). His library is listed by Edward Burbidge in G.E. Duffield (ed.), *The Work of Thomas Cranmer* (Appleford, 1964) pp. 341–65.
10. For the Prayer Books of 1549 and 1552 I have used the Everyman edition, *The First and Second Prayerbooks of King Edward the Sixth* (London, 1910) (hereafter referred to as *Prayerbooks*).
11. I mean that the speech remains Mrs Thatcher's because she delivers it, even if it was actually written by someone else.
12. H.A. Wilson (ed.), *The Order of the Communion* (1548) (London: Henry Bradshaw Society, 1908) vol. 34. Geoffrey Cuming has demonstrated that Cranmer took many phrases from Hermann von Wied's *Simplex ac pia deliberatio* (1545): see his *The Godly Order*, (London: Alcuin Club, 1983) pp. 68–81. He prints an English translation in *A History of Anglican Liturgy*, 2nd edn (London, 1982) (hereafter Cuming, *History*) pp. 286–304.
13. Cranmer, *Defence of the True and Catholic Doctrine of the Sacrament* (London, 1550) V 10 and V 13. I have taken these extracts from G. Dix, *The Shape of the Liturgy* (Westminster, 1945) pp. 648–55.
14. The further extracts are from *Defence*, V 9 and I 16; cf.Dix.
15. Cuming, *History*, p. 51; C.S. Lewis, *English Literature in the Sixteenth Century excluding Drama* (Oxford, 1954) (hereafter Lewis) p. 217.
16. *Rhetorica ad Herennium*, III.15.26–7. Characteristically Quintilian gives a very detailed account of gestures suited to the orator, in *Institutio oratoriae*, 11.3.65–149.
17. See, for example, the tables in Cuming, *History*, pp. 49, 53.
18. Evan Daniel, *The Prayer-Book, Its History, Language and Contents*, 22nd edn (London, 1909) p. 96.
19. Ibid., p.172.
20. Ibid., p. 338 (with a useful table).
21. *Prayerbooks*, p. 348; Daniel, *The Prayer-Book*, p. 98.

22. Reference in Cuming, *History*, pp. 76–7, 362.
23. *Prayerbooks*, pp. 34, 200, 198. This prayer is from the 1549 Prayer Book, but was dropped in 1552 and 1559.
24. See the works on medieval rhetoric listed in note 7 above. Also: H.M. Schaller, 'Ars Dictaminis, ars dictandi', in *Lexicon des Mittelalters*, I (Munich, 1980) pp. 1034–9; L.D. Rockinger, *Briefsteller und Formelbücher des elften bis vierzehnten Jahrhunderts* (Munich, 1863) repr. 2 vols (New York, 1961). There is now an immense literature on the connection between the flourishing of the letter-writing manual (*Ars dictaminis*) and early humanism. See R. Witt, 'Medieval "Ars Dictaminis" and the Beginnings of Humanism', *Renaissance Quarterly*, 35 (1982) pp. 1–35. Some Renaissance letter-writing manuals are: Erasmus, *De conscribendis epistolis*, in *Opera omnia* (Leiden, 1703) repr. (Hildesheim, 1961) I.521–36; J.L. Vives, *De conscribendis epistolis libellus* (Paris, 1547); A. Day, *The English Secretarie* (London, 1625).
25. *The 2 Books of Homilies* (Oxford, 1859) pp. 7–15.
26. Some Renaissance textbooks are concerned exclusively with the figures: Susenbrotus, *Epitome troporum ac schematum et grammaticorum et rhetorum* (Zurich, 1541); Mosellanus, *Tabulae de schematibus et tropis* (Antwerp, 1529); Sherry, *A Treatise of Schemes and Tropes* (London, 1550). They are digested in L.A. Sonnino, *A Handbook to Sixteenth Century Rhetoric* (London, 1968).
27. 'graunte us that we maye in suche wise heare them, read, marke, learne, and inwardly digeste them;'
28. See page 117 above.
29. For example: doubling, Epiphany 3 and 4, Easter 4; transfer of words, Lent 5; filling out, Christmas day first communion (1549), Lent 2.
30. Cuming, *The Godly Order* (see note 12 above) pp. 78–80.
31. One might equally well question whether the artistic prose that Fisher and Ascham wrote offers the right sort of comparison. Other examples which might be considered are: dialogues, educational and otherwise, translations from Latin (but probably not those of elaborate stylists), examples of fifteenth-century prose and Bible translations. One would need to make a survey of early Tudor prose as a preliminary to choosing comparators. Cranmer is compared to the Bible translations in Stella Brook, *The Language of the Book of Common Prayer* (London, 1965).
32. 'Owre father which arte in heaven, halowed be thy name. Lete they kyngdome come ouer vs. Thy wyll be fulfilled as well in earthe as it is in heauen. Geue vs this daye ower sufficiente fode. And forgeue vs ower trespasses as we forgeue them that trespas ageinste vs. And lede vs not into temptacion, but delyure vs from theuel spirit. Amen.' Quoted from Cuming, *The Godly Order*, p. 50.
33. The change was to omit 'as well' from 'Thy wyll be done (as well) in yearth, as it is heauen'. The successive revisions to Joye's version culminating in Cranmer's are set out in Cuming, *The Godly Order*, p. 50.
34. J. Dowden, *The Workmanship of the Prayer Book*, 2nd edn (London, 1902) pp. 195ff.

35. Geoffrey Cuming points out that the English Primers translate fewer of the collects, and translate them much less well; *The Godly Order*, pp. 51–6.
36. Dowden's example (note 34 above), which will do as well as any, begins: 'A Prayer for the estate of Christ's Church: to be used on Sundays(1580)'.

> O Gracious God and merciful father, thou that art the God of all comfort and consolation: we poor and wretched sinners acknowledge against ourselves that we are unworthy to lift up our eyes to heaven: so horrible and great are the sins that we have committed against thee both in thought, word and deed. But thou art that God whose property is always to have mercy, and thou hast extended thy mercy unto us in thy beloved Son our saviour Christ Jesus, in whom thou hast loved us before the foundation of the world was laid: and to the end thou mightest advance thine own mercy in a good and happy time has called us, by the preaching of the blessed and holy Gospel, to repentance, preferring us before many and great nations to be a people consecrate unto thee, to hold forth thy righteousness, and to walk in obedience before thee all the days of our lives. In this persuasion of faith and by him, good Father, we present ourselves before thee, renouncing all our sins and corruptions, and trusting only in him and his righteousness beseeching thee for his sake to hear us, and to have mercy upon us . . .

This is about an eighth of the whole prayer. See *Liturgies and Occasional Forms of Prayer set forth in the reign of Queen Elizabeth*, ed. Rev. William Keatinge Clay (Cambridge: Parker Society, 1847) vol. 27, pp. 576–9.
37. Cranmer's sermons may be found in H. Jenkyns (ed.), *The Remains of Thomas Cranmer* (Oxford, 1833); J.E. Cox (ed.), *The Works of Thomas Cranmer* (Cambridge: Parker Society, 1844–6).
38. J.E.B. Mayor (ed.), *The English Works of John Fisher*, Part 1, Early English Texts Society, Extra Series, vol. 27 (London, 1876). The 'Mourning Remembrance of Princess Margaret' will do as an example, pp. 289–310, and perhaps the second section in particular, pp. 289–303.
39. R. Ascham, *The Scholemaster*, in *English Works*, ed. W.A. Wright (Cambridge, 1904) pp. 289–310, for example pp. 189–95.
40. Lewis, p. 195.
41. J. Shelly, 'Rhythmical Prose in Latin and English', in *Church Quarterly Review*, 74 (April 1912) pp. 81–98; A.C. Clark, *Prose Rhythm in English*(Oxford, 1913); O. Eton, 'English Prose Numbers', in *Essays and Studies*, 4 (1913) pp. 29–54; G.C. Richards, 'Coverdale and the Cursus', in *Church Quarterly Review*, 219 (April 1930) pp. 34–9. The highly impressionistic G. Saintsbury, *A History of English Prose Rhythm* (London, 1912) is still as good as anything on English prose rhythm generally; see also I.A. Gordon, *The Movement of English Prose* (London, 1965).
42. Lewis, pp. 218–20.

43. What I have heard about Cardinal Quinones suggests that his liturgical work might usefully be investigated from a rhetorical point of view.
44. For Hermogenes see D.A. Russell and M. Winterbottom (eds.), *Ancient Literary Criticism* (Oxford, 1972) pp. 561–78; G. Kustas, 'Function and Evolution of Byzantine Rhetoric', in *Viator*, 1 (1970) pp. 55–73, *Studies in Byzantine Rhetoric* (Salonika, 1973); J. Monfasani, *George of Trebizond* (Leiden, 1976) especially pp. 271ff.
45. See Daniel J. Sheerin's essay in this volume on the Liturgy of St John Chrysostom, Chapter 3.
46. The most important texts are *Phaedrus, Gorgias* and *Protagoras*.
47. *De doctrina Christiana*, II.40.60–42.63.
48. I am much indebted to Ronald Jasper and Geoffrey Cuming for criticism, help and encouragement in writing this paper. I thank them, and also Keith Hoskin, who listened to some ideas for it, Martin Warner, who read a draft, and Sue Wallington, who obtained many of the books I needed. Books which I have found particularly helpful were F.E. Brightman, *The English Rite*, 2 vols (London, 1915) and G. Dix, *The Shape of the Liturgy* (Westminster, 1945).

5

Thomas Cranmer, Translator and Creative Writer

Geoffrey Cuming

The thirty years before the appearance of *The Book of Common Prayer* in 1549 were marked, from the liturgical point of view, by an outburst of translation into the vernacular. First and foremost, William Tyndale in the 1520s and Miles Coverdale in the 1530s produced translations of the Bible which resulted in 1539 in the licensed version known as the 'Great' Bible, to which Cranmer wrote a preface in which he set out the reasons for the use of the vernacular. Even more relevant to the texts of the services was the series of reforming Primers which began in 1530 with the publication of George Joye's *Hortulus Animae* and continued up to the fully official *King's Primer* of 1545. Manuscript primers in English had been available for many years to those who could afford to pay for them, but no tradition of polished translation had been created. C.S. Lewis provides a number of examples of their infelicities.[1] The reforming books, of which about fifty different issues have been recorded, contained the traditional Hours of Our Lady in English, and therefore the first printed versions in English of the canticles and several of the collects which would finally appear in *The Book of Common Prayer*.

Between 1530 and 1545 small changes were introduced in different editions, resulting in a gradual approach to the standards of the Prayer Book.[2] Compare the collect of Whit-Sunday from the 1530 translation with the version in *The King's Primer* and Cranmer's final polishing in *The Book of Common Prayer*:

> O God, which has instructed the hearts of faithful men with the lightening of thy Holy Ghost; grant us to savour aright in the

110

same Spirit, and to rejoice evermore of his holy consolation, which livest and reignest in the same Spirit ever.

O God, which by the information of the Holy Ghost, hast instructed the hearts of thy faithful, grant us in the same Spirit to have right understanding, and evermore to rejoice in his holy consolation. Through Christ our Lord.

God, which as upon this day hast taught the hearts of they faithful people by the sending to them the light of thy holy Spirit; grant us by the same Spirit to have a right judgement in all things, and evermore to rejoice in his holy comfort; through the merits of Jesus Christ our Saviour; who liveth and reigneth with thee in the unity of the same Spirit, one God, world without end.

It is noticeable that Cranmer in *The Book of Common Prayer* version uses words of Anglo-Saxon rather than Latin derivation, replacing 'instructed' by 'taught' and 'information' by 'sending light'. The substitution of 'comfort' for 'consolation' provides both a stronger word and a link with 'the Holy Ghost', the 'Comforter'.

Thus a part of the Prayer Book was already in English when Cranmer started work on the first English rite. All the early Reformers had begun by translating some or all of the traditional services, though they quickly abandoned the process in favour of original composition. Cranmer, however, twenty years later, clung more closely than any of them to his original. From the purely theological point of view he no doubt would have liked to follow their example more fully than he did (or had time to?). Politically, however, it was wise to retain at any rate an outward appearance of continuity, though the sound of the English language in the new rite must have destroyed most of the traditional flavour that is apparent to the reader.

In a famous passage in a letter to Henry VIII Cranmer describes his approach to the translation of the medieval 'processions'. Since it applies equally well to his treatment of all liturgical forms, it is worth quoting at length:

Forasmuch as many of the processions in the Latin, were but barren, as meseemed, and little fruitful, I was constrained to use

more than the liberty of a translator: for in some processions I
have altered divers words; in some I have added part; in some
taken part away; some I have left out whole . . . and some
processions I have added whole, because I thought I had better
matter for the purpose, than was the procession in Latin . . .[3]

One obvious feature of Cranmer's work is the psychological need
which he seems to have felt to use someone else's work as a
starting point. He several times takes an existing prayer or exhortation and translates the opening words fairly literally, then gradually slips into new composition. A good example is Cranmer's
preliminary study for the Prayer Book, *The Order of the Communion*
of 1548, where in each of the exhortations he starts by following
the opening sentence of one of the exhortations in Hermann von
Wied's *Consultation* with some closeness. Here is the beginning of
the second Exhortation:

> Quandoquidem Carissimi in Domino Dei gratia cras Sacratissi-
> mam Domini nostri Jesu Christi Coenam celebrabimus, in qua
> nobis carnem suam in cibum, et sanguinem in potum dedit, ad
> confirmandam fidem, et vitam vere Christianam.

> Dear friends, and you especially upon whose souls I have cure
> and charge, on . . . next I do intend by God's grace to offer to all
> such as shall be godly disposed the most comfortable Sacrament
> of the body and blood of Christ.

He then writes an exhortation of five hundred and twenty words
which reads like a new composition, though in fact sixty-seven
words appear also in Hermann, and these are scattered throughout the exhortation. It would seem to have been less trouble to
make a close translation of Hermann or to compose a completely
new exhortation; but the text suggests that Cranmer either steeped
himself so thoroughly in Hermann that little phrases stuck in his
mind even when writing a new piece, or that he translated Hermann and then revised it so thoroughly that only sixteen per cent
of the original remained.

Another example is the very first sentence of the 1549 book:
'There was never anything by the wit of man so well devised, or so
surely established, which, in continuance of time, hath not been
corrupted.' The first twelve words are literally translated from the

Preface of the Breviary of Francesco Quinones (1535), but this then continues: 'which could not later be rendered more perfect by the added insight of many'. This is the exact opposite of Cranmer's continuation.

Cranmer also seems to have felt the need to insert a quotation from the New Testament at an early point in his exhortation or prayer as justification for what he was about to say. In this, of course, he was a child of his time. His treatment of his sources varies between the Latin and the German, that is, traditional or Reformed. The Latin forms are usually expanded and 'unpacked', the German abbreviated or toned down. The word '*mereor*' is often omitted, and the idea of 'remembrance' is stressed more than in the original Latin, both in the interests of Reformed theology. So, too, the word 'mercy' and its cognates appear a good deal more often than the Latin warrants.

Cranmer's style also varied, as with most writers, according to the genre in which he was writing, whether liturgical, doctrinal or epistolary. His doctrinal style is clear and uncomplicated, with sentences of moderate length:

> The eating of Christ's Flesh and drinking of his Blood is not to be understanded simply and plainly as the words do properly signify, that we do eat and drink him with our mouths; but it is a figurative speech spiritually to be understanded, that we must deeply print and fruitfully believe in our hearts, that his Flesh was crucified and his Blood shed for our redemption.[4]

C.S. Lewis describes writing of this sort as 'devastatingly praiseworthy'.[5] In his letters Cranmer allows himself half-humorous conceits, such as: 'that he may repair unto me again with speed, for further furtherance and final finishing of that we have begun'.[6] As he himself was aware, he had no gift for versification: his version of *Veni, creator Spiritus* in the Prayer Book Ordering of Priests confirms his estimate of his abilities in this field:

> Come, Holy Ghost, eternal God, proceeding from above,
> Both from the Father and the Son, the God of peace and love.

Even within the liturgical genre Cranmer uses different styles for collects and exhortations. The famous doublets ('erred and strayed', 'acknowledge and confess') are found in only sixteen out of eighty-four collects of Sundays and saints' days, whereas they are frequent in exhortations, serving as a kind of aural underlining, making the point more emphatically than a single verb would have done. It is possible that he picked up this mannerism from Martin Bucer, who was even more prone to it.[7]

Cranmer's style shows evident traces of Latin constructions and figures of speech. The use of the relative clause is forced on him by the demands of the collect form, but he often sounds as though he were thinking in Latin. Indeed, G.G. Willis claimed to find consistent use of the Latin *cursus* in the 1549 book but not in 1552, and deduced from this that Cranmer was not the author of the latter book. The presence of *cursus*, however, depended on its being so widely defined that almost every *clausula* exemplifies some form of it. Lewis believed that there was sufficient evidence of *cursus* in *The Book of Common Prayer* to suggest that its use was deliberate, but he felt that 'it does not hold the secret of the Prayer Book's music'.[8] D.L. Frost, however, writes that 'most modern scholars have concluded that the *cursus* appears with insufficient frequency in the Prayer Book to be more than the result of chance'.[9]

Another example of the influence of Latin is Cranmer's placing of an adverb or pronoun before an infinitive in order to avoid splitting it. This is quite a natural order in Latin, but in English the adverb or pronoun would normally come later in the sentence. These two examples are often misread by the officiant:

> We humbly beseech thee most mercifully
> to receive these our prayers . . .
> and also daily endeavour
> ourselves to follow the blessed steps . . .

In each case the adverb/pronoun goes with the following verb, not the preceding. Cranmer's use of the relative pronoun often suggests Latin rather than English usage:

> Lord, we beseech thee mercifully to hear us,
> and unto whom thou hast given an hearty desire to pray . . .
> Into the which holy estate . . .

So does his use of participles:

> that it, being lightened by the doctrine . . . may attain . . .

Latin prose is probably responsible for some long and complicated sentences, such as this from the Visitation of the Sick:

And for what cause soever this sickness is sent unto you;
Whether it be to try your patience for the example of other,
and that your faith may be found, in the day of the Lord,
laudable, glorious, and honourable, to the increase of glory,
     and endless felicity:
or else it be sent unto you to correct and amend in you
     whatsoever doth offend the eyes of our heavenly Father:
know you certainly that,
if you truly repent of your sins,
and bear your sickness patiently, trusting in God's mercy for
     his dear Son Jesus Christ's sake,
and render unto him humble thanks for his fatherly visitation,
submitting yourself wholly to his will;
it shall turn to your profit,
and help you forward in the right way that leadeth unto
     everlasting life.[10]

On the other hand Cranmer will only occasionally use a word in its Latin sense ('Prevent us. . . .') and does not import Latin words wholesale as, for instance, Jeremy Taylor does a century later. When he wants, he can write in a simple monosyllabic style:

Let your mind be without desire to sin,
repent you truly of your sins past,
have an earnest and lively faith in Christ our Saviour,
be in perfect charity with all men,
so shall ye be meet partakers of those holy mysteries.[11]

Midway between these two examples comes the Exhortation at the beginning of Morning Prayer, where the lengthy sentence is much more clearly articulated than that from the Visitation of the Sick, but more tightly constructed than that from Holy Communion. It is only half the length of the former, and breaks down into four clauses of roughly equal length, each following on naturally from the preceding clause.

As well as the doublets mentioned above, Cranmer is fond of triplets. These generally express different aspects of the same idea:

'Direct, sanctify, and govern . . .', but may form a logical sequence: 'Begun, continued, and ended in thee . . .'. And there is one famous quartet: 'Read, mark, learn, and inwardly digest them'. (As this is prefaced by 'hear them', it should perhaps be described as a quintet.) Cranmer made much use of antithesis, sometimes in a simple, direct form:

> (not) unadvisedly, lightly, or wantonly . . .
> but reverently, discreetly, advisedly, soberly,
> and in the fear of God.

Or again: 'not weighing our merits, but pardoning our offences'. He would also use it in the form of chiasmus. Perhaps the best example is in the Canon of 1549: 'a full, perfect, and sufficient sacrifice, oblation, and satisfaction', which must be construed as: a full satisfaction, perfect oblation, and sufficient sacrifice'. It is not just familiarity which suggests that Cranmer's figure is superior.

It is in the collects that Cranmer is generally held to have produced his finest work. Here he sometimes sticks closely to the original in his translation, sometimes translates so freely that the result is better described as an adaptation. The clearest example of the latter process is the collect of Lent 2:

> Almighty God, which doest see that we have no power *of ourselves to help ourselves*: keep thou us both outwardly in our bodies and inwardly *in our souls*, that we may be defended from all adversities *which may happen* to the body, and from *all* evil thoughts *which may assault and hurt* the soul . . .

The words in italics were added or substituted by Cranmer. He unpacks 'outwardly' and 'inwardly' and replaces '*mundemur*' ('may be cleansed') by 'assault and hurt', thus continuing the military metaphor of defence. An inspired rewriting is to be found in the collect of trinity 12, where the literal translation woul be: 'who dost exceed the merits and prayers of thy suppliants by the abundance of thine affection'. Cranmer transforms this into: 'which art always more ready to hear than we to pray, and art wont to give more than we either desire or deserve'. The thought is the same, but its expression is clothed in much more memorable language. This is done largely by substituting verbs for nouns. Another example is Lent 3, where '*vota humilium*' becomes 'the hearty desires of thy humble servants'. Cranmer has to add a noun to *'humilium'*, so he adds an adjective to *'vota'* to balance the phrase, throwing in an alliteration for good measure. Similarly, in Trinity 6 *'bona invisibilia'* is rendered 'such good things as pass man's understanding'.

The best example of Cranmer's own compositions is probably the Collect of Advent 1. It is based on the antithesis of the First Coming of Christ and His Second Coming. Cranmer begins, as so often, with a quotation from the New Testament, here the Epistle of the day, which already contains a pair of antitheses:

that we may cast away	the works of darkness
and put upon us	the armour of light.

Then he balances the two Comings:

in the time of this mortal life	in the last day
thy Son Jesus Christ came	he shall come again
to visit us	to judge both the quick and the dead
in great humility	in his glorious majesty.

The last two lines are actually arranged in chiasmus:

visit	humility
majesty	judge.

Next, Cranmer wants to relate the past event and the future event to the present, which he does by emphasising that we are *'now'* in the time of the First Coming. All this is enclosed in yet another chiasmus:

now in the time of this mortal life	we may rise to the life immortal.

This makes its effect despite its members being separated by two or three lines of vivid imagery. Besides these literary devices, the collect sets out clearly the work of Christ in relation to our salvation.

An interesting example of redrafting is to be found in the Collect of the Sunday next before Easter. In *The King's Book* (1543) Cranmer had written:

He did . . . suffer this cross and this kind of death for our example, that we should follow the steps of him in patience and humility.

This becomes:

to suffer death upon the cross, that all mankind should follow the example of his great humility.

'Follow the example' is then clumsily repeated in order to introduce 'patience'.

Sometimes Cranmer will produce a mosaic of phrases from different sources, as in the Prayer of Humble Access. This prayer contains possible echoes of the Liturgy of St Basil, the Book of Daniel, the Gospels St Mark and St John, the Hereford Missal, the 1544 Litany, St Thomas Aquinas, Florus of Lyons and Paschasius Radbert. Another example is the third collect of Good Friday. This is built up on the basis of three phrases from the *Orationes sollennes* traditionally said on Good Friday (though for one of them Cranmer may have gone direct to Ezekiel 33:11). Round these are woven phrases from the Sarum collect *in die jejunii*, the 1544 Litany, Romans 9:27 and John 10:16.

To sum up, it may be said that though Cranmer's Latin education sometimes thwarted his expressed intention, he usually succeeded in finding 'such a language and order as is most easy and plain for the understanding, both of the readers and hearers'.[12]

Notes

1. C.S. Lewis, *English Literature in the Sixteenth Century* (Oxford, 1954) p. 216.
2. A full text of the canticles and collects concerned will be found in C.J. Cuming, *The Godly Order* (London, 1983).
3. Cranmer, 7 October 1544, in *Miscellaneous Letters and Writings*, ed. J.E. Cox (Cambridge: Parker Society, 1846) p. 41.
4. Cranmer, *Defence of the true and catholic Doctrine of the Last Supper*, III, 10.
5. C.S. Lewis, *English Literature in the Sixteenth Century* (Oxford, 1954) p. 195.
6. Cranmer, *Miscellaneous Letters and Writings* (Cambridge, 1846) pp. 366–7.

7. D.L. Frost, 'Liturgical Language from Cranmer to Series 3', in R.C.D. Jasper (ed.), *The Eucharist Today* (London, 1974) p. 156, has a good discussion of doublets.
8. Lewis, op. cit., pp. 217–20.
9. Frost, op. cit., p. 151.
10. Frost, op. cit., p. 157.
11. From the first Exhortation of 1549 Holy Communion, altered for the worse in 1552 and 1662.
12. From the Preface of 1549.

I am indebted to Dr Ronald Jasper for several useful suggestions.

6

Liturgical Language in a Sociolinguistic Perspective

David Crystal

THE SOCIOLINGUISTIC REVOLUTION

In recent years there has been something of a revolution in the field of linguistic study. The established tradition, which can be traced back to the grammarians and philosophers of ancient Greece, Rome and India, and which continues in the present century in the work of De Saussure, Bloomfield and Chomsky, focuses on the most tangible and manifest aspects of language – its formal structure, and the meaning which this structure encapsulates. Thus we find an emphasis on the description and analysis of such domains as syntax (sentence structure), morphology (word structure, with particular reference to word-endings, or accidence), the lexicon, phonology (the pronunciation system of a language) and graphology (the writing system of a language). In different periods and countries this focus has varied: for example, the early Sanskrit linguists (notably Panini) placed particular stress on accurate and detailed phonological analysis; the Stoic philosophers were much concerned with the investigation of word classes (the 'parts of speech'); the Arabic linguists of the early Middle Ages provided early and excellent examples of lexicography; and the nineteenth-century comparative philologists meticulously plotted changes in sounds and words. But the shared concentration is on matters of formal description – a concentration which could also be seen, in due course, in the predilection for parsing and clause analysis in the study of the mother tongue in schools, and in the so-called 'grammar-translation' method in foreign language teaching.

In the 1960s, however, things changed. Formal grammar virtually disappeared from schools and examinations in Britain, the USA and several other countries, and was replaced by the investigation of the way language was being *used* in the various contexts of daily life – the English of advertising, of science, of radio commentaries, of the press or indeed of the classroom itself. New 'communicative' approaches to foreign language teaching were devised, which drew attention to the kind of situations likely to be most relevant and useful to the language learner, such as requesting, thanking, complaining and instructing. And throughout the various domains of linguistic enquiry there developed a concern to see language not solely in terms of sounds, words and structures, but in terms of the *social situations* in which language was used. The focus switched from the forms of language to the functions language performed in society – and thus to the characteristics of those who used language and of the setting in which linguistic activity took place. 'What kind of people use what kind of language on what kind of occasion?' Such questions drew attention to the fact that language was not a monolithic, homogeneous entity used identically by all, but was dynamic, flexible and diverse. Observe language in society, it was pointed out, and the variety of expression is the most striking feature of all, and the one which attracts most public interest and comment – regional and social accents and dialects, occupational slang and jargon, upper- and lower-class pronunciations, formal and informal standards, male and female differences, and much more. Only by focusing on this variety, it was argued, is it possible to provide a convincing, coherent account of language.

This change in direction is often summarised by the term 'sociolinguistics'. Sociolinguistics is that branch of linguistics which studies the relationship between language and society. It observes the range of language varieties which exist, and relates these to patterns of social structure and behaviour – such as age, sex, caste, social class, regional origin and formality of setting. No sociolinguist is content simply to identify a pattern in phonology, grammar or lexicon; rather, this pattern must be seen in the light of who uses it, when, where and why. The range of the subject is vast, from large-scale decisions about language planning (such as which language should be used as a standard in an emerging nation) to the way language is used as a marker of dominance or soldarity in small group debates and discussions.[1]

LITURGICAL LANGUAGE

The changes which have taken place in religious language since the 1960s require a similar broadening of perspective if the distinctiveness of contemporary liturgical language is to be appreciated. Here too there has been a revolution – indeed, no imposed linguistic change has ever affected so many people at once as when Latin was replaced by the vernacular in Roman Catholic Christianity. A similar impact, but on a smaller scale, was felt when the Series III texts were introduced into the liturgy of the Church of England. The main result of these changes was to alter the perceived distinctiveness of liturgical language. Regardless of whether one welcomed or objected to the new genres, there was a widespread claim – which is still to be heard – that there was no longer any distinctiveness about liturgical language. The language of the new liturgy was called 'everyday', 'mundane' and 'lacking in variety' (to take just three comments made by various correspondents to a religious newspaper). For some, this was a good thing. For others, it was a disaster. But how far are the arguments founded on fact? *Is there anything distinctive still about liturgical language?* If so, how can this distinctiveness be defined, and what implications does a sociolinguistic perspective have for contemporary participants in liturgical events?

Any answer to the question of whether linguistic distinctiveness still exists depends on which frame of reference one adopts. From a narrow, formal linguistic point of view, the answer probably has to be 'no', or perhaps 'very little', as can be seen by drawing a contrast between English-language extracts from the two periods. A generation ago, the liturgical linguistic norms in much of the English-speaking world involved a large number of low-level lexical and grammatical usages that were very plainly idiosyncratic to this genre, such as the following:[2]

- special grammatical words and inflections: *thou, thee, ye, art, wilt, unto, -(e)th, -(e)st, spake, brethren,* etc.
- special lexical words: *thrice, behold, vouchsafe, whence, henceforth, thence,* etc.
- vocative (naming) syntactic structures with *O: O God, who . . .*
- vocative structures without *O*, especially adjective plus noun in direct address (*eternal Father, . . ., dear Lord*) or noun with a postmodifying relative clause (*God who in thine infinite goodness . . ., Lamb of God, who takest away . . .*)
- imperative or subjunctive verbs with subject expressed: *go thou . . ., do we sit . . ., glory be to the Father, praise be . . .*
- unusual word order, often following an archaic or Latin con-

struction: *he, having eaten, went . . ., whom, when he saw, he walked . . ., Father Almighty, a treacherous foe and cruel*
- distinctive idioms: *who livest and reignest, through the same Jesus Christ . . .*

Many of these words and constructions were formally restricted to the domain of religious language, or were extremely rare outside that domain. For example, the use of an adjective with a noun used vocatively is hardly ever found elsewhere, apart from such restricted settings as letter openings (*Dear Sir*) and stereotyped greetings among certain professions (for example, the actor's *dear boy*).

Today many of the most distinctive features have gone, in the revised formal Christian liturgies. There is no doubt that modern liturgical styles use far fewer distinctive grammatical features, as the following extracts from the new Roman Catholic rite show:

> Be faithful to your people, Lord, we pray, and do not cease to protect us. Guard us always and defend us, for we have no hope apart from your grace.
>
> (Collect, 5th Sunday of the Year, Nat. Lit. Comm. Text)

> Deliver us, Lord, from every evil, and grant us peace in our day. In your mercy keep us free from sin and protect us from all anxiety, as we wait in joyful hope for the coming of our Saviour, Jesus Christ.
>
> (Order of Mass)

Only the religious vocabulary and theme mark this language as distinctively 'religious': the grammatical constructions used could be found in many other domains of formal English language use. Individual prayers and prayer-openings and -endings do of course sometimes retain elements of archaic syntax (as in the Lord's Prayer or the Hail Mary), but the bulk of the language we encounter in a liturgical celebration nowadays is not of this kind. Only the vocative constructions remain as a testimonial to the previous linguistic liturgical age.

Is there, then, any basis for the notion of 'liturgical language' in contemporary society? Only if we replace the traditional focus on forms by a focus on functions – in other words, by moving from a narrowly linguistic to a sociolinguistic perspective. From this point of view the liturgical setting provides a number of highly distinctive features, for which there is no parallel elsewhere in linguistic behaviour. Taken together, these constitute the genre's continuing linguistic identity.

A FUNCTIONAL APPROACH

A basic feature of any sociolinguistic approach would be to determine the range of functions that liturgical language can be said to perform. Classifications vary, but it is common to find an initial analysis of language functions, or purposes, into eight main types.

1 Informative

The communication of ideas is the normal use of language, in everyday settings. We use language in order to give others information that is new or unfamiliar to them. This is sometimes called the 'ideational' or 'referential' use of language. Many people think of it as the *only* role that language performs, but this is to ignore several other important functions (see 2–8 below).

Example: Three people were seriously injured in an accident on the M4 this afternoon . . .

2 Identifying

Our choice of language will always signal to others our personal, ethnic, regional or social identity – who we are and where we are from, and the social role we are currently adopting. To be a policeman (doctor, priest, believer . . . .) is to *speak* like a policeman (doctor, priest, believer . . . .). To some theorists, indeed, this is the primary function of language.

Example: I was walking along Seton Road in a westerly direction when I observed the accused . . .

3 Expressive

The language we might use when standing alone in front of a painting, or haranguing the elements, or after banging our thumb with a hammer, is plainly expressive of our emotions rather than

being communicative in any strict sense. It often uses utterances that are strictly non-sensical (as in the use of interjections that are little more than noises, such as *ah, yukkk*) or that rely on the prosodic aspects of language (intonation, loudness, tone of voice).
Example: Oh, what a shot! Brilliant!

4 Performative

When someone names a ship or makes a promise, the use of the words is taken to express a deeper reality: the ship is not named until the appropriate words are spoken, nor is a promise made without the use of the word *promise* or its equivalent. There are hundreds of 'performative speech acts' (as they were called by the philosopher J.L. Austin) and their analysis is a major theme in contemporary research into language use.
Example: I now pronounce you man and wife . . .

5 Historical

In all cases of record-keeping (in law, history, business, science) language is being used to summarise the past and preserve it. It therefore requires a degree of explicitness and organisation which tries to anticipate the unforeseen demands that will one day be made of it.
Example: The compound was tested under three conditions . . .

6 Aesthetic

Spoken or written language can be enjoyed purely as a formal display, as in the use of poetic rhythms, calligraphy or the nonsense verse used by children in street ball-games. This is the nearest we get to language being used purely for its own sake – for fun.
Example: (*children skipping*) I like coffee, I like tea, I like radio, and
           TV . . .

7 Heuristic

We often find ourselves speaking aloud while we are thinking out a problem, or jotting notes down in order to organise our ideas. Language can help our thought processes, it seems; and, according to some, rational thinking is impossible without language.

Example: Now, if I multiply it by six, and add four, and take the
           total away from the figure in that column . . .

8 Social

When we pass a comment on the weather or inquire routinely after
someone's health, just to be polite, we are engaging in a purely
social use of language – what the anthropologist Malinowski called
'phatic communion'.
Example: Lovely day for ducks, Mrs Jones!

Classifications of this kind must be used cautiously. They are not
necessarily exhaustive, and the interpretation of each notion is to
some extent a matter of definition. Moreover, any *real* use of
language will display elements of several functions in different
degrees. A poem, for example, may be simultaneously informative, aesthetic and an expression of identity. Indeed, complex uses
of language are complex precisely because they operate at several
functional levels at once. But analytic schemes of this kind are
nonetheless of value, despite these remarks. Above all, they draw
attention to the functional complexity of linguistic behaviour and
thus help us to avoid over-simple analyses of language, or analyses
which focus on a single function (such as informativeness) to the
exclusion of the others.

    How does liturgical language fare when seen in the light of these
criteria? It is immediately evident that no one of these functions
will satisfactorily explain the range of linguistic behaviour which
takes place during a liturgical event. Moreover, the functions often
cited as central to liturgical language – informativeness and histor-
icity – have only limited explanatory power. Such a focus is
inevitable, given the concern to preserve the integrity of a religious
tradition in the words of the liturgical celebration, but it is important not to let the importance of these factors blind us to the
co-occurring existence of other linguistic functions that are also of
considerable import in explaining the structure and impact of the
liturgical event. We can see this if we examine each criterion
separately, using the features of the Roman Catholic Mass as
illustration. See Table 1 on pages 128–9.

1 Informative?

Only a tiny part of the Mass is genuinely informative, in the sense of providing information that would be totally new to the regular Mass-goer. Most of the components are to a greater or lesser extent items that are repeated in successive liturgical events. Those that vary, weekly or daily, include the Antiphon, Collect, Post-communion prayer, Biblical readings and Responsorial psalm. (In the larger time-scale of the annual liturgy, of course, these are repetitive too.) Small sections of the Preface and Canon vary according to the feast day, and the Blessing may alter on special occasions. The Canon itself, along with the response at the Con-secration, appears in one of four versions, giving a limited 'sur-prise value'. There is rather more unpredictability in the Bidding prayers – though these vary enormously in character (in some chur-ches the same ones are repeated weekly; in others they are varied and spontaneous). The components which provide the greatest po-tential exposure to novel language are the Homily and the Parish notices (items which are routine only in Sunday Masses) – though again there is always the possibility that the information value of these discourses is lessened through weekly repetitiveness.

For the rest, the utterances are repeated without variation week by week, day by day. Being wholly predictable, they convey no information (in the strict, information-theoretic sense of the word). The practical problem this raises is all too common: linguistic familiarity breeds contempt, in the form of automatic listening and inattention, and it takes a considerable effort of will (as well as auspicious circumstances, such as the absence of extraneous noise like a crying child or a celebrant with an obscure regional accent) to maintain concentration and to motivate a renewed appraisal of the meaning of what is being said. The experience of realising that a significant part of the event has passed one by is common enough.

People often admit to failing in the fullness of their participation, therefore, but it should be noted that this is failure at only one functional level. And what has to be appreciated is that repeated language should not be judged solely in informative terms. Con-sider the following exchanges:

(1) A It's raining.   (2) A Lovely day.
     B Yes, isn't it awful.   B Yes, lovely day.
     A It's raining.   A Lovely day, yes.

Table 1. Functional linguistic units in the Roman Catholic Mass

Liturgical item	Primary function*	Speech mode	Non-verbal activity
Entry antiphon	1	Unison	Stand
Sign of the cross	2	Dialogue	Stand
Introductory greeting	2	Dialogue (priest and people)	Stand
Introduction to the Mass	1	Monologue (priest)	Stand
Penitential rite	3	Dialogue (priest and people)	Stand
Absolution	4	Dialogue (priest and people)	Stand
Kyrie	3	Dialogue (priest and people)	Stand
Gloria	3	Unison	Stand
Collect	1	Monologue (priest)	Stand
Bible reading	1/5	Monologue (priest/lay reader)	Sit
Responsorial psalm	1/5	Dialogue (priest/lay reader and people)	Sit
Bible reading	1/5	Monologue (priest/lay reader)	Sit
Gospel acclamation	1	Unison	Stand
Gospel opening	5	Dialogue (priest and people)	Stand
Gospel reading	1/5	Monologue (priest)	Stand
Gospel closure	2	Dialogue (priest and people)	Stand
Homily	1	Monologue (priest)	Sit
Creed	2	Unison	Stand
Bidding prayers	1	Dialogue (priest/lay readers and people)	Stand
Liturgy of the Eucharist	3	Dialogue (priest and people)	Sit
Lord God we ask you. . .	3	Monologue (priest)	Sit

Event		Type	Posture
Pray brethren. . .	3	Dialogue (priest and people)	Stand
Prayer over the gifts	1	Monologue (priest)	Stand
Lift up your hearts. . .	3	Dialogue (priest and people)	Stand
Preface	5	Monologue (priest)	Stand
Sanctus	3	Unison	Stand
Canon	5/3	Monologue (priest)	Kneel
Consecration	4	Monologue (priest)	Kneel
Response at Consecration	2	Unison	Kneel
Canon (continues)	5	Monologue (priest)	Kneel
Lord's Prayer	2	Unison	Stand
Prayer	3	Monologue (priest)	Stand
Lord's Prayer (conclusion)	2	Unison	Stand
Prayer	3	Monologue (priest)	Stand
Sign of peace	2	Dialogue (between individuals)	Stand
Prayer	3	Silent monologue (priest)	Stand
Agnus Dei	3	Unison	Stand
This is the Lamb of God	2	Monologue (priest)	Kneel
Lord I am not worthy	3	Unison	Kneel
	3	Silent monologue (priest)	Kneel
The body of Christ	2	Dialogue (priest and individual)	Move
		Silent prayer (individuals)	Kneel/Sit
Prayer	3	Monologue (priest)	Stand/Sit
Parish notices	1	Monologue (priest)	Stand/Sit
Blessing	4	Dialogue (priest and people)	Stand
Dismissal	2	Dialogue (priest and people)	Stand

* See text for typology.

In (1), A's second utterance makes sense only if we read something in – for example, that A has left the washing on the line and wants B to go and get it. In this example the repetition has pragmatic force: it is a cue to action. In (2) the repetition has a phatic force: it promotes social rapport, maintaining good relations between the participants. Similarly, the weekly or daily recitation of a dialogue which is totally familiar can be fully understood only if we see it as operating on other levels than the informative. And at these levels the notion of participatory failure is really inappropriate.

2 Identifying?

A great deal of liturgical language is an expression of the religious identity of the participants. The language which seems to manifest this function most clearly includes: the sign of the cross, the introductory greeting (*The Lord be with you/And also with you*) and subsequent uses of this formula, the Creed, the responses at the Gospel and the Consecration, the Lord's Prayer (given the context of its institution), the Sign of peace, the Prayers said while presenting and giving the Communion host, and the Dismissal. In each case the use of the language expresses the participant's willingness to be part of the event, and provides an affirmation of identity with the body of the Church as a whole. Simply to be physically present, and to utter the language, is enough to satisfy this criterion, even though one's mind might wander during the performance – in much the same way as the carrying of banners in a public march about the situation in, say, South Africa identifies the motivation of the participants, even though, while walking, the participants may at times be talking to each other about the price of soap-flakes.

From the point of view of this criterion the predictability of liturgical language is a strength, not a weakness. Union speech provides an ideal mode for the expression of solidarity, as does the coincidence of verbal and non-verbal activity (see below). Any departure from the expected dialogue norms is psychologically disturbing – as when a visiting priest inadvertently introduces a different form of words from the one the congregation is used to, and is given an uncertain or absent response.

It should also be noted that, to express identity, the language does not even have to be meaningful, in the accepted sense. The use of meaningless language (meaningless, that is, to some or all of the lay participants) is in fact common to many forms of religious behaviour around the world. It can be illustrated in Christianity in such varied forms as the use of Latin in twentieth-century services, the choice of an old biblical translation where parts of the language no longer make sense, or the use of glossolalic utterance in neo-pentecostal meetings, where the primary function of the language is to act as an index of the strength and sincerity of the speaker's conviction.

3 Expressive?

In a sense, the whole of liturgical language is expressive of the emotions. It could hardly be otherwise, with God as the deeper-level interactant. To see the liturgy as a drama in which all actively participate – in the case of the Mass, as a re-enactment of the sacrifice which is at the centre of Christianity – motivates a heightened awareness and excitement which can imbue everything that is said with an emotive force. But there are several utterances in the Mass where the *primary* force seems to be to express depth of personal feeling and commitment, with reference to deep-rooted motives such as sorrow, praise, love and petition. These are the penitential rite (*I confess* . . . .), the Kyrie, Gloria, Sanctus and Agnus Dei, the liturgy of the Eucharist up to the opening part of the Preface (*Blessed are you, Lord God* . . ., *Lift up your hearts* . . . .), part of the Canon (see below), the Prayers for peace, and the sequence during the giving of Communion. It is no coincidence that among these are the pieces most commonly set to music.

Not only are these items repetitive in the sense of weekly or daily recurrence, they are the items which also contain the most internal repetition. This is most noticeable in the Kyrie, where the repetition of *Lord have mercy* raises exactly the same functional question as that posed by examples (1) and (2) above. The repetition cannot carry a straightforward information value, but must be judged in other terms – here, in terms of expressive force. Exactly the same are the repetitions in the Sanctus (*Holy, holy, holy* . . ., *Hosanna in the highest*) and the Agnus Dei (*Lamb of God* . . . .). Rather more subtle are the lexical, grammatical and phonological (primarily rhythmical) repetitions in the Gloria and (less overtly) in the Confiteor:

> we worship you,
>   we give you thanks,
>   we praise you . . .
> For you alone are the Holy One,
>   you alone are the Lord, you
> alone . . .
>   in my thoughts and in my words,
>   in what I have done and in
> what . . .

No other parts of the Mass present such a degree of internal parallelism.

4 Performative?

There are three places in the Mass where the function of the language is purely performative (given the theological context of Catholic Christianity): the giving of absolution in the Penitential rite, the act of Consecration and the final Blessing. In other theological contexts, of course, there could be debate over whether a performative interpretation is permissible, involving such long-standing questions as the nature of forgiveness and the real presence. It would also be possible to argue that several other realities are brought into being through the language, such as a stengthening of belief through saying the Creed, or an increase in sorrow for having offended God through saying the *I confess . . .*, but these effects are less certain, being dependent on the volition of the participants rather than on the formal powers invested in the priest.

5 Historical?

There are no cases in the Mass where the language is being used primarily for purposes of record-keeping, with future users in mind. Liturgical language, as religious language generally, typically looks backwards, not forwards, in its concern to display continuity with a doctrinal or devotional tradition. It is different from most other varieties of language in this respect: the meaning of the language used forms part of a religious frame of reference which, in certain cases, reaches back over many centuries. The careful attention paid to the translation of standard liturgical texts is the clearest evidence of this. The only other domain which shares this concentration on the past – a diachronic frame of reference for the interpretation of synchronic events – is that of the law.

There are therefore several utterances in the liturgy whose purpose is to identify with the historical tradition – which is hardly surprising, given the need to affirm the identity of Christ within the scheme of salvation. The Biblical readings must be seen in this light, as must the Preface and most of the Canon. For example, apart from the pronouns of direct address, the language of the Preface for Pentecost is primarily historical:

Today you sent the Holy Spirit on those marked out to be your children by sharing the life of your only Son, and so you brought the paschal mystery to its completion. Today we celebrate the great beginning of your Church when the Holy Spirit made known to all peoples the one true God, and created from the many languages of man one voice to profess one faith . . .

Throughout the Canon the historical orientation is a major theme, preserved in a clear-cut frame of reference where there is recurrent emphasis on people, places and times – the three dominating themes of history (see Table 2). This long prayer (here shown in the version known as the Roman Canon) systematically and explicitly covers those people and issues to be borne in mind during this part of the Mass, and relates them to the central performative act. The language is persistently spatio-temporal:

remember . . ., in union with . . ., the day before . . ., when supper was ended . . ., celebrate the memory . . ., as once you accepted . . ., remember . . .

and historico-personal:

N. our pope . . ., your people . . ., all of us gathered here . . ., Mary . . ., Joseph . . ., the apostles and martyrs, Peter and Paul, Andrew, and all the saints . . ., your people and your ministers . . ., your servant Abel . . ., Abraham . . ., Melchisidech . . ., those who have died . . ., John the Baptist, Stephen, Matthias, Barnabas, and all the saints . . .

Half the sentences function in this way. The remainder are mainly expressive – in particular the opening and concluding sequences (the latter with marked internal parallelism: *Through him, with him, in him* . . . .). At the very centre of the Canon is a combination of

134   *Language and the Worship of the Church*

Table 2.   Functional linguistic analysis of the Canon
of the Roman Catholic Mass

We come to you Father with praise . . .	Expressive
Through him we ask you to accept and bless . . .	Expressive
We offer them for your holy catholic Church . . .	Historical
We offer them for N. our Pope . . .	Historical
Remember, Lord, your people . . .	Historical
Remember all of us gathered here . . .	Historical
You know how firmly we believe . . .	Expressive
We offer you this sacrifice . . . for ourselves and . . .	Historical
We pray to you . . . for our wellbeing . . .	Expressive
In union with the whole Church, we honour Mary . . .	Historical
We honour Joseph . . . the apostles and martyrs . . .	Historical
May their merits and prayers gain us . . .	Expressive
Father, accept this offering from your whole family . . .	Historical
Grant us your peace . . .	Expressive
Bless and approve our offering . . .	Expressive
Let it become for us the body and blood . . .	Expressive
The day before he suffered . . .	Historical
He broke the bread . . .	Historical
Take this, all of you, . . .	Performative
When supper was ended . . .	Historical
Again he gave you thanks . . .	Historical
Take this all of you, . . .	Performative
Let us proclaim the mystery of faith	Identifying
Unison response	Identifying
Father we celebrate the memory . . .	Historical
We, your people and your ministers, recall . . .	Historical
Look with favour . . . as once you accepted the gifts . .	Historical
Almighty God, we pray that your angel . . .	Expressive
Then, as we receive from this altar the sacred body . .	Expressive
Remember, Lord, those who have died . . .	Historical
May these, and all who sleep . . .	Historical
For ourselves, too, we ask some share . . . with John . .	Historical
Though we are sinners . . .	Expressive
Do not consider what we truly deserve . . .	Expressive
Through Christ our Lord . . .	Expressive
You fill them with life . . .	Expressive
Through him, with him . . .	Expressive

NOTE: Paragraph divisions are as printed in the ICEL[3] text. Sentences
within paragraphs are indented.

performative and identifying functions, in the form of the act of Consecration and the immediately following unison Response.

6 Aesthetic?

There are no examples of language with a purely aesthetic function in the basic structure of the Mass – though it must be appreciated that this example does not include the use of musical settings (plain chant, hymns and so on), where such a function would be clear. As far as spoken language is concerned, it could be argued that the meaning of liturgical language is always paramount (at least potentially), so that this criterion would hardly ever apply. A possible exception is the unison recitation of a litany of saints' names, where ignorance of the identity of some of the saints invoked would not affect the dramatic impact conveyed by the prayer's pace and rhythm. There may be others.

However, although liturgical utterances are not primarily designed for their aesthetic appeal, the importance of this consideration has always loomed large in work on liturgical language – notably in the attention committees pay to considerations of rhythm and euphony in their choice of words and grammar. And when people are critical of liturgical translations they invariably comment on them from an aesthetic point of view, stressing the importance of the 'poetry' of language. The problem, of course, is that no one has ever been able to agree on what features of language count as euphonious or poetic, and arguments based on these supposed criteria tend to degenerate into confrontations of personal taste.

7, 8 Heuristic? Social?

There seem to be no examples of these functions of language in the Mass. Doubtless language as an instrument of thought is primary within the category of silent prayer – though many great spiritual thinkers have stressed the importance of trying to empty the mind of everything, including language, in order to find God. Doubtless, also, much of the Sign of peace is purely phatic in character. Indeed, the risk of having meaningful language degenerate into phatic noise is ever present. But these are matters of performance: no part of the Mass has been designed with these criteria in mind.

This analysis helps to identify one of the most significant features of liturgical language, as encountered in specific religious settings: no other domain of language displays such a juxtaposition of distinct linguistic functions. Of the eight main functions of language, no fewer than five are to be found represented in the illustration of the Mass, with a sixth (the aesthetic) extremely relevant. Apart from the language of literature (which is always an exception, because of its function as a commentary on the whole of human experience), there is no other variety of language which displays such functional diversity.

This point also emerges when we analyse the various categories of speech activity in greater detail. As many as four major types of activity are represented: unison, monologue (usually by the priest; sometimes by a lay reader), dialogue (usually between priest and people, but sometimes between lay reader and people, priest and individual, individual and individual, and also between individual and God). (Most other speech events involve only one of these activities; for example, conversation is dialogue, news-reading is monologue.) Moreover, the priest's monologues vary in terms of their status as spoken or written language (reading aloud, prepared speech, speech from notes, and so on), and also in terms of formality (such as informal sermon versus formal prayer). (Again, there is a contrast with most other speech events, where the mode and formality are constant throughout; for example, conversation is informal and spontaneous, radio news is formal and scripted.) The changes in pace, mood and rhythm form part of the dramatic structure of the liturgical event and underscore the conceptual differences which the event is designed to convey. Even the reading of extracts from the parish bulletin, with its 'what's on?' character, has its place, reminding participants of the place of the Church in the world and of the need to maintain an ongoing relationship with God outside the liturgical setting.

The analysis in Table 1 also draws attention to several other identifying characteristics of liturgical language. In particular, there is the formal correlation which takes place between verbal and non-verbal activity. Thus certain utterances are said (or listened to) while standing, sitting, kneeling, with arms outstretched, holding certain objects and so on. The verbal and non-verbal events are simultaneous and are mutually defining (in the sense that it is necessary, while saying X, to do Y and not Z). It is worth pointing out that such formalised combinations of language and body-movement are highly restricted in other domains. Examples would include shaking hands while expressing a greeting or leave-taking, or providing acquiescent performance while undergoing a medical investigation (*Say ah* . . .). Only liturgy requires a ritual pattern of participation using complementary verbal and non-verbal behaviour which (a) persists over an extended period, and (b) involves such a wide range of body-movements and orientations.

The use of unison speech is itself a highly distinctive linguistic activity. There are no other social occasions where this activity is so carefully structured, and where a written text can be followed. Football crowds chant fragments in unison, as do supporters at political conventions (*Four more years!*), but these occasions lack the structure which is present in the liturgical setting. The highly conventionalised speed, rhythm, volume level and intonation are the main formal features of unison speech, and these provide the vocal complement to the distinctive prosody of the celebrant. Taken together, in fact, the prosodic features of liturgical events constitute their primary formal identity and provide a continuity between old and new liturgical style.

The use of silence becomes meaningful and distinctive in liturgical events, in a way that is not found elsewhere. Periods of silence are encountered during the act of Consecration, following communion and at other climactic points. Here the limitations of the verbal mode are intuitively felt, and the only alternative to silence is to underline the significance of the moment by other means, such as the sounding of a bell, the use of incense or the playing of music. In conversation, by contrast, lapsing into silence is inadvertent and discomfiting (in our own culture, at least);[4] on the radio it is a state of affairs to be avoided at all costs; in a court of law silence from a witness may be interpreted as contempt. But in liturgy silence is positive and creative.

A further difference from other linguistic domains is the importance of the time-frame within which the liturgical language takes place. We have already seen the importance of a diachronic perspective in the long term; but there are constraints which operate in the short term too. Normally the time-frame of an utterance is of only indirect relevance to what we say. If we wish to discuss a film, talk about holidays or complain about an ache, we can use the same language whether it is Monday or Tuesday, January or February, 1989 or 1990. But these changes in temporal perspective are highly significant in the liturgical domain. The choice of the readings and certain prayers depends on which day it is (such as prayers for a certain feast-day), which part of the year it is (such as the sequence of readings over several weeks in Advent), or even which year it is (such as the three-year cycle of biblical readings in the liturgy of the Mass). No other domain imposes such temporal constraints on its utterances.

THE PROBLEM OF LANGUAGE CHANGE

It should be clear that liturgical language preserves a high level of distinctiveness when examined from a sociolinguistic point of view. Although many of the low-level formal features of this variety have disappeared (the distinctive word-endings, grammatical words and so on), the major functional choices and contrasts in the language have been preserved and remain as distinctive as ever. In addition, there has been no change in the reliance on prosody as a means of signalling the special nature of the occasion and the shared purpose of the participants. Unison speech, and the special intonation, rhythm and tone of voice adopted by individual speakers, combine to act as the main linguistic features that formally distinguish liturgical from other kinds of speech event.

This perspective needs to be borne in mind whenever liturgical committees face up to the task of revision, in the context of linguistic change. Language change is ongoing and inevitable. It refers to any developments which cause the forms or functions of a language to alter over time, and it is a complex, multi-faceted phenomenon. Under the heading of changes in form we find the following types:

- *phonological change* affects the pronunciation of vowels and consonants, or aspects of the prosody; a clear example (of the latter) is the alteration in the way some words are stressed, such as the move from *balCOny* in the early nineteenth century to modern *BALcony*, or the current change from *CONtroversy* to *conTROversy*
- *graphological change* affects the conventions of the writing system; a current example is the gradual replacement of certain verbs

ending in *-ise* by *-ize* (*summarize, realize,* etc.)

- *grammatical change* affects the processes of word or sentence construction; this is less noticeable in current English, but can be sensed in areas of controversy, such as the disputes over split infinitives or the placing of *hopefully* in a sentence
- *lexical change* affects the selection of vocabulary and is always the most noticeable area of language change; the development of a set of words ending in *-friendly* during the 1980s provides a current example (*user-friendly, customer-friendly,* etc.).

Under the heading of functional change would be found the development of new varieties of the language, alterations in the pattern of use we associate with a variety, and the emergence of new attitudes to the way in which language is used. In relation to the first of these the most important development in the present century has been the growth of varieties of media language, such as sports commentary, news-reading and advertising language. In relation to the second we find the development of informal styles of programme presentation on the BBC or the changes in government publications as a result of pressure from the Plain English campaign. And in relation to the third we find increasing sensitivity to the use of any language felt to be sexist, racist or misleading – areas which have each been the target of government legislation in Britain.

Liturgical language is inevitably affected by all of these changes, both formal and functional. Religious language is in the world, and of the world, and any changes in linguistic form or function which take place in the language in general will have consequences for the kind of language adopted in the liturgical domain. This can be seen most clearly at present in the pressure on liturgical committees for changes in language that is widely perceived to be sexist – for example, replacing *came to save all men* by *came to save everyone.* These questions cannot – or at least should not – be discussed with reference to a single functional level only. All too often, liturgical language changes are debated with reference only to the first of the factors listed above (the informative) or to the fifth (the historical) or the sixth (the aesthetic) – the extent to which a change alters the meaning of the text or renders it aesthetically unacceptable. The question of sexist language cannot be satisfactorily addressed solely in these terms, however: the issue is primarily one of sexual identity (the second factor in the list). Many women feel excluded from full involvement in the liturgical service by the use of such language. It is true, at the *informative* level, that (to quote one newspaper correspondent) 'it doesn't make any difference' to alter *all men* to *everyone* in the above example; but at the *identifying* level it makes all the difference in the world.

The same issues arise as we broaden our perspective to consider the identity of individual liturgies within Christianity and their underlying theologies. The tradition of debate here has been to focus, once again, on the points of substance as identified in informational and historical terms. However, for some time now there have been signs of change in this respect, with these factors being supplemented (not, of course, replaced) by a recognition of the important role of the identifying function of language. We can see it when people remember to take the social and emotional aspects of language into account, as when liturgical texts are examined to determine whether there are words and phrases which would damage the growth of relationships between religious groups (such as the elimination of the phrase *perfidious Jews* in the Easter liturgy). But we can see it above all in relation to the ecumenical movement.

A typical statement is that of the Anglican/Roman Catholic International Commission, which envisages 'full organic unity', with the two Churches living in communion as sister Churches, each with its own 'theological, liturgical and other traditions', and each thus retaining its identity.[5] The critical question, as always, is how to operationalise this 'unity within diversity'? As far as language is concerned, the approach of this paper suggests that unity could be interpreted in relation to the underlying structure of the two liturgies as defined in functional terms. Such unity is not at all obvious if we look only at the surface level of formal linguistic features. Here, the different formulations of grammar and vocabulary, and to some extent the different subject matter, cause us to see the two liturgies as being far apart. A functional approach draws them together, while allowing for differences as features of the desired diversity.

The existence of low-level differences is immediately apparent as soon as texts are placed in parallel. There are over thirty points of lexical, grammatical or graphological difference in the opening of the Gloria, for example:

Roman Catholic and Anglican (new)

> Glory to God in the highest
> and peace to his people on earth.
> Lord God, heavenly King,
> almighty God and Father,
>   we worship you, we give you thanks,
>   we praise you for your glory.

Anglican (Book of Common Prayer)

> Glory be to God on high,
> and in earth peace, goodwill towards men.
> We praise thee, we bless thee, we worship thee,
> we glorify thee,
> we give thanks to thee for thy great glory,
> O Lord God, heavenly King, God the Father Almighty.

On the other hand, when the two orders of service are compared from a functional point of view using standard published formats (see Table 3),[6] the parallelism is remarkable. The differences are few, and can be grouped into three types:

1 Differences of sequence (shown by the lines between the columns), none of which have any major structural effect; the only item which moves considerably is the Notices (and even this is more apparent than real, as many RC priests position them before or after the Creed anyway).
2 Items which have no equivalent (shown by blank lines).
3 Items which have a functional difference, of which there seem to be only three instances:
   (a) The RC Entry antiphon is obligatory, and varies with the Mass; it thus has to be considered informative. By contrast, the CE Opening is optional, and partly sung; it would thus seem to be more expressive. (The differences between the two services in respect of their singing traditions have not been considered in Table 3.)
   (b) The RC Introduction to the Mass is clearly informative, being provided in the priest's own words; the CE Introductory Invocation is an expressive request: *Almighty God . . . cleanse the thoughts of our hearts . . .*

Table 3. Roman Catholic and Anglican services: functional analysis

Roman Catholic Order of Mass		Church of England Order of Holy Eucharist (New)	
Liturgical item	Primary function	Liturgical item	Primary function
Entry antiphon	1	Entry sentence and hymn	1/3
Sign of the cross	2		
Introductory greeting	1	Introductory greeting	2
Introduction to the Mass	3	Introductory prayer	3
Penitential rite	4	Penitential rite	3
Absolution	3	Absolution	4
Kyrie	3	Kyrie	3
Gloria	3	Gloria	3
Collect	1	Collect	1
Bible reading (Old Testament)	1/5	Bible reading (Old Testament)	1/5
Responsorial psalm	1	Psalm	1
Bible reading (New Testament)	1/5	Bible reading (New Testament)	1/5
Gospel acclamation	1	Gradual	1
Gospel opening	5	Gospel opening	5
Gospel reading	1/5	Gospel reading	1/5
Gospel closure	2	Gospel closure	2
Homily	1	Homily	1
Creed	2	Creed	2

Notices	1
Intercessions	1
Penitential rite	3
Peace	1
Offertory	3
Yours Lord is the greatness . . .	1
Lift up your hearts . . .	3
Preface	5
Holy, holy, holy . . .	3
Canon	5/3
Consecration	4/5
Acclamation	2
Canon (continues)	5
Lord's Prayer	2
Fraction	2
Agnus Dei	3
Draw near and receive . . .	2
The body of Christ . . .	2
The blood of Christ	2
Sentence	1
Post-communion prayer	1
Notices	1
Blessing	4
Dismissal	2

Bidding prayers	1
Offertory	3
Lord God we ask you . . .	3
Pray brethren . . .	3
Prayer over the gifts	1
Lift up your hearts . . .	3
Preface	5
Holy, holy, holy . . .	3
Canon	5/3
Consecration	4
Response at Consecration	2
Canon (continues)	5
Lord's Prayer	2
Prayer	3
Lord's Prayer	2
Prayer	3
Sign of peace	3
May this Mingling . . .	3
Agnus Dei	3
This is the Lamb of God	2
Lord I am not worthy	3
Silent monologue (priest)	3
The body of Christ	2
Communion prayer	1
Parish notices	1
Blessing	4
Dismissal	2

(c) Whether the act of Consecration should be given the status of performative or historical utterance raises, in a novel guise, the classical issue of transubstantiation.

It would, I imagine, be agreed that points (a) and (b) in this list are minor; and we are therefore faced with a most striking functional correspondence underlying the utterances of the two services – a correspondence which markedly contrasts with the diversity of formal features referred to above.

An analysis of this kind suggests the importance of a functional perspective. Without it, liturgical development will remain bogged down in the kind of disputes over points of detail which bedevilled discussions of liturgical reform in the 1960s. I recall the questionnaire studies of the time, when people were presented with parallel texts and asked to indicate their preferences, in order to determine whether there was a 'majority style'. In an examination of several hundred such documents which I carried out in 1967 on behalf of the Roman Catholic International Committee on English in the Liturgy, the responses were *never* identical. Innumerable individual differences precluded any clear generalisations about preference. At the time, given the climate of linguistic opinion with its emphasis on formal analysis, this kind of exercise seemed the sensible thing to do. In retrospect the attention to large numbers of linguistic minutiae seems misplaced. Given the diversity of linguistic functions, and the inevitability of language change, there is no likelihood of devising a liturgical language which is equally acceptable to everyone, or even to a majority. There are too many factors involved: age, sex, regional background, social background, temperament (such as whether one is radical or conservative in linguistic taste) and a range of random personal factors (such as whether one has a preference for a particular translation). Agreement is likely only at a deeper, functional level.

Questions of linguistic choice are never straightforward, when couched purely in formal terms. Should we use *thou* or *you*? syntactic construction A or B? rhythmical structure C or D? There are no simple generalisations to be found at this level. A personal decision about *thou*-forms, for example, will relate to such factors as age, regional background (*thou* being still being in use in some dialects) and temperament, as well as to the linguistic context in which it appears. To take just one example of this last point: replacing *thy* in a highly conventionalised context such as *Hallowed be thy name* is much more problematic than replacing it in the context of a less familiar prayer such as *We ask for thy blessing*. . . .. There are many people who would not object to *We ask for your blessing* . . ., but they would balk at *Hallowed be your name*.

The sociolinguistic approach emphasises that surface-level differences of this kind are not the be-all and end-all of liturgical language. The linguistic distinctiveness of the liturgy is best defined at a deeper level, in terms of an aggregate of functions, and it is these which provide the variety with its identity. At this level it is possible to demonstrate a continuity between the different stages of liturgical development, and it may also be possible to show an underlying unity beneath the superficial diversity of different liturgical traditions. The level of sounds, words and sentence patterns should no longer be seen as the only level at which issues of language change can be debated. To restrict the arguments to this level is to fail to see the (functional) wood for the (formal) trees.

One of the merits of the sociolinguistic model, therefore, is that it pays proper attention to the complex range of factors involved in language change, and in particular to the factor of social identity. Language rarely changes of its own volition (though it used to be thought that this was so). Language changes because society changes – not only in the obvious sense that new concepts give rise to new vocabulary, but more fundamentally, in that new social structures generate new linguistic identities. All aspects of linguistic form are affected: phonology, graphology, grammar and lexicon. We subconsciously alter our speech in subtle ways to sound more like those we admire, and to distance ourselves from those we dislike. The principle can be summed up in an old rhyme: 'The chief use of slang is to show that you're one of the gang'. It isn't just slang, of course: pronunciation, grammar and other aspects of vocabulary are also affected. But the important point to appreciate is that 'gang' here refers to far more than a crowd of street urchins. It subsumes any social group: footballers, Liverpudlians, scientists, lawyers . . . or Christians.

Notes

1. Recent introductions to sociolinguistics include: P. Trudgill, *Sociolinguistics: an introduction*, 2nd edn (Harmondsworth, 1983) and R. Wardhaugh, *An introduction to sociolinguistics* (Oxford, 1986), the latter including a discussion of performatives and related notions (chapter 12). Functional classifications of language are discussed in several works, especially those which stress the ethnography of communication, such as D. Hymes, *Foundations in sociolinguistics: an ethnographic approach* (London, 1977). Matters of analysis are well illustrated in M. Stubbs, *Discourse analysis: the sociolinguistic analysis of natural language* (Oxford, 1983) and also in K.R. Scherer and H. Giles (eds), *Social markers in speech* (Cambridge, 1979).

2. This is part of a classification used in my 'A liturgical language in a linguistic perspective', in *New Blackfriars* (December, 1964) 148–56, whose title I have modified for the present chapter. For a more general statement of the role of language in relation to religion, in the context of the 1960s, see my *Linguistics, language and religion* (London, 1965).

3. ICEL: Roman Catholic International Committee on English in the Liturgy.

4. The cultural differences in the value of silence are well illustrated in D. Tannen and M. Saville-Troike (eds), *Perspectives on silence* (Norwood, 1985).

5. ARCIC, *The Final Report* (1982) p. 91.

6. I have not been able to take account here of local differences in liturgical practice; nor has it been possible to ascertain preferences regarding optional elements (i.e. those where the rubric states that a certain element 'may' be said).

7

Philosophy, Implicature and Liturgy

Martin Warner

Glory be to the Father, and to the Son: and to the Holy Ghost;
As it was in the beginning, is now, and ever shall be:
   world without end.

Alternatively,

Glory to the Father and to the Son: and to the Holy Spirit;
as it was in the beginning, is now: and shall be for ever.

The Lesser Doxology provides an important touchstone for Christian worship. Its scriptural basis lies in a conflation of the ascription of worth to (worship of) God and the Lamb in the Book of Revelation 5 (and analogous ascriptions of praise at the close of several of St Paul's Epistles) with the Trinitarian formula of Our Lord's final charge to his disciples recorded in St Matthew's Gospel. Its regular use goes right back to the early Church. As far as the contemporary Church is concerned, the essay on 'Theology of Worship' in one of the best known recent ecumenical works in English on liturgy, *The Study of Liturgy*, points out that 'almost all collects begin with an ascription of praise to the Father, make petition through the Son and conclude with a mention of the Holy Spirit', maintaining that these phrases, together with the Doxology which concludes the Eucharistic prayer, serve to 'remind us that the aim of the whole liturgy is entrance into communion with God, a communion in the divine life and love that constitute the Trinity'.[1]

If Mgr Crichton is even partially correct, then the ascription of praise to the Triune God in the Doxology would appear to be an

147

example of what has been called a 'benchmark situation', a paradigmatic case or stereotype that fixes the linguistic meaning of
predicates used to construe it² – in this case the predicates associated with Christian liturgy and, indeed, with Christian worship.
The sentences used in such ascriptions, on this account, provide
touchstones against which any account of Christian liturgy and its
language may be tested. Whether these sentences should indeed
have the authority I have suggested is a matter for theology rather
than philosophy – though I should not have chosen them if I had
not thought their claims for touchstone status to be plausible – but
I hope that the thought-experiment of taking seriously their expression of a Trinitarian norm will have liturgical significance even
to those who reject their authority – or indeed that of the Trinitarian norm itself.

                                    I

The ramifications of ascribing benchmark status to the utterance of
these sentences are, I think, far-reaching, but to show this I wish to
use certain tools drawn from contemporary work in the philosophy of language – and for this purpose, also, my opening
provides a useful example. When I read a version of this paper to
the Centre for the Study of Literature and Theology at the University of Durham my starting with an ascription of glory to God, as I
had expected, made a significant proportion of my audience dis-
cernibly uneasy. Tense muscles began to relax when I gave an
alternative version, and all was back to normal when I used that
reassuringly academic term 'Lesser Doxology'. Although everyone
understood, in a sense, every word I uttered from the start, the
same is not true for understanding what I meant by them, and this
distinction between word meaning and utterer's meaning provides
us with a useful first step towards unravelling the notion of
'understanding'. The tension arose from a perceived disparity
between utterance and context. That there should have appeared
to be such is itself a culturally relative matter: the translators of the
1611 Authorised Version of the Bible tell us without embarrass-
ment that when they assembled together 'they prayed to the Lord',
and it is a function of the secularisation of our culture that it is the
conjoining rather than the separation of religious observance and

academic scholarship that seems odd. However, in the experience of most of us, the context in which we normally encounter the Doxology is that of public worship, and seminars not only belong to a different sphere of activity but to one so different that the words of public worship can only play a proper role in it when safely and clearly identified as enclosed within inverted commas; the flouting of this convention leads either to bafflement or to uneasy suspicions of religious imperialism or related types of bad form.

Context, in other words, plays a crucial role in our understanding of utterances. Some types of utterance are so stereotypically associated with a particular range of contexts that their utterance in an apparently different one drives the hearer to reinspect the current context, in case the speaker is attempting to indicate that it should be understood differently from the way in which it appears; conversely, the hearer can be led to reinterpret the utterance in a non-standard way which allows for its appropriateness to the perceived context. Linguistic inertia leads one to attempt to construe the words according to the stereotype, but when the verbal or other context renders such construals unacceptable, the phenomenon of linguistic force comes into play to force adaptations of meaning.

The vocabulary I have just used derives from J.F.Ross's *Portraying Analogy*, and I have taken some liberties with it, as Ross restricts his account of inertia and force to verbal contexts; hence he could not unreasonably be construed as excluding considerations concerning the relations between linguistic expressions and their users – the province of pragmatics – in favour of a purely semantic account. However, in my paper 'Philosophy, Language and the Reform of Public Worship' I have given reasons both for thinking that in general the venerable trichotomy between syntax, semantics and pragmatics is somewhat myth-eaten, and that Ross's work in particular is best not construed in terms of it; after all, benchmark situations are of importance for him in locating linguistic inertial frames and they clearly fall within the province of pragmatics. The significance of operating with the wider notion of 'context' will become apparent if we relate the apparatus I have sketched to other accounts of the relation between expression and context which are unambiguously contributions to pragmatics.

A famous example of the bearing of context on interpretation is provided by Paul Grice:

A is writing a testimonial about a pupil who is a candidate for a philosophy job, and his letter reads as follows: 'Dear Sir, Mr. X's command of English is excellent, and his attendance at tutorials has been regular. Yours, etc.' (Gloss: A cannot be opting out, since if he wished to be uncooperative, why write at all? He cannot be unable, through ignorance, to say more, since the man is his pupil; moreover, he knows that more information than this is wanted. He must, therefore, be wishing to impart information that he is reluctant to write down. This supposition is tenable only on the assumption that he thinks Mr. X is no good at philosophy. This, then, is what he is implicating.)[3]

The terms 'implicate' and 'implicature' are constructed after the analogy of 'imply' and 'implication'; the latter are truth-functional notions to be analysed according to standard logical principles, but implicatures stretch wider than mere implications, for they are context-dependent, often in non-conventional ways; even if the implications of what is said are entirely innocent it does not follow that the implicatures are. For a further Gricean example consider the differences between the implications and the implicatures of the following:

Suppose that A and B are talking about a mutual friend, C, who now working at a bank. A asks B how C is getting on at his job, and B replies, *Oh quite well, I think; he likes his colleagues, and he hasn't been to prison yet.*[4]

Grice's own account of implicature is concentrated on 'conversational implicatures' which arise from talk exchanges. His overall idea is that in conversation a 'Co-operative Principle' is normally operative: 'Make your conversational contribution such as is required, at the stage at which it occurs, by the accepted purpose or direction of the talk exchange in which you are engaged.'[5] This principle gives rise to four categories under which fall certain more specific maxims and sub-maxims; the categories concern informativeness, veracity, relevance and manner of expression. My utterance of p may be said to implicate q when there is reason to presume that I am observing the Co-operative Principle and recourse to q is required in order that my utterance of p may be made consistent with this presumption. Thus when I find you beside your obviously immobilised car and you tell me that you are out of petrol, if I reply 'There is a garage round the corner' I implicate that

I think it at least possible that the garage is open and has petrol to sell; otherwise I infringe the maxim 'Be relevant'.

Figures of speech typically enter discourse through an apparent and obvious flouting of a maxim, such as 'Try to make your contribution one that is true', so that we are forced to take what is said non-literally if we are to suppose the Co-operative Principle to hold; it can hardly be literally true, of the Almighty, that 'thou shalt be safe under his feathers', let alone in a context where you are afraid of 'the arrow that flieth by day'. On this account, even if what is asserted is given by truth conditions and its implications are truth-functional, what is said, together with the assumption that the Principles of Conversation are being adhered to, determines what is implicated in a non-truth-functional manner;[6] the utterance, moreover, is only understood when the implicatures are grasped.

Grice's approach has been subject to a number of extensions and modifications, of which I shall mention only two. (His terminology also is often, as here, simplified.) David Holdcroft has explored the possibility of applying Grice's principles to all discourse types, not merely conversational exchanges. Clearly the Co-operative Principle will need modification, but a generalised version of it appears to have a surprisingly wide range of application. Holdcroft's version is as follows:

> Make your contribution to the discourse such as is required, at the stage at which it occurs, by the purposes you have in entering into, or which you have accepted as the purpose of, or which are the generally accepted purposes of, the discourse in which you are a participant.[7]

As one might expect, acceptance of this generalised version of the Principle seems to involve the acceptance of different sets of maxims in different cases, but the sets have a great deal in common. Holdcroft's own taxonomy has as its first *principium divisionis* whether only one or more than one person speaks; in the former case an addressee may or may not be intended, and where it is intended – as in this lecture or a sermon – there may be an 'institutional' context which itself sets constraints on what count as the 'accepted purposes' of the discourse. As Holdcroft points out:

> The situation may be unhappy if an invited speaker does not stick to an agreed topic, or talks in an inappropriate way on an

agreed topic. So that there is always an element of consent on the part of the audience, even on occasions when it says nothing; a point which has an important bearing on the question of whether the Principles of Conversation apply on all such occasions.[8]

The relevance of this to my earlier discussion of my opening sentences is not accidental and should need no labouring.

The case where more than one person speaks is more complex. Here we may distinguish between cases where the roles of speaker and addressee are interchangeable and those where they are not. Where they are, the participants' discourse rights may be unequal, as when we catechise, interview or interrogate; or they may be equal. In the latter case the interests of the participants may be opposed – as in bargaining or quarrelling – or not opposed – as in a consultation, discussion or chat. Here, of course, the most difficult problems arise where interests are opposed, especially where discourse rights are unequal and hence the notion of 'co-operation' at its most problematic. Clearly a maxim like 'try to be as informative as possible', which might generate implicatures in the context of a friendly chat, is hardly appropriate in a negotiating situation. In the limiting cases we need not merely to take account of institutional contexts (respect for the law may in general be in our interests, even if not in this particular case) but also to make a distinction 'between accepting that certain rules and maxims shall apply on a given occasion, and conforming with the rules and maxims that it has been agreed should apply',[9] a distinction also important where only one person speaks, perhaps falsely, to vilify or glorify another. There remains the case where more than one person speaks, but the roles of speaker and addressee are not interchangeable; examples would be a joint report to a third party, a chorus, a hymn or, of course, common prayer. Holdcroft dismisses the last category as 'of slight interest',[10] which for his purposes it probably is, but in the light of our present concerns it is worth further consideration.

In the essay I cited earlier, immediately after his declaration that 'the aim of the whole liturgy is entrance into communion with God', Crichton goes on:

> In the liturgy there is a vertical movement, the out-going of man to God. But there is also a horizontal movement. Liturgy is

celebrated *with* others and the relationships between the members of the worshipping community are of the highest importance.[11]

This suggests that even in the purest cases of common prayer, as when priest and people say the Lord's Prayer together, the inter-communal relationships of the speakers are as important as that between the speakers and the addressee, God. If the 'aim' of liturgy is as stated, and the inter-communal relationships in its celebration 'are of the *highest* importance', then presumably that importance is related to the aim: our relationships with each other affect our capacity to enter into communion with God – a thoroughly scriptural, indeed Dominical, claim. The role of different speakers in this context, however, may be different (the priest or president may lead and the others follow) and even their interests may not be in all relevant respects identical (consider their respective roles in the context of a healing service or, indeed, the solemnisation of matrimony). This suggests that there may be a complex interplay of implicatures depending on the different roles of the various speakers *vis à vis* both themselves and the addressee. This does not seem to be merely a peculiarity of liturgy or common prayer. Consider a joint report where the different authors represent differing interests or expertise: the implicatures associated with the one may not be identical with those associated with the other, each may be aware of this, and yet all prepared to put their names to the report because they can live with the variant implicatures. The term commonly given to this practice is 'compromise', and it appears to be one not wholly alien to the work of the Church of England Liturgical Commission.

In the instance of Christian worship the case is to some degree simplified by the presumption that the interests of speakers and addressee are not opposed, or to be more accurate (for the notion God's 'interests' is a difficult one) that the interests of the speakers are not opposed to the will of the addressee; the presumption is less clear in non-Christian worship and, of course, even in the context of Christian worship one's perceived interests may not conform to the Divine will. But the simplification has its attendant complications when one reflects that, if the aim of the liturgy is 'entrance into communion with God', this is likely to involve the discipline of attempting to align one's perception of one's interests with His will, and the language used may have a role here;

consider the impact on a Victorian servant-child, brought up on a not unknown variant of the Catechism, of discovering that the concluding clause of the Duty Towards Neighbour is not 'to do my duty in that state of life to which God has called me' but rather 'to do my duty in that state of life, unto which it shall please God to call me'. But even if the interests of speakers and addressee are, with the qualifications noted, not at odds, this need not be the case *among* the speakers even when conjoined in the same act of worship – and rival acts of worship are hardly unknown.

So far, of course, I have assumed that in the Liturgy the roles of speaker and addressee are not interchangeable. This is an over-simplification, for there is more to liturgy than common prayer in its simplest form. Not only are the roles of priest or president and congregation separated, but they typically say different things: versicle and response, after all, exemplify a ritualised talk exchange, and there are many other types of liturgical interchange. In such cases the model of speaker and addressee being interchangeable, with frequently unequal discourse rights, in an institutional context where interests are taken not to be opposed would seem attractive, but for the fact that standardly the versicle or equivalent is not directed to the respondent but to God, who is not part of the talk exchange. The combination of a 'vertical', Godward movement with a 'horizontal', communal one complicates any account of the linguistic principles governing Christian worship. Indeed, I take it that this interplay governs what is presumably the basic principle governing liturgical revision: the rite must aspire to be worthy of God while speaking to the condition of the worshippers in a manner that integrates the two concerns – for the condition of the worshippers needs itself to be transformed in a Godward direction not least through participation in the rite.

This proposed transformation itself further complicates the linguistic model, for my assumption that in liturgy God remains silent can itself be challenged; God, it is said, may speak through the voice of preacher or scripture reader and reply to our prayers in other ways in the sacraments in a transforming manner. Against this it may be urged that whatever place may be given to perceived divine response in extempore prayer, it is of the essence of liturgical prayer that it be formalised, and where this is the case the model of a talk exchange is inappropriate. The problems of identifying divine responses to prayer are notorious – thunderbolts falling on York Minister apparently do not count – and the ritual framework of the liturgy provides a secure framework free from such anxieties. But of course analogous considerations could be urged against regarding any piece of ritual, including the move from Exhortation to Confession, as a talk exchange – which would be a desperate move. A liturgical text is only intelligible to the extent that its linguistic patterns formalise ones recognisable in less formal contexts, and hence take account of the appropriate implicatures and implications; the fact that a response is written in does not prevent it from being a response. But if this is right it should be noted that responses by God are also, as it were, written in – at least through presupposition; 'we most heartily thank thee, for that thou dost vouchsafe to feed us', said after Communion, or 'seeing . . . that this Child is by Baptism regenerate', said after the baptism of an infant, provide examples. This suggests that the linguistic model needed for liturgy is a complex one involving interchange between a number of different speakers and respondents with different types of roles, rights and interests in a highly institutionalised framework.

Complexity, however, is only bought at a price: if this model has to be dovetailed with the Gricean one of open-ended sets of maxims and sub-maxims falling under one or other of four interconnected categories, there is a danger of losing touch with psychological reality. Fortunately recent work on the borderlands of psycholinguistics and philosophy has addressed this problem, and one of the most impressive recent treatments – Dan Sperber and Deirdre Wilson's *Relevance* – attempts to organise our understanding of communication, cognition and non-demonstrative inference round the concept of 'relevance' – which for Grice was only one of his four categories. The basic idea is best grasped in the context of the communication of information, though it can be extended to others; most of our information is old and lodged in our memory, part of our standing representations of the world, and most of our new information is entirely unconnected with the old and can only be added to these representations as isolated bits and pieces – involving too much processing for too little benefit; but some new information does connect with the old in such a way that when they are put together further new information can be derived which could not have been gained without this combination. As Sperber and Wilson put it: 'When the processing of new information gives rise to such a multiplication effect, we call it *relevant*. The greater the multiplication effect, the greater the relevance.'[12] The degree of relevance, of course, is always relative to a context, so we have two extent conditions:

an assumption is relevant in a context to the extent that its contextual effects in this context are large;

and

an assumption is relevant in a context to the extent that the effort required to process it in this context is small.[13]

Assessing relevance is therefore a matter of balancing contextual effects against processing effort. The so-called 'Principle of Relevance' asserts that 'every act of ostensive communication' (which includes most linguistic communication) 'communicates the presumption of its own optimal relevance',[14] and this principle is used to explicate in psychologically plausible terms the proposed model of communication and with it the implicatures of non-demonstrative inference.

This is not the place to go into the strengths and weaknesses of the Principle of Relevance on its own ground, but the framework provided can help to illuminate some of our own concerns. The conception of degrees of relevance can help us to see how the implicatures of an utterance can vary in strength, from those where they must be supplied if the interpretation of an utterance is to be consistent with the Principle of Relevance, through cases where the hearer is strongly encouraged but not actually forced to supply them, through further cases where the encouragement is weaker and the range of relevant implicatures wider, to the limiting case where there is no encouragement to supply any particular implicatures and the hearer 'takes the entire responsibility for supplying them himself'.[15] Thus if Peter asks Mary 'Would you drive a Mercedes?' and she replies 'I wouldn't drive ANY expensive car', the strongest implicatures are 'a Mercedes is an expensive car' and 'Mary wouldn't drive a Mercedes' – they are necessary to make her response relevant. Rather weaker is 'Mary wouldn't drive a BMW', and if Peter were to reflect that people who would not drive an expensive car would not go on a cruise either and accordingly infer 'Mary would not go on a cruise', he would be at the weakest end of the range of implicatures. These examples, it is suggested, show that there may be no cut-off point between assumptions strongly backed by the speaker, and assumptions derived from the utterance but on the hearer's sole responsibility. The fiction that there is a clear-cut distinction between wholly determinate, specifically intended inferences and indeterminate, wholly unintended inferences cannot be maintained. Relevance theory offers a way of getting rid of this fiction without sacrificing clarity of conceptual framework.[16]

On this model the psychological processes by which implicatures are reached determine their relevance, which affects their plausibility – and where we have to choose between them, that requiring greatest effort is regarded as the least plausible. Thus 'a speaker aiming at optimal relevance will leave implicit everything her hearer can be trusted to supply with less effort than would be needed to process an explicit prompt',[17] but this presupposes some assumptions about the degree of mutual understanding between speaker and hearer – relevance is at least a two-place relation ('what is relevant to one person may not be relevant to another')[18] – thus the form used to convey the information reveals these assumptions, 'there is no entirely neutral style'. That primarily associated with poetry is one in which utterances achieve most of their 'relevance through a wide array of weak implicatures',[19] which is presumably why T.S. Eliot thought it appropriate to add his notes to the published version of *The Waste Land* – he was not entirely assured about the contextual resources and processing abilities of the wider public. The conclusion drawn is that:

In general, the wider the range of potential implicatures the greater the hearer's responsibility for constructing them, the more poetic the effect, the more creative the metaphor. A good creative metaphor is precisely one in which a variety of contextual effects can be retained and understood as weakly implicated by the speaker. . . . The surprise or beauty of a successful creative metaphor lies in . . . condensation, in the fact that a single expression . . . will determine a very wide range of acceptable weak implicatures.[20]

If this general approach is right, then it has important implications for the notion of style. As Sperber and Wilson insist:

Generally, the most striking examples of a particular figure, the ones singled out for attention by rhetoricians and students of style, are those which have poetic effects [through a wide array of weak implicatures]. These poetic effects are then attributed to the syntactic or phonological construction in question. However, . . . a repetitive syntactic pattern does not invariably give rise to noticeable stylistic effects. The same is true of all the figures of style identified by classical rhetoric.[21]

This may help to explain the perennial attraction of the attempt to separate style from meaning. For example, Ronald Jasper, then Chairman of the Church of England Liturgical Commission, roundly declared in *The Eucharist Today* that 'in addition to questions of meaning and translation there are also questions of style'.[22] In my paper 'Philosophy, Language and the Reform of Public Worship' I suggested that if meaning is understood as something construable in terms of a set of co-ordinates independent of style it must be understood as fully explicable in terms of truth conditions or their analogues, after the manner of the programmes of formal semantics, and that this was not merely implausible in terms of linguistic theory but devastating for theology. In a subsequent communication Dr Jasper perceptively commented:

Perhaps your interpretation of 'style' may not be the same as mine. I am thinking mainly in terms of rhetorical devices – the use of the cursus, chiasmus, asyndeton, alliteration and so on. Clearly there must be occasions when the use of a word in terms of meaning may conflict with the use of that word in terms of style, e.g. a wrong combination of syllables. But I still think the two things are distinct and pose their own problems!

If style is construed simply in terms of devices, without reference to intended effect or construable implicatures, then Dr Jasper is clearly right even on the most 'pragmatic' interpretation of 'meaning': the reordering of an utterance to avoid alliteration need not change its meaning. But of course these 'devices' were originally developed in terms of ancient psychological theory, and the significance of the distinctions drawn was related to the effects of the different devices to be expected in terms of such theory; part of the value of the sort of work I have sketched is that it promises to reintegrate stylistic considerations into broader linguistic and cognitive theory, and when this is done the separation of style from meaning no longer seems so attractive an option. If we consider stylistic devices in terms of their point, taking into account intended effect and the strong and weak implicatures they sponsor, we find that shifts in the implicature mix relevant to given contexts involve difference in meaning.

Let us take one of Grice's maxims under the category of Manner, 'Be brief (avoid unnecessary prolixity)';[23] in discussing the way that different discourse types may involve the acceptance of different sets of maxims in different cases, David Holdcroft remarks that 'ones relevant to an address to the emperor might include "be circumlocutionary"'[24] and thus run counter to Grice's maxim; it is easy to see how this point could be reformulated in terms of the Principle of Relevance. Now consider the following:

> O Lord our heavenly Father, high and mighty, King of kings, Lord of lords, the only Ruler of princes, who dost from thy throne behold all the dwellers upon earth; Most heartily we beseech thee with thy favour . . .

This is indeed circumlocutionary and sounds remarkably like a petition to the emperor; it is very different in respect of prolixity to that other address to 'Our Father, which art in heaven'. The use of the imperial titles and reference to God's throne help place the register we are in and the relevance of this register becomes apparent when we realise that it is the opening of the Prayer for the Queen's Majesty: 'Most heartily we beseech thee with thy favour to behold our most gracious Sovereign Lady, Queen Elizabeth . . .' Were the prayer to resolve itself in a significantly different way there would be likely to be a clash of implicatures, because the relevance of the circumlocutionary stylistic device employed would be problematic. And of course for those without historical awareness and having republican sympathies or a reduced conception of monarchy this type of rhetoric might be unacceptable even if the prayer resolved itself in a reference to the president or a Scandinavian sovereign; *The Alternative Service Book*, one notices, removes the circumlocution. 'What do you mean by talking like that?', we might be asked, and the conception of 'meaning' thereby presupposed might quite reasonably be construed as ordinary linguistic meaning, with its attendant implicatures; the objection that this was a matter of style rather than meaning would not merely be an evasion but actively misleading.

We may now be in a position to appreciate some of the interest of my proposed extension of Ross's account of linguistic inertia and force to take account of extra-linguistic as well as linguistic context. In order to take account of the relevant phenomena we need to vary the classical semantic account of meaning as a function from sentences (or terms or predicates) to possible states of affairs (or individuals or sets of individuals) by considering context fully, but not as just another index (speaker, time, place and so on). Such a move, as we have seen, blurs the semantics/pragmatics distinction and reintegrates style with meaning. On this account metaphor, for example, appears to be inevitable and ineradicable. In metaphors the normal linguistic meanings of the words used are not cancelled, but the normal contexts standardly presupposed for their application are here clearly not so presupposed; the reader's or hearer's task is to see the appositeness of the application despite the fact that the context of application is untoward, and the need to render such a context relevant forces meaning adaptations (with concomitant implicature shifts) from the norm. The notion of a 'normal' context is given by 'benchmark situations' which stereotypically fix the linguistic meaning of predicates used to construe it. According to Ross some discourse is 'craftbound', that is, skill in action is necessary for a full grasp of the discourse,[25] and religious discourse falls into this category, for 'religion is taught to modulate living' and 'living in God . . . is the object of the craft of Christian doing'.[26] In craftbound discourse the basic vocabulary is anchored to benchmark situations such as 'Scripture stories' that 'structure and stabilize the central meaning relationships',[27] and the destabilising 'force' is provided by the varying contexts in which this vocabulary is placed. If 'the aim of the whole liturgy is entrance into communion with God', then it would appear that Christian worship, like other religious discourse, is craftbound on Ross's criteria, and liturgical writing will need to take account of this, attempting to facilitate that transformation of the worshippers through worship which I discussed earlier. In this task attention to the variety of relevant linguistic and extra-linguistic contexts, with their attendant implicatures and stylistic constraints, will be as appropriate in constructing the words of the rites as will attention to those words' truth-functional implications.

II

I suggested at the outset that the liturgical utterance of the Lesser Doxology has benchmark status, hence the unease at hearing it in a non-liturgical context, and I traced its scriptural source to, *inter alia*, Revelation 5. But the context of that source is the vision which opens in the previous chapter with its worshipping beasts: 'Holy, holy, holy, Lord God Almighty, which was, and is, and is to come.' This, of course, takes us back to Isaiah 6 (not to speak of Ezekiel) with the seraphim who cry 'Holy, holy, holy is the Lord of hosts: the whole earth is full of his glory', to a scripture story which is standardly interpreted as paradigmatic, providing a benchmark situation, for Christian worship. In his discussion of the concept of worship Ninian Smart argues that the experience which worship tries to express is the numinous (the object of worship is thus perceived as awe-inspiring)[28] and that the vision of Isaiah in the Temple is a prime example of the numinous.[29] There are, of course, other aspects to be taken into account: worship is relational, it typically involves ritual which both expresses the superiority to the worshipper of the focus of worship and participates in or sustains its power, and it involves praise of the focus of worship which is conceived as transcending any particular manifestation;[30] it will be noted that in all respects Isaiah's Temple vision fits the characterisation.

If this scripture story does provide such a benchmark, then it is appropriate to note that Isaiah's immediate response to the numinous is as follows:

> Woe is me for I am undone; because I am a man of unclean lips, and I dwell in the midst of a people of unclean lips: for mine eyes have seen the King, the Lord of hosts.

It is only after this response that his 'sin is purged', burnt out as by a live coal, and he is thereby enabled so to enter into communion with God as to become his agent and mouthpiece; the narrative structure of this benchmark story appears to be important for its intelligibility (a consideration not without its relevance to discussions of the relation between narrative and liturgy).

Bearing this in mind it is instructive to note that the 1958 Lambeth Conference which gave impetus to the whole process of Prayer Book revision sponsored in its Report the recommendation that 'the present corporate expressions of penitence need to be modified both in length and language' (1.47 and 2.81), which appears to be Anglican code for 'shortened and weakened'; the early revisions carried out this coded injunction, until the objections of worshippers caused the expressions of penitence to be strengthened (though hardly to Cranmerian stringency). Of course this recommendation had a context: we were on the eve of what has become known as the 'permissive society', with influential theologians quoting Freud and criticising the notion of guilt. But it also had quite strong implicatures: either liturgical activity is distinct from worship proper, or contemporary Christian worship should diverge from the scriptural norm; if the latter, this is either because of the distinctively Christian transformation of the Jewish tradition (God is to be conceived of and addressed as 'Abba, Father') or because of something distinctive about contemporary society (humanity has come of age). Contemporaries not crediting any of these implicatures might not unreasonably have reflected on a weaker, probably unfair and certainly unintended implicature: episcopal eyes have never seen the King, the Lord of hosts. The objections of the worshippers, presumably, concerned the conception of God, of our present condition and of the relation between them enacted in the revised liturgy, and if 'the aim of the whole liturgy is entrance into communion with God' these are important matters.

This example helps to point up the importance of the cognitive element in worship. Smart rightly points out that 'stating descriptions is not a primary aspect of any worship', and that what appear to be descriptions (such as 'telling God at Easter that he has raised his Son up from the dead') have a performative character (celebrating or representing the event) which gives their primary significance; he concedes, however, that 'it can prove embarrassing if the words descriptively are not *true*'.[31] If one asks why this should be so, the question becomes part of a more general enquiry concerning why truth matters in religion (for such benchmark stories help fix the meaning of the terms we predicate of God).

The problem that this enquiry addresses dominates Saint Augustine's *Confessions*, and his answer has been generally taken as authoritative: 'How can one pray to you unless one knows you? If one does not know you, one may pray not to you, but to something else.'[32] In other words, a false understanding of God may distort one's spiritual life, cut one off from the true God and so bar the way to salvation. Augustine believed this to have been his own situation while he was still a Manichee. Sound doctrine provides a channel pointing in the right direction in which our spiritual lives may safely flow and deepen. But the relation is to a certain extent reciprocal. My ability to respond to the doctrine as true, or even understand it, is partly a function of my own experience, activity and spirituality. Thus Augustine opens the story of his first or 'intellectual' conversion with the words, 'With you to guide me, I entered into the innermost part of myself, . . . and saw with my soul's eye (such as it was) an unchangeable light shining above this eye of my soul and above my mind'.[33] The story of the *Confessions* up to that point has been the story of how his mind had so developed that this was possible. One's ability to discern spiritual truth is a function of one's life and experience.

To some extent, no doubt, this is the case with many forms of truth. One cannot fully accept or even understand the theory of special relativity without a certain degree of acquaintance with physics; both the discourses of religion and of physics are craft-bound. But the extent varies with the subject matter in question. Aristotle, notoriously, held that a young man was not a fit hearer of lectures on ethics, 'for he is inexperienced in the actions that occur in life' (1095a), but he made no such proviso for lectures on physics. Theological discourse, in as much as it is concerned with the deepest things of all, is still further along this spectrum than is ethics. In religion, we are told, the way, the truth and the life are different aspects of the one unity; if this is so, then one's life of prayer and worship is likely to be internally related to one's belief structure. *Lex orandi, lex credendi*; confessing oneself before God as a 'miserable sinner' (even in the Tudor sense of the word) in whom there is 'no health' has implicatures which render more credible than do the weakened formulations the claim that 'Thou art of purer eyes than to behold evil, and canst not look upon iniquity'. Reciprocally, the move to weaken the corporate expressions of penitence may be not wholly unrelated to the decline in the belief in the reality of hell. Similarly, if style affects implicature, then stylistic changes in the language of worship may have far-reaching consequences for the faith of the worshipping community.

'Liturgy', I take it, designates the prescribed public worship of the Church, as contrasted with private devotion on the one hand and extempore prayer on the other; for convenience, all my examples are taken from the public worship of the Church of England.

The institutional associations of the term go back not only to its origin in denoting public works but to its Septuagint associations with the services of the Temple (where, of course, Isaiah had his vision). 'The Liturgy', in my usage, refers to the Eucharist, understood as the Dominically authorised act of public worship. The texts which prescribe such public worship stand to it in the same relation as does text to performance in the performing arts; and in analogous manner to the way in which a proper assessment of a score or dramatic script can only be carried through by reference to its potentialities in performance, so a liturgical text is to be judged by reference to its capacities in the context of prescribed institutional worship.

At a somewhat trivial level, though one which appears to cause a good deal of mutual irritation between priest and people, the giving of the Peace in many congregations involves an element of the extempore which breaks with the liturgical (and hence prescribed) character of the congregational experience of the rest of most services and is thus disruptive of that pattern of worship; the experience of the Liturgy as a whole, and therefore of the giving of the Peace within its context, is of course different for the priest: thus what in the text is peace can in practice be an occasion of discord. Of greater historical importance are the traditions of allegorical interpretation of the Liturgy stemming from Amalarius: congregations appear to have found difficulty in relating spiritually to the *muthos* at the heart of the rite and so responded positively to its presentation in such a way that the events of the sacred narrative could be seen as discernible within it; it has been plausibly argued that modern drama evolved out of this tradition.[34] Amalarius' writings were pronounced heretical in his own lifetime, and Mgr Crichton speaks for liturgical orthodoxy today when he urges that we should have 'nothing to do with the allegorizing of the writers of the ninth and subsequent centuries, least of all [those] for whom the Eucharist became a sacred drama'.[35] On the other hand, as O.B. Hardison points out, they 'answered a strongly felt need for an interpretation of the Mass which emphasized its immediate, as against its historical, significance', especially with respect to those 'for whom historical details and theological subtleties [were] meaningless'.[36] No doubt there are serious objections to presenting or interpreting liturgy as allegorical drama, but it remains important for the liturgical reviser to take account of the 'felt needs' such treatments were responding to.

More generally, it would appear that it is the nature of Christian worship that should determine good liturgical practice, and the various stylistic and scholarly tools available to the modern liturgiologist are properly subordinate to its demands. Such a claim appears to be in conformity with the position of Fr Hugo Rahner, for whom the Christian 'mysteries' as focused in ritual have from Classical times involved a principled blend of 'common archetypal elements', Revelation and cultural borrowings;[37] the archetypal elements are those relating to all worship, Revelation provides the distinctively Christian contribution to liturgy, while cultural borrowings are capable in principle of rendering it culturally accessible and relevant. If this approach is on the right lines, then the possibilities of tension between these three elements may help us understand some contemporary disputes. I shall take just two types of example of such conflict.

First, there may be tension between the archetypal elements and one's understanding of Revelation. Thus Mgr Crichton opens his discussion of worship by claiming that it is 'a reaching out *through* the fear that always accompanies the sacred to the *mysterium* conceived as *tremendum* but also *fascinans*, because behind it and in it there is an intuition of the Transcendent';[38] Christian worship, he claims, 'does not deny the values to be found in more primitive kinds of worship. It purifies them, puts them into an entirely new context, and enhances them.' However, when he comes to 'the ground-pattern of all Christian worship', we are told that 'the glorifying of God, the response in faith which issues into praise, thanksgiving, and supplication is exactly what we are doing in worship';[39] the 'fear that always accompanies the sacred' seems to have dropped out of sight. Presumably this objection might be met with the contention that, for the Christian, God is love and 'perfect love casteth out fear'; however, such a move not only presupposes that the fear of which St John speaks is the same as the awe described by Otto, which might be difficult to sustain, but indicates that Christian worship is so far removed from other forms of worship that a central archetypal element is not so much purified as eliminated. Given such a theology one may reasonably ask whether there is not now equivocation over the word 'worship', and whether a liturgy developed in the light of it is capable of meeting the needs that the more 'primitive' types of worship address.

Second, there may be difficulties in harmonising Revelation with

cultural accessibility, both spatial and temporal. From a geographi-
cal point of view the needs and culture of different groups even
within a single country may be so diverse as to lead to pressure for
different types of liturgy in, for example, the urban areas of Britain
and in the suburbs; against such pressures for inculturation one
might object that to risk dividing the Church on class lines is to
endanger the catholicity of the Church – setting at nought both the
Credal affirmation of the Holy Catholic Church and that of the
Communion of Saints.

From a temporal standpoint most attention has been directed to
the divergence in implicatures of words and images in the context
of scripture or of the early Church from those of our own time;
thus J.L. Houlden complains of 'modern liturgy-making' that
'there has been little sign of any serious attempt to consider
whether these words and images still carry their former vividness
or are intelligible expressions of what is to be said'.[40] This problem
has been accentuated by the fact that the Liturgical Movement has
sought to return to the scriptures and the liturgical models of the
patristic period as possessing normative status, thus often by-
passing the traditions of the intervening centuries; in parallel
fashion those who set the terms of reference for the *New English
Bible* abandoned the old Authorised Version principle in Biblical
translation of attempting to improve on previous efforts, 'to make
a good one better', and instead aimed for 'a completely new
translation'. However, it may be objected to such practices that
'liturgy is a public act by which the worshippers identify themselves with a continuing community'[41] and that to ignore the most
recent centuries of the life of that community is to take less than
seriously the doctrine of the Communion of Saints. Less doctrinal
considerations point in a similar direction: David Frost, a member
of the Liturgical Commission which produced the *Alternative Service Book 1980*, declared that 'following old liturgical practice, our
new material is a tissue of scriptural allusion';[42] but if allusion is so
important the Principle of Relevance requires that it can be pro-
cessed easily and hence that allusions should be readily recognisable – a requirement ignored by the proliferation of 'completely
new' translations without cultural roots in regular liturgical use. In
this connection it may be worth pointing out that the translators
of the *New International Version* 'sought to preserve some measure
of continuity with the long tradition of translating the Scriptures
into English' (page vi).

Such objections are hardly alien to what the *Book of Common Prayer* in its Preface characterises as 'the wisdom of the Church of England': as R.T. Beckwith has pointed out, the idea that the recovery of the worship of the primitive Church was the aim of the compilers of the first prayer books of the Church of England is a mistaken one, and Cranmer himself was concerned to avoid unnecessary change.[43] Early models can be accorded a certain normative status without being thereby treated as unalterable stereotypes, and if intermediate traditions are allowed their own authority it may be possible to take account of the mediating contexts they provide in bridging the gaps of implicature between the first century and today; the rival claims of 'Lead us not into temptation' and 'Do not bring us to the time of trial' in the liturgical versions of the Lord's Prayer are not unconnected with this issue. More generally, as Hans-Georg Gadamer has argued, cultural artefacts are always read by us in the context of tradition, and the attempt to ignore that fact is to invite hermeneutic misrepresentation.[44]

III

It is with respect to the attempts of liturgical revisers and Biblical translators to harmonise fidelity to normative originals with contemporary cultural accessibility that the notion of implicature has its most obvious applications in the present context. I shall conclude by considering two types of example, that of translation and that of doctrine.

In a recent powerful study of language, poetics and biblical interpretation Stephen Prickett contrasts two opposing models for translation: 'paraphrase' and 'metaphrase'. As a representative of the former he cites Eugene Nida, one of the influential figures behind the *Good News Bible*, for whom

> translating consists in producing in the receptor language the closest natural equivalent to the message of the source language, first in meaning and secondly in style. . . . By 'natural' we mean that the equivalent forms should not be 'foreign' either in form (except of course for such inevitable matters as proper names) or meaning. That is to say, a good translation should not reveal its nonnative source.[45]

It is easy to find instances of biblical translation where this principle is not observed. For example, the ASB's Liturgical Psalter substitutes in Psalm 150 'Praise him in the blast of the ram's horn' for Coverdale's 'Praise him in the sound of the trumpet'; C.H. Sissons's ironically tart comment is worth quoting: 'Ah, Coverdale, we must tell him; at least we moderns know it *was* a ram's horn, and do not mix it up with any instrument we have actually heard in the twentieth century.'[46] Further, writing of the *Jerusalem Bible*, Ian Robinson objects: 'If the twenty-third Psalm is to begin "Yahweh is my shepherd, I lack nothing", the Psalter is a foreign text, not part of the English Bible',[47] thereby putting in question Nida's parenthesis. For a positive use of the principle of equivalence the opening of the twenty-third Psalm again provides an instructive example: I am informed that in a recent translation of the Psalter into one of the American Eskimo languages, where there is no 'natural' word for sheep or shepherd, the solution chosen was one which could be literally translated 'The Lord is my seal-pup keeper'.

Prickett, however, argues for metaphrase ('turning an author word by word, and line by line, from one language into another')[48] rather than paraphrase, on the ground that the ideal of paraphrase denies the creative function of language: 'it is not equivalencies, but *dissimilarities* that force the modification and change necessary to accommodate new associative patterns of thought'.[49] He instances Elijah's 'still small voice', literally 'a voice of thin silence', and criticises the domestication of this boundary-breaking concept to contemporary naturalistic categories in contemporary translations: 'the soft whisper of a voice' (*Good News Bible*), 'a low murmuring sound' (*New English Bible*), and 'sound of a gentle breeze' (*Jerusalem Bible*). Of these he comments:

> Not one of these three major modern translations manages to suggest an inherent peculiarity about the event that might indicate a quite *new* kind of experience. . . . The modern mind cannot have an event that does not fit into one of the two categories [*either* miraculous *or* natural]. Yet such rationalism would seem to strike right at the heart of the original story.[50]

The difference between metaphrase and paraphrase is, he argues, crucial: 'metaphrase aims to render the original in all its starkness and oddity, it does not imply *mastery*. Paraphrase implies, at least in some degree, comprehension – in the ancient and full meaning of the word.'[51]

That a significant difference is here being pointed to seems clear; what is less clear is exactly how it should be drawn and evaluated. The differences in the types of example instanced are striking: that which leads Sisson to support 'equivalents' ('trumpet' rather than 'ram's horn') is one where insisting on the alienness of the instrument seems religiously irrelevant or intrusive – what matters are the implicatures, which scholarship can help us to master, and those of the trumpet in our culture are perhaps as close as we can get to those of the ram's horn for the psalmist (though clearly a number of culture-specific implicatures are bound to be lost); on the other hand the alienness of the still small voice, together with its apparent disruption of the patterns of expectation so far established in the story, is far from religiously irrelevant – it is these implicatures rather than those of a 'soft whisper' on which attention needs to be fixed. But if 'relevance' is to be invoked in this context norms are needed by which it is to be established, and these must be primarily theological: the notion of a religiously neutral translation of the Bible seems to be something of an *ignis fatuus*.

However, the contrast between paraphrase and metaphrase may sometimes be difficult to draw. The case of proper names is instructive, despite the way that Nida dismisses them in a parenthesis which Prickett omits. Insisting on 'Yahweh' for the Tetragrammaton certainly establishes a 'nonnative source', as Robinson complains, and hence presumably exemplifies what for Prickett is metaphrase, but whether the traditional 'The LORD' is metaphrase or paraphrase is less clear; partly, no doubt, it depends on how seriously one takes the Jewish aversion to uttering the Tetragrammaton in establishing the text to be translated. It is clear, however, that the implicatures of 'the LORD' are to a contemporary ear different from those of 'Yahweh', and theological considerations should decide which are the more important; even the no doubt inaccurate 'Jehovah' also has its merits from the point of view of cultural accessibility, both in the light of the sound pattern of the English language and of the implicatures established by tradition.

Similar considerations apply in the case of the new versions of the Lord's Prayer. The claims of cultural accessibility appear to have won greater support than usual here, largely because the religious power and importance of tradition are in this instance at their most obvious, but even in the traditional 'Rite B' version the pull of the normative originals is still evident. To some this is objectionable: Sisson remarks that it 'varies from the true English version only by tiny verbal changes so silly that no one but a pedant could have thought of making them at all',[52] but even a sympathetic examination reveals oddities. The switch from 'which art' to 'who art' is presumably motivated by the twin (challenge-able) considerations that hiatus is less offensive to the contemporary ear than to the Tudor and that the distinction between 'which' and 'who' is stronger now than it was then. The latter considera-tion might be thought to be important if the retention of 'which' inculcated a less than personal view of God, though any strong implicature of that nature would seem to be blocked by the word 'Father'; the Greek of Matthew, however, has a masculine article rather than neuter pronoun (if the lack of accent is to be trusted) and this seems to have decided the matter.

The substitution of '*on* earth as it is in heaven' for '*in* earth as it is in heaven' is more interesting. The Greek certainly changes the prepositions (*epi* earth, *en* heaven), but although 'on earth' is perfectly possible the implicatures in Classical and New Testament Greek are associated with 'on (*epi*) earth' being importantly differ-ent from 'under (*hupo*) the earth'; on the other hand, in contempor-ary English the implicatures of 'on earth' take account of space travel, hence the possibly apocryphal child who described the Ascension as 'just another blast-off'. The traditional 'in earth' captures the point that we are concerned with the sphere of earthly things, not with a part of the solar system: for twentieth-century ears, being within the sphere of earthly things has only the weak-est of Ptolemic implicatures. In a curious way what Sisson calls 'pedantry' is perhaps not pedantic enough – more attention to the implicatures both of the original Greek and of contemporary dis-course might have led the revisers in this instance to have found in the traditional word precisely that mediating element between normative original and cultural accessibility they were presumably seeking.

But the tension between these two poles goes beyond issues of translation to those of doctrine itself. I opened by presenting the ascription of praise to the Triune God in the Doxology as a 'bench-mark situation' and the Doxology itself as a touchstone against which any account of Christian liturgy and its worship may be tested. If this is right, an account of liturgical language which blocks Trinitarian implicatures in worship is defective. The problem here was seen with some clarity by Cardinal Newman, but if the line of argument I have developed is correct his proposed solution is seriously flawed. In the *Grammar of Assent* he writes as follows:

> Religion has to do with the real, and the real is the particular; theology has to do with what is notional, and the notional is the general and the systematic. Hence theology has to do with the Dogma of the Holy Trinity as a whole made up of many propositions; but Religion has to do with each of those separate propositions which compose it, and lives and thrives in the contemplation of them.[53]

Worship is part of religion, not of theology, thus the permeation of the Liturgy with Trinitarian formulae puts the onus of proof on Newman to show that the Doctrine of the Trinity is not within the province of religion. His case, of course, rests on the distinction between the notional and the real, and this in turn depends on his distinction between the 'strong' apprehension of 'concrete' things and the weaker apprehension of abstractions. No doubt the phenomena he instances to support this distinction go some way towards doing so, but they hardly show that the distinction is absolute, and the way implicatures enable the mind to move easily and in principled fashion between different levels of discourse in a manner impossible for truth-functional implications must put in doubt the existence of any such middle wall of partition. Further, the best contemporary work on the doctrine of the Trinity, for example that of David Brown, interprets it in terms of models – as indeed did Saint Augustine long ago – and models mediate between the concrete and the abstract. It may be that it was, at least in part, a defective theory of language that led Newman to the bizarre conclusion that the Divine Trinity is an abstraction inaccessible to religion.

But if the language of worship is to be faithful to the Trinitarian norm while remaining culturally accessible its implicatures need to be handled with some care. Merely incorporating or multiplying Trinitarian formulae will of itself be inadequate, for they are liable to remain inert markers of theological orthodoxy – 'vain repetitions'; Newman was pointing to a real difficulty. Linguistic inertia is liable to leave them tied to first- or fourth-century stereotypes, and the linguistic force required to make them live imaginatively and transformingly in the minds of the worshippers can only come from the context in which they are set – and here the linguistic context is crucial. Thus language which addresses the Triune God in such a manner as, through its implicatures, either to confound the Persons or to divide the Substance is liable to weaken the ability of the worshippers to transform the doctrine from mere theology into the stuff of worship. Conversely, forms which preserve in their implicatures and style the need to think of the Triune God in terms of models which inevitably fall short of the reality may help to safeguard that sense of the *mysterium tremendum et fascinans* which we have seen to lie at the heart of worship as such.

How this may be done, however, is not the province of the philosopher.[54]

Notes

1. J.D. Crichton, 'A Theology of Worship', in *The Study of Liturgy*, eds Cheslyn Jones, Geoffrey Wainwright and Edward Yarnold (London, 1980) p. 19.
2. J.F. Ross, *Portraying Analogy* (Cambridge, 1981) p. 212.
3. H.P. Grice, 'Logic and Conversation', in *Syntax and Semantics*, Vol. 3: *Speech Acts*, eds P. Cole and J.L. Morgan (New York, 1975) p. 52.
4. Ibid., p. 43.
5. Ibid., p. 45.
6. David Holdcroft, 'Speech Acts and Conversation – I', in *The Philosophical Quarterly*, 29 (1979) p. 128.
7. Ibid., p. 139.
8. Ibid., p. 130.
9. Ibid., p. 139.
10. Ibid., p. 131.
11. Crichton, op. cit. (see note 1) p. 19.
12. D. Sperber and D. Wilson, *Relevance: Communication and Cognition* (Oxford, 1986) p. 48.
13. Ibid., p. 125.
14. Ibid., p. 158.
15. Ibid., p. 199.
16. Ibid., p. 199.
17. Ibid., p. 219.
18. Ibid., p. 252.
19. Ibid., p. 222.
20. Ibid., p. 236–7.
21. Ibid., p. 223.
22. R.C.D. Jasper (ed.), *The Eucharist Today* (London, 1974) p. 3.
23. Grice, op. cit. (see note 3) p. 46.

24. Holdcroft, op. cit. (see note 6) p. 141.
25. Ross, op. cit. (see note 2) p. 158.
26. Ibid., p. 167.
27. Ibid., p. 158.
28. Ninian Smart, *The Concept of Worship* (London, 1972) p. 51.
29. Ibid., p. 22.
30. Ibid., p. 51.
31. Ibid., p. 27.
32. *The Confessions of St. Augustine*, trans. Rex Warner (New York, 1963) I, 1.
33. Ibid., VII, 10.
34. See O.B. Hardison Jr, *Christian Rite and Christian Drama in the Middle Ages: Essays in the Origin and Early History of Modern Drama* (Baltimore, 1965).
35. Crichton, op. cit., p. 14.
36. Hardison, op. cit., p. 38.
37. H. Rahner, 'The Christian Mystery and the Pagan Mysteries', in *Pagan and Christian Mysteries: Papers from the Eranos Yearbooks*, ed. Joseph Campbell (New York, 1955) pp. 152–5.
38. Crichton, op. cit., p. 5.
39. Ibid., p. 9.
40. J.L. Houlden, 'Liturgy and Her Companions: A Theological Appraisal', in Jasper, op. cit. (see note 22) p. 173.
41. J. Wainwright, 'The Understanding of Liturgy in the Light of its History', in *The Study of Liturgy*, p. 504.
42. D.L. Frost, *The Language of Series 3*, Grove Booklets (Bramcote, 1973) p. 11.
43. R.T. Beckwith, 'Thomas Cranmer and the Prayer Book', in *The Study of Liturgy*, p. 72.
44. Hans-Georg Gadamer, *Truth and Method*, trans. William Glen-Doepel (London, 1975).
45. Stephen Prickett, *Words and The Word: Language, Poetics and Biblical Interpretation* (Cambridge, 1986) p. 31; Eugene A. Nida, 'Principles of Translation as Exemplified by Bible Translating', in *On Translation*, ed. R.A. Brower, Harvard Studies in Comparative Literature No. 23 (Cambridge, Mass., 1959) p. 19.
46. C.H. Sisson, *Anglican Essays* (Manchester, 1983) p. 53.
47. Ian Robinson, *The Survival of English: essays in criticism of language* (Cambridge, 1973) p. 46.
48. Prickett, op. cit., p. 29.
49. Ibid., p. 32.
50. Ibid., pp. 6–9.
51. Ibid., p. 30.
52. Sisson, op. cit., p. 48.
53. J.H. Newman, *An Essay in Aid of a Grammar of Assent*, 1870 (Westminster Md, 1973) p. 140.
54. This discussion is a sequel to the author's 'Philosophy, Language and the Reform of Public Worship', in *Philosophy and Practice*, ed. A. Phillips Griffiths (Cambridge, 1985).

8

The Language of Hymns: Some Contemporary Problems

J.R. Watson

Of all the sounds which are associated with churches, liturgies and worship, that of the hymn is probably the most instantly recognisable as religious noise. There is a particular kind of hymn-ness about a hymn, a preference for rhythms and cadences of a certain kind, an absence of surprise, a recognition of familiarities in tune and words: G.K. Chesterton, it is said, wrote 'O God of earth and altar' in that particular metre of 7.6.7.6.D. because he thought that all hymns were written to the tune AURELIA. And clearly there exists a strong sense of what a hymn is in the popular imagination: it is the kind of thing which is sung on the radio and on television, or the well known hymns which are traditionally used at weddings and funerals.

Hymn-writers practising the craft today have to bear this in mind. They must decide at some point how far to follow this expected pattern, and how far to experiment with new patterns of words and music. They are perpetually working in the shadow of their predecessors, and especially that of the compilers of *Hymns Ancient & Modern* (1861). The power of that book, itself a gathering-up of many previous strands, established for a century or more the major canon of English hymnody, apart from the non-conformist denominations, each of which held to a tradition grounded in its own writers. *A & M* even took the best of these, such as Isaac Watts and Charles Wesley, into itself, to produce a collection which proved immensely influential and durable.

This hymn book, and others which followed it, established the normative idea of hymnody for a hundred years, in spite of what Bernard Manning referred to (with regard to *A & M*) as 'the wretched versification, doubtful grammar, and questionable theo-

174

logy thereof'. He went on to describe the *English Hymnal* as not much better:

> stuffed out with second-rate creaking translations of Greek and Latin hymns, fusty as a second-hand Lewis and Short, more like the meritorious exercises of the classical sixth than Poetry, the handmaid of Piety.[1]

The durability of these major books was helped by the fact that there was little new writing, except in *Songs of Praise* (1925) (with writers such as Eleanor Farjeon, Jan Struther, Geoffrey Dearmer and Percy Dearmer), until the time of the second world war and after; at that time Albert Bayly began to write hymns, and his example was followed by others, such as Fred Pratt Green and Timothy Dudley-Smith. The principal hymn books of most denominations were given supplements during the 1960s and 1970s: *Hymns and Songs* for the Methodists in 1969, *100 Hymns for Today* for the Anglicans in the same year, *Praise for Today* (Baptist, 1974), *New Church Praise* (United Reformed Church, 1975), *New Catholic Hymnal* (1971), *Broadcast Praise* (1981) for the *BBC Hymn Book* of 1951. Entirely new hymn books also appeared, such as *With One Voice* (originally published as *The Australian Hymn Book*, 1977).

New hymn books begat other new hymn books, and two of these, *Hymns for Today's Church* (1982) and *Hymns & Psalms* (1983), will be referred to in some detail here. They represent two ways of responding to the present situation: one radical, the other fairly conservative but with a substantial sprinkling of new elements. Both books have in common a very proper impatience with sectarianism, and are ecumenical in tone and in content; both contain a number of hymns by new writers, who are representative of what has come to be known as an 'explosion' of hymn-writing. It has been characterised by an almost overwhelming desire to make hymnody new, to cast off the traditional image of hymns and their place in worship, and to use hymns to express something about the contemporary world. When this new and rapidly developing art is seen alongside the current changes in liturgical practice, from the *Book of Common Prayer* to the *Alternative Service Book, 1980*, it is clear that an unfamiliar practice has taken the place of the recognisable and traditional.

It is an unfamiliar practice, but not an unfamiliar art: it seems generally accepted that there is an increasing place within the liturgy for singing hymns, for that active participation of a congregation, for the sound of many voices as against the single voice of the priest, for the musical word as opposed to the spoken word, for ecstasy and emotion as well as prayer and argument. One of the most interesting examples of a new approach to a familiar medium is *Hymns for Today's Church*, a striking and radical attempt to construct a hymn book which would seem to be appropriate for the present time and place. In their preface to the words edition, the committee responsible for the texts, chaired by Michael Saward, had some very significant points to make about the problems and opportunities with which they were presented.

They noted, first of all, how difficult it was to shake off the heavy influence of the last century. The committee had hoped to encourage new writers, but many of the submissions consisted of 'pastiche Victoriana, new minted for the 1970s'. The new hymns which were selected were therefore those which, in the opinion of the committee, showed originality, contemporaneity and poetic skill. Sometimes they succeeded triumphantly in finding these:

> When Christ was lifted from the earth,
> his arms stretched out above,
> through every culture, every birth,
> to draw an answering love.

> Still east and west his love extends,
> and always, near or far,
> he calls and claims us as his friends
> and loves us as we are .   (335)

The images are traditional (the stretched-out arms, the claiming as friends) but they have been rethought and made new in Brian Wren's own seizure and expression of them: the verse changes from a spectacular and arresting opening to a moving simplicity at the end of verse 2, where the idea fits neatly and simply into the line. A similar accommodation of the sense to the line, and an equally fine conclusion, comes in verse 3 of Wren's hymn for Holy Communion, 'I come with joy to meet my Lord':

> As Christ breaks bread and bids us share,
> each proud division ends;

> the love that made us makes us one,
> and strangers now are friends. (408)

Hymns such as this are written in simple language; at their best they have a clean and functional simplicity which is restrained, severe and even classical, as in this hymn by Christopher Idle:

> Now let us learn of Christ:
> he speaks, and we shall find
> he lightens our dark mind;
> so let us learn of Christ . . .
>
> Now let us grow in Christ
> and look to things above,
> and speak the truth in love;
> so let us grow in Christ.   (503)

This kind of modernity depends on the avoidance of trite phrases, archaic language or traditional presentation. It is valuable in its ability to speak straight to people; it is based on biblical texts (indeed, it quotes them) but it is not churchy. Its verses are shaped in the rigorous way that hymn verses usually are, and the hymn has a structure in which the first and fourth lines of each verse are repeated; but the total effect is of clarity and good sense.

The sense of the modern is taken further by those writers who are prepared to versify their sense of contemporary suffering and wrong. Sometimes this can be expressed with a powerful and bitter rhetoric, as it is in Fred Pratt Green's hymn 'The Church of Christ, in every age' (*Hymns & Psalms*, 804):

> Across the world, across the street
>   The victims of injustice cry
> For shelter and for bread to eat,
>   And never live until they die.

Here the images are complementary – 'world . . . street', 'shelter . . .bread' – a doubled catalogue of deprivation, driven home by repetition, until the last line surprises by producing an opposition, a paradox which states an unpalatable truth in the strongest terms. The hymn is characteristic of a certain kind of modern hymnody in its openness to pain and misery, and in its

awareness of the need for Christians to *do* something: to work to
alleviate poverty, starvation, ignorance and exploitation. The last
line, in particular, suggests that some people never 'live' (never
have a chance in this life) from their birth right up until the day
they die; it could also be read in the sense that they 'live' after they
die (a recasting of the parable of Dives and Lazarus in modern
terms), though I think that this is a secondary level of meaning. (It
was stronger in an earlier version, which read 'And never live
before they die'.) In either case, the severity of the hymn is not very
well suited to the sweet tune HERONGATE to which it is set in *Hymns
& Psalms*.

In *Hymns for Today's Church* the same engagement with social
problems is found in a hymn by Timothy Dudley-Smith, where the
world is described as

> A home of plenty: clothed and fed
> our sturdy children play;
> while other children cry for bread
> not half the world away . . .
>
> Renew our love, O Lord, and touch
> our hearts to feel and care
> that we who seem to have so much
> so little seem to care.   (332)

Hymns such as these are important indicators of a modern sensibility in worship: a service is likely to be used to call attention to
some problem in the world in addition to the prayers of confession, thanksgiving or adoration. The emphasis is a difficult one to
get right and can lead to some uncomfortable juxtapositions of
mood and sensibility; but the effort is a necessary one. It is found
in the openness of, for example, Fred Kaan's hymn 'For the
healing of the nations' (*Hymns & Psalms*, 402), traditional in
rhythm, tune and pattern, but aware of concerns far beyond the
church walls:

> All that kills abundant living,
>   Let it from the earth be banned;
> Pride of status, race, or schooling,
>   Dogmas that obscure your plan.
> In our common quest for justice
>   May we hallow life's brief span.

The danger with such hymns is that they will cross the frontiers of poetry and become preaching (the last line of this verse, for example, is feeble and tired in metaphor but strong on instruction); but at their best (as in most of the examples quoted) the line is held with a very appropriate decorum. The ancient restrictions of tune, verse and line length have been used – not overcome, but *used*, so that the very restrictions of rhythm and rhyme become exciting in their ability to unite with the words and syntax to drive home the point. Rhymes have always been an integral part of hymns, and sometimes they are enjoyed and exploited, as they are by Michael Saward:

> Through all our days we'll sing the praise
> of Christ the resurrected;
> who, though divine, did not decline
> to be by men afflicted . . .   (145)

This fine beginning is not quite sustained in the verses which follow, but, like all Michael Saward's hymns, this one is full of gusto and energy; there is the strong sense that the author is actually rejoicing in the contemporary possibilities of the hymn form.

This word 'Rejoice' appears in the title of every one of the collections of hymns published during his lifetime by Albert Bayly, although only one of his hymns appears in *Hymns for Today's Church* (there are twelve in *Hymns & Psalms*). This is 'O Lord of every shining constellation', a hymn which anticipates Bayly's other attempts to bring together the concerns of science and religion. The second verse, for example, could not have been written before Rutherford split the atom:

> You, Lord, have made the atom's hidden forces;
> your laws its mighty energies fulfil:
> teach us, to whom you give such rich resources,
> in all we use, to serve your holy will.   (315)

Similarly the theory of relativity is referred to in the opening line of 'Lord of the boundless curves of space' (*Hymns & Psalms*, 372), a hymn which was later adapted and added to by Brian Wren to include a reference to Teilhard de Chardin's 'omega point'.

Bayly was a pioneer of modern hymn-writing, beginning a

decade or so before the great wave of the 1960s. He was felicitously described by Cyril Taylor (a writer of some splendid modern tunes, including the magnificent ABBOT'S LEIGH) as 'the last of the old and the first of the new',[2] and some of his hymns are finely traditional. There is a hymn for baptism, for example, which deserves to be widely known and used:

> Our Father, whose creative love
> The gift of life bestows,
> Each child of earthly union born
> Thy heavenly likeness shows.
>
> Grant those entrusted with the care
> Of precious life from thee,
> Thy grace, that worthy of the gift
> And faithful they may be . . .
> (*Hymns & Psalms*, 372)

Such traditional hymns are still very useful in their unassuming and subtle delicacy; there is a mode of writing which is still strong, side by side with the more striking pieces of hymnological architecture. Indeed, the building metaphor is quite a useful one, for modern hymns are like modern buildings in that the traditional and the innovative are to be found side by side. Bryn Rees is the author of a good traditional hymn, found in *Hymns & Psalms*:

> Have faith in God, my heart,
> Trust and be unafraid;
> God will fulfil in every part
> Each promise he has made.
>
> Have faith in God, my mind,
> Though oft your light burns low;
> God's mercy holds a wiser plan
> Than you can fully know.   (675)

The hymn deals in this way with heart, mind and soul, ending with

> Until I rest, heart, mind, and soul,
> The captive of your grace.

There are some archaic moments here, such as 'oft' in verse 2, but on the whole this is a hymn which presents the need for faith in a way which is unobtrusively effective, like a well made modern building that does not stick out from the other traditional buildings in the street. A certain ebullience is found in another traditionalist-modernist hymn, Colin Thompson's 'Christian people, raise your song', with its use of jaunty rhythms:

> Come to welcome Christ today,
>   God's great revelation;
> He has pioneered the way
>   Of the new creation.
> Greet him, Christ our risen King
>   Gladly recognizing,
> As with joy men greet the spring
>   Out of winter rising.
>   (*Hymns & Psalms*, 601)

The hymns which have been quoted above are not great: almost all of them could be discovered to have some weak line or phrase at some point in the composition. But they do represent useful attempts to write hymns in a medium which adds to the traditional resources of hymnody and which draws attention to modern problems in a contemporary world. More difficult for most readers to accept is the practice of modernising old hymns. There are two reasons for this. The first is that the original hymn and its tune are familiar, and any interference with long-known (and often much-loved) familiarity is hard to accept (though good for us, some would argue). The second is that such modernising sometimes seems to be a superficial altering, a shiny coat of paint over the old shape that we had got used to. Brian Wren, in a lecture to the Hymn Society in 1976, spoke at one point of 'giving faith a re-spray',[3] which indicates an approach that will make some readers uneasy. Wren's new version of 'We plough the fields and scatter' is a good example:

> We plough and sow with tractors
> and bale the new-mown hay
> we reap the fields with combines
> to bring our harvest day . . .
>   (*Faith Looking Forward*, 8)

Now this is quite true: we *do* use tractors and combine harvesters, and balers, and a modern farmer may well find this a better hymn than Jane Montgomery Campbell's translation from the German (first published in 1861). Many readers, however, will find that the older text is a poetic or metaphorical way of describing the processes of seed-time and harvest, and that as such it has a continued relevance; indeed to make the hymn seem up to date is almost too much, like making relevance relevant. The idea is commendable, and Wren is a very fine hymn-writer; but the result here seems insistent, like an over-zealous steward at the church door.

There should, in theory, be no problem about such modernisation. The *Alternative Service Book, 1980*, which encouraged the use of hymns in the liturgy,[4] established a new and a clear liturgical form for the Church of England, using 'you' instead of 'thou', and there seems no reason why hymns should not do the same. And, as the editors of *Hymns for Today's Church* point out, hymns have always been subject to emendation.[5] They argue, sensibly enough, that revision is essential:

> Liturgies and Bibles have been as radically translated as in the sixteenth century, and only the hymns have remained in the language of previous eras. To leave them unrevised in that situation is to create a verbal and cultural gulf which cannot be to the long term advantage of Christians at worship.[6]

For some readers this will seem too dogmatic, just as some of the radical revisions of liturgies and Bibles have seemed insensitive in translation and authoritarian in application. There are many passages of scripture which have been much improved, clarified and brought to life by modern translation; there are others which have been spoiled. To speak of a verbal and cultural gulf in relation to (say) the first chapter of the Gospel according to St John is absurd: 'In the beginning was the Word, and the Word was with God, and the Word was God' is not a sentence that requires improvement or alteration. Similarly with hymns: there are many hymns which can and probably should be improved, but there are also many which are straightforward and simple enough to be capable of crossing any normal 'verbal and cultural gulf'.

In *Hymns for Today's Church* the alterations are principally of three kinds:

1 The change from 'thee' to 'you'. The editors describe this as 'such a liturgical commonplace that no justification seems necessary'.
2 The removal of archaic endings such as '-est' and '-eth'.
3 The removal of emotive or sentimental sections not easily acceptable to modern congregations.

As an example of the first of these, there is Bishop Ken's morning hymn:

> Awake, my soul, and with the sun
> your daily stage of duty run;
> shake off your sleep, and joyful rise
> to make your morning sacrifice. (264)

This works well enough at one level, but we ought to ask whether enough has been gained here to compensate for the loss of the well-loved traditional version. It is also an example of how difficult such modernisations can be, of how intractable problems can arise: the second line, for example, sees each day of life as a stage in the journey, an image which comes originally from the days of stage-coach travel. Similar problems arise with the second class of alteration, the change from '-est' and '-eth':

> The day you gave us, Lord, is ended,
> the sun is sinking in the west;
> to you our morning hymns ascended,
> your praise shall sanctify our rest. (280)

Here a great deal of trouble has been taken to avoid 'The day Thou gavest' and 'at Thy behest'; and this may be an example of a committee imprisoned in the procedures of its own making. Certainly it seems unfortunate, and perhaps tactless, to interfere with the words of such a beloved hymn; although the love of such traditional forms is sometimes interpreted, by the reformers, as a sign of complacency.

It is perhaps better to recast a whole hymn, such as Michael Perry's rendering of Luther's 'Ein feste Burg', which begins 'God is our fortress and our rock'. This version at least avoids the undignified wriggling which goes on in some hymn books (see *Hymns & Psalms*, 661) over Carlyle's translation of verse 4:

> And though they take our life,
> Goods, honour, children, wife,
> Yet is their profit small:
> These things shall vanish all;
> The city of God remaineth.

The problem with this is that women seem not to be included as the singers: it raises the question of gender-based language, which will be discussed below. Perry's last verse ends:

> for even if distress
> should take all we possess,
> and those who mean us ill
> should ravage, wreck, or kill,
> God's kingdom is immortal!   (523)

This is so distant from Carlyle's translation as to avoid any uncomfortable comparisons; the changes to Ellerton's text in 'The day Thou gavest' stay closer to the original (except in line 2) and are therefore more disturbing. So is the new version of 'Come, ye thankful people, come', where 'you' replaces 'thee' and 'ye', and where the editors are anxious to be rid of 'Ere' in line 4:

> Come, you thankful people, come,
> raise the song of harvest home!
> fruit and crops are gathered in
> safe before the storms begin . . .   (283)

The third reform, that of a sentimentality which is unacceptable to modern sensibilities, also raises difficult questions. The problem is, of course, that what is acceptable to some modern sensibilities is unacceptable to others. Sometimes this kind of reform leads to decisions based on ignorance or insensitivity, such as the omission (in *Hymns & Psalms*, 807) of the final verse of John Wesley's translation of his friend Spangenberg's hymn, 'What shall we offer our good Lord':

> We all, in perfect love renewed,
>   Shall know the greatness of Thy power,
> Stand in the temple of our God
>   As pillars, and go out no more.

It was argued in the *Hymns & Psalms* committee, amazingly, that to encourage a congregation to stand in the church as pillars would be wrong after five verses exhorting them to go out and spread the gospel; thus one more metaphor bit the dust, a poetic reading became a literal reading, a hymn lost its crowning last verse and the Methodists lost a part of their poetic heritage.

It is often the old metaphors and symbols that give trouble to the modernisers: like old houses, they are untidy and they get in the way of road-widening. Their replacement by more literal versions, however, almost always loses flavour and poetic life. Cowper's magnificent, violent, tactile imagery is too much for *Hymns for Today's Church*, which changes it to:

> There is a fountain opened wide
> where life and hope begin;
> for Christ the Lord was crucified
> to save us from our sin.   (144)

This is to turn William Cowper into Cecil Frances Alexander ('There is a green hill far away'). More damagingly, it is a replacing of the old poetic vision with a summary of the gospel in traditional and abbreviated form. The transition is from the poet to the preacher, from the figurative and imaginative to the predictable and the religious.

Another example of an attempt to reshape the congregation's responses is found in hymns which describe heaven. It is against all reason to describe heaven as 'up there', and so Heber's morning songs no longer 'rise to Thee':

> Holy, holy, holy, Lord God Almighty!
> early in the morning our song of praise shall be . . .   (7)

and in Charles Wesley's great Ascension hymn Jesus Christ no longer returns 'Glorious to his native skies':

> Hail the day that sees him rise
> to his throne beyond the skies . . .   (176)

This may be a part of 'grown-up' Christianity, but it has lost the poetic vision of the original conception; and 'except ye become as little children' applies to the imagination and to the religious sense as it does to other things.

So the word 'Hark!', which is regarded as archaic, or perhaps sentimental, disappears from 'Crown him with many crowns', and also from Cowper's lovely 'Hark, my soul! it is the Lord', which becomes

> Christian do you hear the Lord?
> Jesus speaks his gracious word;
> gently sounds the saviour's call,
> 'Do you love me best of all?'   (472)

Frequently these alterations destroy an original that was really quite acceptable before, and which in its original form stimulated the poetic imagination. Moreover, we have to be careful about the adjective 'Christian': so often, as Erik Routley noted, 'it has meant a form of lasso with which we hope to capture things within reach which appeal to us, and dress them up our way . . .'[6] Here it seems to be exclusive too. But such changes are not always for the worse. J.S.B. Monsell's hymn, 'O worship the Lord in the beauty of holiness', with its superb first line (the rhythms of which subsequently straitjacket the whole hymn) is considerably improved at one point:

> Low at his feet lay your burden of carefulness,
> high on his heart he will bear it for you,
> comfort your sorrows and answer your prayerfulness,
> guiding your steps in the way that is true.   (344)

The last line here is markedly better than Monsell's 'Guiding thy steps as may best for thee be'; one only wishes that the improvers could have got rid of 'carefulness' (Monsell presumably meant 'care').

To the three kinds of alteration which have been mentioned above should be added the problem of what the editors rather gracelessly call 'linguistic sexism', requiring the removal, wherever possible, of exclusively masculine references. Here *Hymns for Today's Church* takes a moderate line:

We have responded to this with care and sympathy but not to the point of fatuity. Wherever it has been possible to reduce an unnecessarily masculine reference we have done so, including on occasions alterations to our own previously published hymns. The issue is one where moderation seems the wisest course . . . [8]

Curiously, this seems one area where moderation was perhaps not the wisest course (an indication of how difficult the task facing the editors was). Five years later we are becoming more and more sensitive to the use of non-inclusive gender-based language: a hymn such as 'Rise up, O men of God' was dropped from *Hymns & Psalms* for this reason. In recent years, thanks to the writings of theologians such as Sallie McFague,[9] we have become aware of how comprehensively religious language has been appropriated by the male sex during the last two thousand years. So in *Faith Looking Forward* (1983) Brian Wren showed what might be done, in a hymn which ends with the word 'personhood':

> Dear Sister God
>   you held me at my birth.
> You sang my name, were glad to see my face.
>   You are my sky, my shining sun,
> and in your love there's always room
> to be, and grow, yet find a home,
>   a settled place.   (3)

This is a brave hymn, although the uhird verse struggles with the opposition of Christ and capitalism and has a wallowing cliché in line 2:

> Dear Sister God
>   in Christ your love rings true.
> Directors, boards, and bosses lose their sway.
>   Your service, free from servitude,
> draws out a love that, strong to give,
> can struggle, suffer, care, and live
>   a better way.

The line about directors and bosses poses another problem. How far can you go in bringing in modern imagery, the properties of everyday urban life? In the introduction to *Hymns for Today's Church* the editors note that you cannot please everybody: 'those who want "concrete" and "protest" in every hymn will regard us as compromising reactionaries. Those who love pietistic language interspersed with the endless repetition of "Alleluias" will find us much too objective . . .'[10] There is something of a caricature in this, but the editors are clearly aware of the ecclesiastical bullies who impose their taste and opinions upon their congregations, and I have a great deal of sympathy with their moderation and restraint. The whole passage from the preface indicates how great the pressures are: there are certainly groups within the Church who see it as the spearhead of social protest and political reform and for whom traditional hymnody is no doubt a waste of time. Others urge the employment of modern metaphors, drawn particularly from urban life: indeed, the mention of 'concrete' in the introduction may have sprung from a famous hymn of the 1960s, Richard Jones's 'God of concrete', which became widely known not only through the Methodist *Hymns & Songs* (1969), but through its publication in *100 Hymns for Today* (1969):

> God of concrete, God of steel,
> God of piston and of wheel,
> God of pylon, God of steam,
> God of girder and of beam,
> God of atom, God of mine,
> All the world of power is thine.
>
> Lord of cable, Lord of rail,
> Lord of motorway and mail, . . .
> (*100 Hymns for Today*, 33)

This is another brave attempt, and it is certainly a hymn which makes an immediate and almost startling impression, like the new brutalism of 1960s architecture. One of its problems may be the use of the word 'of', which is clearly intended to imply that God is 'in' concrete and steel; it also has the sense of a 'concrete God', which suggests that a metaphorical meaning has crept in to strangle the intended theological one. It is a very interesting example of the uneasy relationship between poetry and theology at the present time, although what it does manage to do is to get away from the God of flowers and fields, the nice country-based God of 'All things bright and beautiful'.

There are certain areas in which modern liturgical practice has clearly influenced modern hymnody and where modern hymns are in joyful co-operation with modern liturgy. These are in the recognition of the importance of the Lectionary: indeed, it might be said that as liturgists have recognised the importance of hymns, so hymnologists have recognised the importance of the Lectionary. This has led to good hymns and other inestimable benefits. It has had a particular effect upon the place of the celebration of the sacraments: non-conformists, especially, have come to see sacramental worship as much closer to the centre of a practising faith than the preaching of the word, which used to be seen as the main purpose of divine worship. A book such as *Hymns & Psalms*, therefore, has much stronger sections on baptism and the Lord's Supper than the *Methodist Hymn Book* of 1933. Examples from Communion hymns by Brian Wren and Colin Thompson have already been quoted; other notable contributions are Fred Kaan's post-Communion hymn 'Now let us from this table rise' (*Hymns for Today's Church*, 419; *Hymns & Psalms*, 619) and the lively unrhyming hymn by 'Peter Icarus' (Luke Connaughton):

> Reap me the earth as a harvest to God,
> Gather and bring it again,
> All that is his, to the Maker of all;
> Lift it and offer it high:
>
> Bring bread, bring wine,
> Give glory to the Lord;
> Whose is the earth but God's,
> Whose is the praise but his?
>   (*Hymns & Psalms*, 623)

An example of the new hymns for baptism is Brian Wren's hymn from *Faith Looking Forward*, written for the tune BUNESSAN:

> Wonder of wonders
> life is beginning,
> fragile as blossom,
>   strong as the earth.
> Shaped in a person
> love has new meaning,
> Parents and people
>   sing at his birth.   (29)

Wren can be shocking, as in 'Dear Sister God', but he is always 'looking forward', and here he expresses tenderness with grace and charm. A similar baptismal hymn, though with more firmness and restraint, is Albert Bayly's 'Our father, whose creative love', which has already been mentioned.

The introduction to *Hymns for Today's Church* refers, as we have seen, to new translations of the scriptures. There is no doubt that much has been lost with the disappearance of the Authorized Version, but there is also no doubt that, for modern hymn-writers, much has been gained by the arrival of new translations, most notably the *New English Bible* New Testament of 1961. The most spectacular example of a phrase from the *NEB* which was lifted bodily into a hymn is Timothy Dudley-Smith's 'Tell out, my soul, the greatness of the Lord' (*Hymns for Today's Church*, 42; *Hymns & Psalms*, 86) from the opening of the Magnificat (Luke 1:46). Sung to WOODLANDS, it has made its way everywhere. Less well known, but equally good, is Ian Pitt-Watson's paraphrase of Psalm 139, which skilfully uses the modern translation in a 10.10.10.10. metre:

> Thou art before me, Lord, thou art behind,
>   And thou above me hast spread out thy hand;
> Such knowledge is too wonderful for me,
>   Too high to grasp, too great to understand.
>
>   (*Hymns & Psalms*, 543)

Hymns such as these, and Fred Pratt Green's 'Christ is the world's Light, he and none other' (*Hymns & Psalms*, 455), have taken their places as permanent additions to the core texts of any new hymn book.

Fred Pratt Green's work is notable, not only for his provision of hymns such as this, but for his command of line, rhythm and (above all) imagery. He is a poet as well as a hymn-writer, whose poetry has gained recognition from some distinguished practitioners (Philip Larkin included 'The Old Couple', for example, in *The New Oxford Book of Twentieth Century Verse*). Metaphor and simile form the cutting edge of Fred Pratt Green's hymns: 'Jesus in the olive grove' is as sharply painted as a Giotto, or (if that sounds too old-fashioned) as a succession of cinema stills; it is a slide-projector account of the Passion:

> Jesus in the olive grove
> Waiting for a traitor's kiss
> Rises free from bitterness.

As he wakes his comrades up,
Torches flicker in the glen;
Shadows turn to marching men.

In that dawn of blows and lies
Church and State conspire to kill,
Hang three rebels on a hill.

Innocent and guilty drown
In a flood of blood and sweat.
How much darker can it get?
                    (*Hymns & Psalms*, 169)

There is little room for anything except the brief succession of images, but their juxtaposition is immensely powerful. They also have political overtones, unmistakably from our own time: the state as a killer, the soldiers closing in, as at the death of Che Guevara. Only in the second part of the hymn does the moral appear:

It is God himself who dies!

which indicates clearly enough Fred Pratt Green's line of descent from Charles Wesley: ''Tis mystery all; the Immortal dies!'. But the twentieth-century hymn surrounds this central exclamation with all the imagery of power politics, and with a technique that is modern in its spare use of words.

Charles Wesley's example can also be seen in the work of Ann Phillips, especially in her use of imagery. Some of Wesley's most remarkable hymns, with his most daring employment of metaphor, are those concerned with the Holy Spirit, and Ann Phillips uses the same metaphors in a new way:

Into a world of dark,
    Waste and disordered space,
He came, a wind that moved
    Across the water's face.

The imagery of this, and of the next two verses, is from Genesis 1:2; there it was the *Spirit* of God which moved upon the face of the waters, and that same spirit descended upon the disciples at Pentecost:

> Into a world of doubt,
>   Through doors we closed, he came,
> The breath of God in power
> Like wind and roaring flame.
>   (*Hymns & Psalms*, 290)

These hymns take their places beside the new liturgies, and complement them, because they express the truth of the gospel in a manner which is timeless in subject matter and yet contemporary in tone and treatment. Ann Phillips' free use of the stanza form, for example, would have been difficult to imagine in a previous age (with certain exceptions, such as Christina Rossetti's 'In the bleak mid-winter'); similarly, rhyme has been dispensed with in some cases. I have already quoted from 'Reap me the earth' by 'Peter Icarus', which is an example of the way in which free verse, the modern movement in poetry towards looser and more expressive forms, has affected hymn writing. So Tom Colvin can write simply 'Jesu, Jesu, fill us with your love':

> Kneels at the feet of his friends,
> Silently washes their feet,
> Master who acts as a slave to them.
> Jesu, Jesu . . .
>   (*Hymns & Psalms*, 145)

This is typical of a certain kind of modern hymnody in its immediate turning from worship to service. The rhythm and melody are free-flowing, from Northern Ghana, where the author was a missionary; now that we live in a global village they are a reminder of the many different influences which are loosening the hymn from its ancient western stereotypes. If Chesterton thought that all hymns were written to the tune AURELIA, we now know differently.

How far this process can go in accompanying liturgical change, and what its effects will be, is difficult to predict. There are many different kinds of church service, and there will always be those who prefer a traditional solemnity, just as there will be those who wish for something more informal. Certainly religion is on offer today in more diverse and more accessible forms than ever before, from the Solemn Eucharist to the chat show of 'Family Worship'. It is safe to say, however, that the best modern hymnody is distinguished by its commitment to the poetic as well as to the contemporary. The worst is contemporary without being imaginative: it sees with a deadly literalism, repeats the same phrases time and again, and denies the relevance of the poetic. Its patronising idea that modern congregations will not understand metaphor (as in the case of the John Wesley translation mentioned above) is a failure to understand the truly poetic nature of religion.

In his preface, dated 1779, to the 1780 *Collection of Hymns for the use of the People called Methodists*, the same John Wesley concluded with a reference to poetry: 'When poetry thus keeps its place, as the handmaid of piety . . .'[11] Wesley was wrong: poetry is not a domestic servant in the house of religion, but a part of the fabric itself. It allows, as Coleridge saw, imaginative perceptions of the deepest truths, often inaccessible to the procedures of reason alone. 'Stories forged upon the anvil of the imagination', writes David Jasper, 'take life far more seriously than do the manipulations of the rational in the human mind'.[12] The metaphors and images of Holy Scripture, as Coleridge saw, were 'the living educts of the imagination', and the poet, using this imagination, 'brings the whole soul of man into activity'.

This is the ultimate criterion by which we ought to judge. Does the hymnody of today bring the whole soul into activity? Does it provide that poetic awareness of the gospel and a sense of the sacramental? Does it sanctify the things of daily life? Peter Redgrove, for example, thinks of poetry as sacred activity:

> Poetry's clearly a branch of religion. For myself, all the things that official religion ought to be about are in poetry. If we had a proper religion, that is, a psychologically useful religion in this country, it would be of course highly poetic.[13]

Redgrove's 'if we had a proper religion' indicates where he stands; he sees, as Coleridge saw and Wesley did not, the poetic needs and imaginative character of our religious apprehensions, most notably through image, metaphor and parable, and the failure of much modern religion to provide for them (though things are not quite as bad as they might appear from the outside, as I have tried to show). If we bear this in mind we must, I believe, applaud the efforts of some modern hymn-writers to engage in *poetic* hymnody, in the perception of religious truths in a new way or of old truths in a fresh way; we may wish, too, to deplore the loss of reserve and the failure of mystery in some modernisations, the authoritarian spirit in which congregations have these imposed upon them (this is the 'you need to change' syndrome) and the shallow triumphalism of some choruses ('He is Lord, he is Lord') or the too easy take-over of the hard-won spirituality of some negro songs ('Kum ba yah, mu Lord, kum ba yah'). Those who use such things might be advised to consider the way in which the audiences at poetry readings are often intent, rapt, engaged, treating a contemporary and secular poet's reading as if it were the voice of a prophet.

Some choruses are very fine, combining as they do well-shaped combinations of biblical phrases, sweetly set to music. The effect of others on modern hymn-writing is likely to be negative, because they employ such non-poetic sensitivities. It is precisely their banalities, their psychological uselessness, which the best modern hymn-writers have attempted so strenuously to avoid. The best modern hymns move us by their poetic activity, deepen our understanding by their imaginative apprehension, and challenge us with their authenticity of feeling. 'Writers can only hope', writes Brian Wren in the preface to *Faith Looking Forward*, 'that their words will be clear enough for people to decide whether to sing or remain silent. Words which provoke that decision are better than those which give a bland bath of feeling.'[14] Perhaps the most notable contribution which modern hymnological practice can make to the liturgical movements of our times is to substitute for the bath of feeling a testimony to a living, thinking, sympathising and imaginative faith, not just for the sake of the Church but for the world.

Notes

1. Bernard Manning, *The Hymns of Wesley and Watts* (London, 1942) pp.33–4.
2. Quoted by Edward Jones in an obituary of Albert Bayly, *Bulletin of the Hymn Society*, No. 161 (September 1984) p.202.
3. *Bulletin of the Hymn Society*, No. 138 (January 1977) p.199.
4. James H. Litton, in his essay 'The Hymn in the Anglican Liturgy', points out that with the coming of the *Alternative Service Book* and the American *Book of Common Prayer, 1979*, the classic prayer book rubrics regarding the use of hymns in worship have been greatly expanded: 'It is clear that these revised Anglican liturgies now recognise music and especially hymns as an integral and necessary part of worship in the Anglican tradition'. See *Duty and Delight: Routley Remembered*

(Carol Stream, USA; Norwich, England, 1985) pp.159–70, especially pp.167–8.

5. This seems to be one of the principal differences between a poem and a hymn: the poem is regarded as inviolate textually – indeed, strenuous efforts are made to recover it as the poet wrote it – whereas the hymn is unfortunately regarded as continually alterable: the whole idea of the hymn as a valid literary form has suffered as a result.

6. 'Words Preface' to *Hymns for Today's Church* (no page numbers).

7. Quoted by Ian Fraser in his essay 'Beginnings at Dunblane', in *Duty and Delight: Routley Remembered*, p.185.

8. 'Words Preface' to *Hymns for Today's Church*.

9. See Sallie McFague, *Speaking in Parables* (Philadelphia, 1975) and *Metaphorical Theology* (Philadelphia, 1982).

10. 'Words Preface' to *Hymns for Today's Church*.

11. The 1779 Preface to the 1780 *Collection of Hymns for the use of the People called Methodists* was printed in full at the front of the *Methodist Hymn Book* (1933) and quoted extensively in the preface to *Hymns & Psalms* (1983).

12. David Jasper, *The New Testament and the Literary Imagination* (London, 1987) p.4.

13. 'Interview with Peter Redgrove', by Jed Rasula and Mike Erwin, in *Hudson Review*, 28 (1975) 377–401.

14. Brian Wren, Preface to *Faith Looking Forward* (Carol Stream, USA, 1983) (no page numbers).

9

Music and the Liturgy

Raymond Warren

Music can have an uplifting effect on a church service – we all know that; yet surprisingly little thought has been given to how it best functions in this regard.[1] Is it merely an adornment of words which would be sufficient in themselves without such adornment? Some liturgists, I believe, would not now think so: they have found it very difficult to find words totally adequate to their task and have suggested a more comprehensive approach, embracing from the outset not only words but also music and action.

At the heart of the matter lies the idea that the liturgy must contain an element of mystery; that is, that which cannot be expressed precisely in verbal prose but not, of course, that which we cannot comprehend at all. This is one of many aspects of the close connection between musical and liturgical thinking. (Another is the problem of having to reject or renew a great inherited tradition.) For music is indeed a mystery in this sense, but this does not mean that it is incomprehensible. Mendelssohn was once confronted with the objection that since one person listening to his 'Hebrides' overture might think it represented clouds moving across the sky and another waves on the sea, there was a lack of precision about music as a mean of communication. He replied that his music was indeed precise and that it was the words and visual images in this case which were imprecise. His reply suggests that music can provide a general experience of which the verbal or visual images may be particular expressions, and if this is so we can regard the musical setting of the words of the liturgy as a general experience of which the words themselves are a particular expression but of which extra-liturgical ideas may be particular expressions too. So the music of the Easter vigil may well also suggest the rebirth of nature in the spring or the change from darkness to light in the dawning of a new day. Music may thus not only express the (in words) inexpressible, but may also be a means of relating the liturgy to the totality of life.

The Easter vigil, the religious experience of rebirth, shows how music can assume and enliven a pattern of experience, and it is with such patterns that this essay is largely concerned. But first there is a more fundamental consideration: the most obvious usefulness of music in worship is its ability to present a mood, attitude or gesture in a direct and immediately comprehensible way and to sustain it for as long as necessary. At the beginning of Luther's great hymn for the Reformation festival *'Ein feste Burg'*, the three reiterated high tonic notes falling a fourth to a cadential roulade on the dominant are an exact musical equivalent of the triumphant certainty of which the words speak: see Example 1.

The melody is powerfully reinforced by Bach's bass line, striding purposefully down the octave to its logical fulfilment at the cadence. The second phrase, in which the melody emulates the earlier bass part by descending the full octave, is given renewed energy by a rising bass line and is, if anything, even stronger. I could go on to show how this is sustained for all eight lines of each verse and with such force that four verses are not too many. The whole hymn will last over five minutes (a sizeable patch of even a Lutheran service) and so make a structurally weighty expression of the theme of the act of worship for which it was written. I believe

Example 1

Words by Luther, tr. Thomas Carlyle   Music arr. J.S. Bach

A   safe stronghold   our   God   is   still, A

trus - ty   shield and   wea - - - pon :

that, whatever style of congregational music we use in church, these same criteria should apply: excellence and appropriateness of both the melody and its musical setting, and due consideration of the weight of each section in relation to the service as a whole. Our example is of excellent word setting; that is, of music simultaneous with the singing of the words. Music can also predispose us to words yet to come, just as a Collect can predispose our interpretation of the following Epistle and Gospel, and perhaps even more potently. The brightness or sombreness of an organ prelude or an opening hymn can determine the mood of much of the ensuing service. It will stay in the memory the longer for being the first thing we hear. At other times music may relate to what has gone before.

The question as to what constitutes an appropriate musical style for worship is as elusive as in the case of verbal style. Certainly the division between sacred and secular is shown in historical perspective to be almost non-existent. Some of the greatest Renaissance church music was based on secular love songs, Monteverdi used contemporary dances in his Vespers, and Bach was able to use the Sarabande, originally described as a lascivious love dance, for some of the most solemn moments of his Passion settings. It could be argued, however, that these examples show a restrained treatment of the secular models, so that there is a compatibility of words and music.

Thus far, I imagine, most of my readers will be broadly in agreement with me, but I must move on to the subject of structures, an aspect of music to which most priests and liturgists are, in my experience, much less sensitive. Just as the spoken liturgy has a shape resulting from the juxtaposition of contrasting parts, a shape enhanced by the way a good precentor can articulate it with appropriate variations of pace and tone, so it is with the music. Indeed, because music does not have the same semantic complications as words its structures are the more directly perceived and, in Mendelssohn's sense, precise. I would guess that, in as far as a congregation is aware at all of a structure in worship, it is more likely that the music rather than the words will have made the greater contribution to this. If the service is felt to have no clear shape this may also be due to inappropriately balanced music.

Some of the problems and possibilities on a small scale can be seen from a brief consideration of how a composer might set the text of the Gloria in the new Anglican and Roman Catholic rites to music. The text is in three clear sections, each of six lines:

> Glory to God in the highest,
> and peace to his people on earth.
> Lord God, heavenly King,
> almighty God and Father,
> we worship you, we give you thanks,
> we praise you for your glory.
>
> Lord Jesus Christ, only Son of the Father,
> Lord God, Lamb of God,
> you take away the sin of the world:
> have mercy on us;
> you are seated at the right hand of the Father:
> receive our prayer.
>
> For you alone are the Holy One,
> you alone are the Lord,
> you alone are the Most High,
> Jesus Christ,
> with the Holy Spirit,
> in the glory of God the Father. Amen.

It will be noticed that the metre is irregular except for the fact that the first two lines can be read as though in regular dactyls:

> Glōrў tŏ Gōd ĭn thĕ hīghĕst ănd pēace tŏ hĭs pēoplĕ ŏn ēarth

Was there the intention behind this regularity of stylising this quotation from the Christmas song of the angels so as to set it apart from what follows? Or should the composer set the whole section as a continuous entity? In either case the musical setting will almost certainly avoid the banality of a repeated dactylic rhythm. If a good musical setting enhances the essential structure of its words it will usually destroy their own musical qualities, though rhyme and alliteration will often come through. Certainly the second of the following settings is preferable: see Example 2.

The words of the first section finish strongly, possibly calling for a musical climax, and we move at once into the very different mood of the second section, a change from ecstatic praise to

Example 2

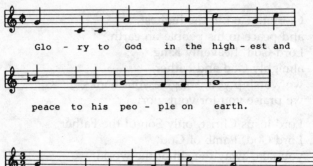

Glo - ry to God in the high - est and

peace to his peo - ple on earth.

Glo - ry to God in the high - est and

peace to his people on earth.

contrite humility which exemplifies a frequently encountered pattern of religious experience (cf. Isaiah 6:1–8). This is just the sort of pattern that music can well articulate, perhaps in this case with changes of dynamics and key but probably not tempo, for too great a contrast would undermine the integrity of a short setting. Lines 3 and 4 could possibly be set to the same music as lines 5 and 6 to give an ABB form for this section, though exactly the same music would not fit because the line 5 words have very different stress patterns from line 3.

The last section of the Gloria returns to the first section's general theme of praise, a common theme which may well suggest a musical correspondence between the two sections so as to give an overall ABA' shape, the dash on the second A implying some modification of the opening material. For example, where the second line of the first section suggested a falling phrase, the corresponding words of the third seem to want to rise, perhaps as in Example 3.

Is such an ABA' structure a true interpretation of the liturgical text, or is the music predisposing us to feel a structure slightly skew to the words? This particular problem is avoided in the plainsong settings and in Merbecke's, which have less strong

Example 3

For you a-lone are the Ho - ly One,

you a - lone are the Lord,

structural implications, and in the more extended eighteenth-
century cantata-like settings,[2] where each line or pair of lines
constitutes a self-contained movement and the principal vehicles
of overall structure, key and orchestration have less specific implications than musical motives such as that used in our example.

If music has a tendency to impose structural patterns on the
small scale of the short Gloria setting, it will also do so on the larger
scale of the whole act of worship; and where that act has itself a
clear form, as in the Mass, it is important that the music should
underline it. We could briefly summarise the Mass as moving from
sections of preparation and the ministry of the word to the climactic sacramental action of the Consecration and Communion, and
this shape can emerge quite clearly in the music when the Ordinary is sung to a single setting. In many of Palestrina's Masses[3] we
can hear the change from the usually syllabic settings of the Credo
to the exultation of the Sanctus and the heightened, more melisma-
tic style of the Agnus Dei, which often has an extra contrapuntal
part to give added richness for this most solemn part of the
worship. Incorporated into this may be some unifying idea, perhaps the liturgical theme for the day, recurring throughout and
giving what Professor Skoglund has described as an overall spiral
effect.[4] When the music is planned as an entity this can be very
simply achieved, as for example in those Palestrina Masses where
every movement is based on the same plainsong hymn.

Unfortunately nowadays the music for parish worship is only
very rarely planned as an entity in this way, and the bizarre
mixture of liturgical music, hymns and anthems heard in most
services is almost certain to obscure the structural intentions of the
liturgical authors. I am not so much thinking of differences of
historical period. As in architecture, and indeed in the words of the

liturgy itself, the old music can live happily alongside the carefully handled new, and in any case church music of many past periods has often been written in a sort of pastiche style, called *stile antico*, rendering such chronological divisions less important. Nor is it just a matter of bad and good, though we must remember that our new music has not yet gone through the natural selective filtering that time tends to apply to the old.

It is dichotomy of style which usually causes the worst musical disruption to the articulation of liturgical form. This may be the composer's fault. There is a unison setting of the Creed which, probably for reasons of achieving musical variety and perhaps to give the choir something more interesting to do, moves into richer four-part choral harmony for the *Et incarnatus*. The effect of this is to accentuate this part of the creed and so to interpret it as being more important than the rest. There is, incidentally, an obverse to this problem, that when the music is fixed, as in a strophic hymn, the words must not change their thrust too much from verse to verse. An unfortunate instance of this comes in the hymn 'Holy holy holy' where, in verse 3, the words 'Though the eye of sinful man thy glory may not see' have to be sung to the same cheerful music as was appropriate in verse 1 for 'Early in the morning our song shall rise to thee'.

To return to the contemporary liturgical scene, the blame for the misuse of music lies less frequently with composers than with those who assemble the music of the service by juxtaposing the incompatible or inappropriate. I recall Merbecke's simple setting of the Creed being quite spoilt by being followed immediately by a Victorian hymn whose fulsome harmonies made the Merbecke seem so archaic as to be an irrelevance. The problem here was also one of scale: the hymn with all its verses was more than twice the length of the Creed and consequently dwarfed it. Curiously, that modern phenomenon, the popular 'chorus', inserted into an other-wise traditional service is generally less destructive. Its slow har-monies and repetitive figurations will make it so different from its musical surroundings as to be almost acceptably incompatible – rather like a marquee on the lawns of a stately home. It is, though, best spaced apart from other music by a decent musical silence on either side, and it must still be said that it generally has the effect of underlining that cultural dichotomy which its insertion into the service was intended to remove. And how is the congregation to interpret the very loud modern French organ voluntary played at the end of an otherwise musically restrained service? It is not, one hopes, a musical symbol of the destruction of what has gone before, but it may well suggest that the congregation is being sent 'out into the world' with a fair bump!

The purpose of this discussion is certainly not to suggest that Victorian hymns, choruses and Messiaen should not be used in church, but only to make the point that their use alongside other kinds of church music can have certain musical consequences. I see no reason why such consequences should not be used creatively, nor indeed why consistently contemporary music should not be organised to fit a liturgical structure as well as Palestrina did it. Indeed, experiments along these lines should be more frequent if our worship is not to degenerate into the archaic.

So much for the interaction of music on music. What can now be said about the relationship of music to the *spoken* word, an important issue at a time when the majority of our services contain such a mixture of media? It may be helpful to look for models outside church music. The problems that arise have been faced by many of the great playwrights who have used incidental music and by the many composers of operetta and Singspiel opera containing spoken dialogue. Indeed, I would suggest that *The Tempest* and *The Magic Flute* should be compulsory set works for all ordinands and future liturgists!

Let us first think about the spoken drama, where, of course, the main articulation of the characterisation and action is effected through the words: to that extent we may think of it as analogous to Low Mass. One common rule for play and liturgy is that changes from the spoken word into sung word and back again must always be handled with care and with a clear purpose behind the changes of level and intensity that they produce. Shakespeare handles such changes with wonderful resource.[5] In his theatrical tradition it would seem that moving into a musical dimension was easy if there was a reasonable dramatic pretext for it, and that a bigger problem, both for him and his actors, was to make the return to speech equally effective: usually a new twist of direction to the drama at such a point will avoid any feeling of anti-climax resulting from the lowering of level. Thus in *The Tempest*, where music has the clear role of signifying the magical dimension, we experience a sense of pleasurable anticipation at the moment we hear the first notes of Ariel's song in Act I, or of the music for the entry of the masque in Act IV. It is the endings of these two little musical scenes which are especially interesting. In the first it is at

the very moment when the music stops that Miranda sees and falls
in love with the bemused Ferdinand, an event of such compelling
dramatic interest that we in the audience shall not think to lament
the loss of the musical dimension.

Ariel [sings]:
Full fathom five thy father lies;
Of his bones are coral made;
Those are pearls that were his eyes:
Nothing of him that doth fade,
But doth suffer a sea-change
Into something rich and strange.
Sea-nymphs hourly ring his knell:
Burden: Ding-dong.
Hark! now I hear them, – ding-dong, bell.
Ferdinand: The ditty does remember my drown'd father:
This is no mortal business, nor no sound
That the earth owes: – I hear it now above me.
Prospero: The fringèd curtains of thine eye advance,
And say, what thou see'st yond'.
Miranda: What is't? a spirit?
Lord, how it looks about! Believe me, sir,
It carries a brave form: – but 'tis a spirit.
Prospero: No, wench; it eats, and sleeps, and hath such senses
As we have, such. This gallant, which thou see'st,
Was in the wreck; and but he's something stain'd
With grief, that's beauty's canker, thou mightst call him
A goodly person: he hath lost his fellows,
And strays about to find them.
Miranda: I might call him
A thing divine; for nothing natural
I ever saw so noble.

(*The Tempest,* I.1)

The Act IV masque ends even more dramatically, when Prospero
suddenly interrupts it, summarily dismissing the dancers in order
to cope with the impending assault from Caliban and his fellows.

The same principles apply to liturgy. The moving into music is
easy and welcome if there is a good reason for it; so the change of
level from speech to chant as we move from Epistle to Gospel
underlines the greater immediacy of Christ's words and actions

there depicted, and later on the moving into chant at the *Sursum Corda* similarly heightens the level as we approach the climactic act of the consecration, which, incidentally, comes roughly at the golden section of the service, about two-thirds of the way through, a proportion widely favoured by musicians to give the most satisfying structural point for a climax. Other moves from speech into music, such as for an inserted hymn or psalm, though generally less purposefully related to the dramatic movement of the service, can nevertheless be effective and welcome. As with the play, the more difficult thing to do well is to get back to speech. The person handling the order of service must realise that the change of medium throws an enormous weight on such moments, a concentration of interest which calls, as in Shakespeare, for a clear and impelling new direction in the first spoken words.

The invitation to prayer in the *Book of Common Prayer* is a splendid example of such a clear new direction: 'Let us pray for the whole state of Christ's church . . .' Hence, in part, the desirability of putting hymns at the structural divisions of the service, where they will have the effect of highlighting the new direction when speech returns. It is in fact just possible for the words following a hymn not to go to something new but to carry on from the hymn: but such words will need to be heightened both in their language and in the way they are spoken. At the offertory in the ASB rite the words 'Yours Lord is the greatness, the power, the glory . . .' can be spoken so as to continue in the uplift of the hymn.

There is perhaps one more lesson to be learned from *The Tempest*. The musical sections from the play discussed above, Ariel's song and the masque, are of quite substantial duration, lasting several minutes each. The fact that the music has had time to establish itself makes it the more necessary for Shakespeare to use a strong dramatic gesture to justify the return to speech. When the music is of less consequence, as for Stephano's songs, there is no such necessity.

Singspiel[6] opera provides the opposite aspect, an art form in which the main thrust of the characterisation and the essential action are conveyed in the music, and here the closer analogy is with High Mass. The tensions of the medium are still felt at the moments of change, but now the other way round. In contexts where the main thrust is musical we tend to welcome changes to the more prosaic speech, and it is in the return to music that the greater dramatic skill is needed. There is the further difficulty for

both composer and performers of relating the musical movements
across the spoken gaps so that the music can be experienced as an
entity. Given well planned music, this is something that many
musicians, both in theatre and church, will do instinctively. In
opera it is often a new situation which can best be the occasion for
the re-introduction of music: the arrival of a new character or a
change of scene will invariably make a new musical beginning
seem quite justified. In *The Magic Flute*,[7] for example, Papageno is
left on stage at the end of Pamina's aria No. 17 for some comic
spoken business with the animals, but a complete change of mood
is effected by the very first chord of the ensuing temple scene's
music. In exactly the same way just a single introductory chord
may be enough in the Mass to articulate the change from the
opening penitential prayers to the joy of the sung Gloria.

Another common operatic way of moving from speech to singing occurs when a single character moves to a more intense level,
perhaps exposing his own innermost feelings by changing from
speech into song. In eighteenth-century Italian opera, where there
was sung recitative rather than speech, this was achieved by
making the recitative more lyrical, more like aria, towards the end,
so that the transition to the new level was smoothly bridged.
Similarly, in the spoken dialogue of Singspiel the language was
raised to approach the condition of poetry just before the music
entered. In the following example (Example 4) from *The Magic Flute*
Pamina's voice naturally becomes more emotional for her last
words to lead into her beautiful aria. In the Mass, too, the preface,
even when spoken, has the heightened quality which enables the
priest to lead us upwards into the exalted music of the Sanctus:
'Therefore with angels and archangels . . .'

The Magic Flute is also worth studying for the way Mozart is able
to preserve the integrity of his musical structures despite the
interruptions brought about by the non-musical spoken dialogue.
Two aspects are of particular relevance to the liturgy. The timings,
long or short, of the spoken dialogue will space out the music and
suggest groupings, just as, say, a long sermon will divide the
music and a whole service into two parts. A short dialogue, on the
other hand, suggests a musical relationship across it. In *The Magic
Flute* between No. 11 (Chorus of Priests, Key C) and No. 12
(Quintet with Papageno, Tamino and the three ladies of the Queen
of the Night, Key G) the priests leave and Papageno and Tamino
have only two short speeches before the three ladies enter and

Example 4

Pamina [speaking]:

Papageno, sag du mir, was ist mit
meinem Freund? Wie? Auch du?
Erkläre mir wenigstens die
Ursache eures Stillschweigens!
   O, das ist mehr als Kränkung,
mehr als Tod!
   Liebster einziger Tamino!

Papageno, tell me, what has happened
to my friend? And you too? At least
tell me the reason for your silence!
   O, that is worse than insult, worse
than death!
   Dearest, my only Tamino!

launch at once into the music of the quintet, which is in the
dominant key of the chorus. Across this short gap we hear the
tension of this dominant relationship quite clearly, expressing in
music the new problem of the arrival of these enemies of Sarastro.
Similarly in the liturgy, when two musical movements are in such
close juxtaposition, any musical contrasts of key or material will
just as surely create tension, which must have a proper justification, such as the dramatic change from Kyrie to Gloria noted
above.

One other Singspiel trick remains to be mentioned. Whereas the
ear will not readily recognise tonal tensions across a wide gap, it
will remember the same key should this return, and a quite long
period of an opera can be unified in this way. In the scene at the
beginning of Act II the Chorus of Priests is in F and so is Sarastro's
aria, the next musical movement. These two movements effec-
tively relate to each other across a page of spoken dialogue to come
together as a larger musical and dramatic unit. Thus in the liturgy,
even if the Gospel is spoken, the sung Doxologies before and after

it will reach to each other across it (if they are a good pair) and so frame the Gospel and by implication heighten it. I think there is no exact operatic parallel to the practice in some churches of having a period of complete silence for the congregation's individual prayer or reflection, though silence is indeed within the dimension of music. One of the effects of such a separation is to consolidate the subsequent grouping. A silence after the Communion tends to separate off the final prayers and so throws more weight on them, giving the final section and its music a clearer coda function.

Let us now try to put some of these ideas together in considering another possible structural aspect of the Eucharist, the recurrence of the idea of God coming into our midst. This is announced early on when we sing the Christmas words of the angels at the beginning of the Gloria, and we have seen how music can help to dramatise this moment. Christ's coming in sacramental form can be regarded as the climax of the whole service, and we have also seen how music can embody this as a climax in its own structure at the Agnus Dei. The pattern of experience at the Ministry of the Word moves towards the same end: in the prophecies and anticipations of the Old Testament reading and the teaching of the New Testament epistle leading to the words and actions of Christ in the Gospel. The sequence with its music is often as follows:

Gloria
Collect
Old Testament reading
Psalm
New Testament epistle
Gradual hymn
The Gospel preceded and followed by Doxologies.

We can assume that one of the liturgical intentions here is to show connections between the readings, related to the theme for the day, and so it is important that the music should reinforce this pattern by showing connections too. This could be done by putting Psalm, Gradual and Doxologies in the same key or mode. However, such a musical scheme would not in itself bring out the pattern of the progress towards the Gospel. That would better be achieved by a progressive key structure, perhaps getting sharper to suggest the building up to the Gospel; for example, Key C for Psalm, G for Gradual and D for Doxologies. The mounting energy of this structure would certainly be clearly heard across the comparatively short spoken interlude of the readings and, if this is felt to be right, the musical director can compensate for the lost tonal unity by giving the musical sections other unifying features, motivic or harmonic.

But what of the relationship to the preceding Gloria? If it were thought right to establish the 'Coming of God' idea we could relate the Doxologies to the Gloria (and later to the Agnus Dei) by putting them in the same key, in which case there would be a tonal tension D–C between Gloria and Psalm, a tension gradually resolved as we approach the Gospel. It may well be felt that the Gospel Doxologies are not long enough to bear the weight of the closure of this tonal scheme: in any case more music may be needed after the second Doxology if the Gospel procession is to have time to return to the chancel. This could be a hymn or organ music, but of course it must be in the same key as the Doxology if our tonal planning is to reflect the liturgical intentions. The foregoing discussion is not, of course, meant to suggest a blueprint for all Mass celebrations, but rather to consider some of the kinds of thinking which should go into our musical planning.

Here, finally, are a few further observations on extra-liturgical musical items: hymns and anthems. When hymns are added to the liturgy it is important that their scale as well as their words and mood and musical key are right. I have sometimes heard the Gloria at the beginning of a Mass dwarfed by a big heavy opening hymn only a minute or two earlier. It would have been better in such a case to have started the service without any music at all, so that the outburst at the beginning of the Gloria could make its maximum effect. Anthems and motets too must be to scale in relation to the whole. One difference between anthem and hymn is that the presence of a separate body of singers in the choir can allow the choir a certain distinction of function over and above its assumed duty of leading the congregational singing. It may sing on behalf of the congregation in choral settings of the liturgy, but may occasionally do something quite different; for example, when the members of the congregation are receiving Communion and so are unable themselves to sing, the choir can get on with its own job of praising God with motets in the sanctuary. This will add further musical weight to this climax of the service.

Hymns, as we saw earlier, best come at the natural dividing points of the service: indeed, in some non-liturgical worship it is the hymns which, by being the pillars, seem to dictate the form of the whole:

Hymn I
Prayers, reading
Hymn II
Sermon
Hymn III, etc.

The first hymn will set the tone for the whole service, but thereafter the natural *modus operandi* of such an ordering is that a hymn is taken to relate to what precedes it. Thus hymn II will relate to the reading, hymn III to the sermon, etc. Overall structure of such a service will not normally amount to more than an episodic treatment of a common theme, but there can be differentiation of emphasis; for example, an appropriate sermon leading into a big hymn like our first Lutheran example would be remembered as the main feature of the service. It even follows that a bad sermon can sometimes be redeemed by a good following hymn, but only on condition that the sermon is fairly short! If it is too long the hymn itself will be structurally dwarfed and so will make a smaller impact. The reverse also holds: a bad hymn or a badly sung one, perhaps because the congregation does not know the tune, can reduce the force of what precedes it.

I must say in closing that these, and indeed probably all of the 'rules' I have suggested, can be broken if the reason and the underlying artistry are strong. Music has always been able to surprise, for it is, as I suggested at the outset, a mystery. We should thank God for that!

Notes

1. An exception is C. Henry Phillips, *The Singing Church* (London, 1945). There are, of course, many fine studies of particular types of liturgical music, notably W. Apel, *Gregorian Chant*, 3rd edn (Bloomington, Indiana, 1966).
2. See C.S. Terry, *Bach's B Minor Mass* (Oxford, 1924).
3. See L. Lockwood, *Introduction to Giovanni Pierluigi da Palestrina: Pope Marcullus Mass*, Norton Critical Scores (New York, 1975).
4. John Skoglund, 'The Communication Revolution and Liturgy', in *Documents of Societas Liturgica*, No. 9 (1969).
5. See the chapter on music in Shakespeare in W.H. Auden, *The Dyer's Hand* (London, 1963).

6. See D.J. Grout, *A Short History of Opera*, 2nd edn (New York and London, 1965).
7. The reader will make better sense of this discussion with a copy of the vocal score of the opera to hand. For a general view of *The Magic Flute* and its Singspiel background E.J. Dent *Mozart's Operas* (Oxford, 1947) is perhaps the best of many studies.

Index

212

DATE DUE